TURGENEV

L E T T E R S

VOLUME   TWO

Edited and Translated by David Lowe

ARDIS

Ardis Publishers
2901 Heatherway
Ann Arbor, Michigan 48104

Library of Congress Cataloging in Publication Data

Turgenev, Ivan Sergeevich, 1818-1883.
　　Letters in two volumes.

　　Includes index.
　　1. Turgenev, Ivan Sergeevich, 1818-1883—Correspondence. 2. Authors, Russian—19th century—Correspondence. I. Lowe, David Allan, 1948-　　. II. Title.
PG3432　1982　　　891.73'3　　　82-18515
ISBN 0-88233-735-1　(v.1)
ISBN 0-88233-736-X (v. 2)

CONTENTS

Acknowledgments

First place in the acknowledgments belongs to the scholars who prepared and annotated the *Complete Collected Works and Letters (Polnoe sobranie sochinenii i pisem)*. But for that edition this collection of translated Turgenev letters would not even have been undertaken. Among the colleagues who have been helpful in elucidating difficult passages in the Russian originals, I have especially imposed on the generous expertise of three Ninas: Professor Nina Perlina of Macalester College and Professors Antonina Filonov Gove and Nina Mitelman at Vanderbilt University. Professor James Engel of Vanderbilt University and Christina Kraus kindly checked over the translations from the German. Very special thanks are due Professor Helena Goscilo-Kostin of the University of Pittsburgh: her careful checking of the manuscript saved me from myself on more occasions that I'd like to admit. Any mistakes that remain in the translations are mine, of course.

David Lowe
Vanderbilt University

For Inna Varlamova

Letter 166 (1305). To P.V. Annenkov.
January 7/19, 1863. Paris.

Paris.
January 7/19, 1863.
Rue de Rivoli, 210.

The news conveyed in your letter surprised me very much, dear Pavel Vasilievich. I'm certain that the rumor is without foundation, because it's absurd.[1] To summon me now (to the Senate), after *Fathers and Sons,* after the younger generation's abusive articles,[2] precisely now, when I've broken forever—practically in public—with the London exiles,[3] i.e., with their mode of thought, is an absolutely incomprehensible fact. No one here has spoken to me of this—no one, beginning with our present Ambassador, Budberg,[4] whose acquaintance I made at New Year's, and ending with our former Ambassador, Kisilyov,[5] at whose home I dined a few days ago. It goes without saying that if summoned, I'll go immediately—it's silly even to add that it will be with a clean conscience; only one thing will be unpleasant—a winter journey, which in view of my poor health doesn't promise any pleasure; well, and it wouldn't be exactly fun to leave my daughter here either. But up until now I haven't heard anything from anyone, and I hope that this will all turn out to be a false rumor. I still have the self-confidence to think (what a Gallicism!) that my way of thinking must be known both to the Emperor and to our government officials.

But if I have to go, then I'll also be consoled by the fact that I'll see you and other good friends. As you say, I am unaware of any imprudent or rash act on my part; my whole life is there for all to see, and I have nothing to hide.

Until we meet, if not now, then in April...

Letter 167 (1329). To Gustave Flaubert.[1]
March 7/19, 1863. Paris.

> Paris.
> Rue de Rivoli, 210.
> March 19, 1863.

Dear Monsieur Flaubert,

Your letter made me blush just as much as it gave me pleasure—and that's saying a great deal. Such praise can make one proud—and I would like to have merited it. Be that as it may—I'm very happy to have pleased you—and I thank you for having told me so.

I'm sending you a book of mine that just appeared;[2] I'm publishing another one and will send it to you as soon as it comes out.[3] You can see that I will no longer have any mercy on you.

Are you planning to come to Paris before the summer? I would be so happy to continue the acquaintance with you that has begun under such good auspices and—on my part I'm certain of this—which could wish nothing better than to become a very close friendship...[4]

I clasp your hand with all of what I already feel for you—and beg you to believe in my most cordial regards.

> J. Tourguéneff

Letter 168 (1348). To Ye. Ye. Lambert.
April 27/May 9, 1863. Baden-Baden.

> Baden.
> Schillerstrasse, 277.
> April 27/May 9, 1863.

Dear Countess, I arrived here about a week ago, but didn't get myself firmly situated, find an apartment, and so on, until today. I was already planning to write you—if not 14 pages, then the usual 4—when your long letter suddenly arrived and, of course, in spite of its merciless severity, accelerated my intention. I'll say a few words of explanation, not justification.

You condemn me as a person (in the sense of a political figure, a citizen) and as a writer. In regard to the former, you are right—in the latter, no, I don't think so. You're right in saying that I'm not a political person and in asserting that the government has no reason to fear me; my convictions have not changed since my early years—but I have never been and never will be involved in politics: that business is alien to me and uninteresting, and I pay attention to it only as much as is necessary for a writer called upon to paint pictures of contemporary life. But you're wrong in demanding of me in the literary arena that which I can't give, fruit that doesn't grow on my tree. I have never *written for the people*. I have written for that class of the public to which I belong—beginning with *Notes of a Hunter* and concluding with *Fathers and Sons;* I don't know of how much use I've been, but I know that I've moved unswervingly toward one and the same goal—and in that regard I don't deserve reproach. You think that it's only because of laziness, as you say, that I don't write simple and moral stories for the people; but how do you know that I haven't tried something like that twenty times—and finally abandoned it, because I became convinced that it's not for me, that I *don't know how* to do that. This is precisely where the weak side of the brightest people who are *not* artists shows itself: having grown accustomed to arranging their whole life in accordance with their own will, they can't understand that an artist often is not free in his own offspring—and they are ready to accuse him of laziness, epicureanism, and so on. Believe me: people only do what it is given to them to do—and to force oneself is both useless and fruitless. That is why I'll never write a story for the people. For that one needs quite a different disposition of mind and character.[1]

I swear to you that I also do not think that I live abroad exclusively out of a desire to enjoy hotels and so on. Up until now circumstances have arranged themselves such that I can only spend five months a year in Russia; and now it's gotten even worse. I hope that you'll believe me when I tell you that it is precisely now that I would like to be in Russia to see from close up what's transpiring there and what I profoundly approve of.

I still haven't given my daughter in marriage, but she's written you herself. Forgive me for forgetting to thank you for the marvellous album which reached my daughter intact and now graces her table. I would be very happy if you were advised to take a trip abroad—then I would have a chance to see you.

Be well, write me indignant letters if you wish, and be assured that I love you with all my heart and treasure your friendship. I clasp your husband's hand firmly.

Your Iv. Turgenev

11

Letter 169 (1356). To N.V. Shcherban.[1]
June 2/14, 1863. Baden-Baden.

Baden-Baden.
June 2/14, 1863.
Schillerstrasse, 277.

Dear Shcherban, first of all, thank you for the journals that you sent, and secondly—I have a request. Could you please subscribe to Aurelieu Scholl's *Nain Jaune*[2] for me, from its initial issue on, and have it sent to me here, of course. Subscribe for six months. I don't know how much it costs, but I doubt that it's very much. I'll be very obliged to you for this.

I just read your article in *Nord*[3] about the spurious "Secret Decree of the Tsar"[4]—and applauded you. There isn't any filthy slander that they wouldn't impute to us, and thank the Lord for those who protest. But we can't avoid war, especially now, after the taking of Pueblo.[5] And to tell the truth, I'm beginning to wish for war: it's the only solution—and one way or another we'll extricate ourselves from the vile bog in which we're sitting up to our ears.

I read almost all the pieces in *The Contemporary* (I especially liked Stasov's passionate, energetic article about the exhibit[6]), but—pardon me!—I could hardly get through Chernyshevsky.[7] His style arouses physical revulsion in me, like worm seed. If this is—I won't even say art or beauty—but if this is intelligence and something worthwhile—then all I can do is crawl under a bench somewhere. I hadn't yet met an author whose characters *stank:* Mr. Chernyshevsky turns out to be such an author. But let's not speak of this subject anymore: I'll only note that Mr. Chernyshevsky involuntarily reminds me of a naked, toothless old man who alternately babbles like a baby, wagging his unwashed behind for beauty, or swears like a carter, belching and spitting.

Well, enough!

I can tell you that yesterday I finished a short story that's not a story—Lord knows what it is—under the title of "Phantoms," for *Time.*[8] It's the same "Phantoms" on whose account, if you recall, Katkov and I nearly fell out when *The Russian Messenger* was starting up.[9] Now I intend to really get down to work on my long novel.[10]

In conclusion, be well. I send you my cordial regards and clasp your wife's hand.[11]

Your devoted

Iv. Turgenev

P.S. Should I send back the journals or not?

Letter 170 (1368). To A.I. Herzen.
June 10/22, 1863. Heidelberg.

Heidelberg.
July 22, 1862.

Dear Alexander Ivanovich, I just read the issue of *The Bell* in which the "French and English mustard" and so on are mentioned. Thank you for not believing that vulgar joke[1]—but it seems to me that you would have expressed yourself more definitely if you hadn't believed it at all. Not a single offensive or mocking word about the Poles has come from my lips— if only because I haven't yet entirely lost an understanding of "the tragic." No one is in a mood for laughter now.

I broke off correspondence with you for reasons well known to you— besides which, who would want to exchange letters such as our last ones?[2] Our opinions are too far apart, and what's the point of irritating each other to no purpose? I am not now suggesting a resumption of that correspondence, but I would be very much obliged if in the next issue of *The Bell* you published the statement that "We have received positive corroboration that the words attributed to Mr. Turgenev were an utter falsification."[3]

I'm writing to I.S. Aksakov today.[4] I'm deeply wounded by this filth with which my solitary, practically underground life has been bespattered.

I wish you tranquillity such as is possible—and in the name of our past I beg you not to consider me capable of a mean word or deed.

Iv. Turgenev

P.S. I live in Baden-Baden, Schillerstrasse, 277—and I've come here only for a day, in order to consult a doctor.

Letter 171 (1371). To Moritz Hartmann.[1]
July 28/August 9, 1863. Baden-Baden.

Baden-Baden.
Schillerstrasse, 277.
August 9, 1863.

My dear friend, begging your pardon for the delay, I'm enclosing my photograph and a few biographical details. My life has been very ordinary. I was born November 9, 1818, in Oryol (in Russia)—I studied for a year at Moscow University, and then three years at Petersburg—in 1838 I made my first trip abroad and studied philosophy, philology, and history in Berlin until 1840—in Berlin I spent an entire year in the same house and almost in the same room with Bakunin.[2] In 1843 I wrote my first poems and served for a very short time in the Ministry of Internal Affairs. My poems were bad, and so was my service. From time to time I wrote poetry of reflection, without sonority or inspiration, with petty details, and I was ready to finish with literature altogether when, at the end of 1846, at the request of my friend Belinsky, I wrote the first sketch of *Memoirs of a Hunter* for his newly-founded journal. It was a success—many others followed it—and thus I became a story writer and novelist. I lived abroad from 1847 to 1850—in 1848 thought of settling in France permanently, but returned to Russia—and in 1852 was punished by Emperor Nicholas by a nearly two-year exile. The occasion for that was an article about Gogol, who had just died: they wanted in this way to intimidate young writers. Since then I've been writing novellas—long and short—and have lived by turns in France, Germany, and Russia, but you know that as well as I do. I had two brothers; the younger one died long ago. Voilà tout [that's all].

I hope that this letter finds you still in Stuttgart. Gerken's brain is in a very bad way;[3] his mother-in-law[4] hasn't arrived yet.

I send my regards to your wife[5] and a cordial handshake to you. At the same time I'm sending you *Pères et enfants.*[6]

Your

I. Turgéneff

Letter 172 (1396). To P.V. Annenkov.
November 19/December 1, 1863. Paris.

Paris.
December 1/ November 19, 1863.

Dear Pavel Vasilievich, the lamentable story of my money[1] has finally been played out to the end, not without considerable loss to my own pockets. Here's what happened: the lyric poet Fet, having received the money from my uncle, put off sending it for a long time, all the while trying to decide how best to send it to Baden—since there are no bank arrangements *directly* to Baden. (That historic pronouncement belongs to the sagacious Botkin office in Moscow.)[2] There really are no banks with direct links to Baden, but in Baden there are at least a dozen bankers who greedily watch over every note of exchange, even if it's for Valparaiso—not just for Paris. In his reasoning, which reached the Gordian knot and Sesostris (his own words—I'll show you the letter)—he had just about decided on Frankfurt.. but they have *florins* there... that might not be convenient for Turgenev (honest to God!). So the days passed—I was expiring—and in Petersburg the exchange rate up and crashed. Then the lyric poet Fet, completely losing his head, rushed to a banker by the name of Vogan or Vogau (it's spelled differently on the two notes of exchange)—and, throwing himself at his feet, implored him to take 100 rubles per 350 francs (even during the Crimean War the exchange rate was never that bad!), which the latter agreed to, since at the same moment Akhenbakh[3] and other bankers were giving 367—and sent me the money à trois mois de date [valid for three months], moreover, identifying me as M. Furguheneff. The result of these Sesostrisian cogitations was pure loss. All of this would be funny if it hadn't cost me money. It's a lesson for the future: don't entrust financial matters to lyric poets. There's one consolation—added material for a comic depiction of the state of Russian society. Read this to Botkin— he'll have a good laugh.

Perhaps Khanykov will show up in Petersburg before this letter arrives; he'll tell you that I'm planning to gallop along after him. Unfortunately, I caught a cold at the farewell dinner given for that same Khanykov—and sat in my room for three days—as a result of which I'll arrive in Petersburg three days later than I had planned. I'm going to Baden the day after tomorrow; I'll collect my things, and after two or three days there I'll set out for Petersburg, where I plan to arrive before November 30. And so, we'll see each other soon, but here are two more requests for you.

Keep all the letters, money, and so on that you receive from my uncle

15

until my arrival. Thank Tyutchev for me for his having dealt with Zakhar and having provided that mortal with 110 rubles.[4] That was very nice of him; I'll pay him back the money as soon as I return. Yes, one more point. Tyutchev and many other friends advise me not to publish "Phantoms"— ask Dostoevsky (if he hasn't done it yet) not to announce it and not to say that such-and-such a piece by so-and-so will appear.[5] When I arrive in Petersburg I'll consult with you—and then we'll see...

Letter 173 (1404). To A.A. Krayevsky.[1]
December 3/15, 1863. Baden-Baden.

> Baden.
> Schillerstrasse, 277.
> December 3/15, 1863.

Monsieur,

This letter will be delivered to you by Mme Clara Schumann, of whose admirable talent you doubtless are aware. She is coming to Russia for the second or third time—and all friends of good and great music ought to wish that she be more and more satisfied with our public's reception of her. Your position gives you a greater opportunity than anyone else to facilitate this, and I do not doubt that you will do that eagerly, which doesn't prevent me from appealing to our long-standing friendship. I will consider any services that you can render Mme Schumann as a personal favor, and I beg you to accept my thanks in advance, along with the expression of my sincere devotion.

> Iv. Turgenev

Letter 174 (1438). To Pauline Viardot.
February 3/15, 1864. Petersburg.

No. 15

St. Petersburg.
Hôtel de France.
Monday, February 3/15, 1864.

Dear good Mme Viardot! I received your letter from Leipzig with the variants of "The Bird";[1] but you probably already know that Bodenstedt[2] sent me a complete translation; and of course that's the one we'll use. The first six romances have already been printed. Iogansen[3] swears that the rest of them will be printed by the end of next week. I'm leaving Petersburg—again, si Dios quiere [if God wishes]—*Wednesday,* February 19/March 2, i.e., a little more than two weeks from now. Never has time dragged by so slowly for me. I'm trying to work so as to make it go more quickly.

Yesterday we had a meeting of our Society for the Assistance of Writers in Need. We were expecting trouble from the impatient ones, those who, thanks to me (I first introduced the word in *Fathers and Sons*), are called "nihilists" here; they find us too reasonable; but everything went off splendidly; moderates were elected to the committee (I was elected a member of the committee and chairman of the review commission). Then we had a dinner in honor of our deceased confrère Druzhinin; we talked a lot without saying anything special; we ate and drank a great deal, I especially, for which I paid with rather poor health (you recognize me, don't you?). Today I've only had a cup of tea and am going to bed hungry as a dog, with an empty stomach that I'm not about to feed.

I just finished correcting the proofs of my "Fantasy."[4] The die is cast. Whether they curse it or praise it is a matter of indifference to me; and you won't doubt that when you find out that the issue of the journal in which it will be published will come out when I'm already in Baden. You are there already; perhaps you just arrived, and my thoughts follow you and accompany you at the moment of your return to your dear nest.

Don't be too proud—just a little bit longer, and I'll be doing the same thing. Please don't forget to check on the position occupied by the civil servant in charge of cases of insolvency.[5] From Paulinette's letter that I just received I see that this marriage means much more to her than she used to say—or perhaps even think. Oh, pink tricot, how difficult it is to catch you!

I spent the evening at the home of Mme Vinogradskaya,[6] with whom

17

Pushkin was once in love. In her honor he wrote a number of poems that are recognized as some of the best in our literature. In her youth she must have been very beautiful, and even now, for all her good-heartedness (she's not bright), she has maintained the manners of a woman who is used to having men like her. She keeps the letters that Pushkin wrote her like relics; she showed me a half-faded pastel depicting her at age 28: she is pale, blonde, with a gentle face, naive grace, and remarkable good-heartedness in her gaze and smile . . . she looks a little like a Russian chambermaid such as Varyusha. In Pushkin's place I wouldn't have written verses to her. She apparently wanted to meet me very much, and since yesterday was her saint's day, my friends offered her up to me instead of a bouquet. She has a husband who is twenty years younger than she: it's a pleasant family, a little touching even, and at the same time comical.

Farewell until Wednesday . . . and then, in two weeks . . . Be well; give everyone a thousand kind regards from me. I kiss your hands, very tenderly.

Your I. Turgenev

Letter 175 (1458). To A.I. Herzen.
March 21/April 2, 1864. Paris.

Paris.
Rue de Rivoli, 210.
Saturday, March 21/ April 2, 1864.

After returning from Russia I hesitated for a long time before writing to you in regard to the remarks in *The Bell* about "the grey-haired male Magdalene whose teeth and hair fell out from repentance" and so on. I admit that that remark, clearly referring to me, wounded me.[1] That Bakunin, who borrowed money from me and because of his womanish chatter and empty-headedness put me in a very unpleasant position (he simply destroyed other people)—that Bakunin, I say, spread the most banal and vile slander about me—that's in the nature of things—and since I've known him for ages and ages, I didn't expect anything else. But I didn't suppose that in just the same way you would sling mud at a person whom you've known almost twenty years, only because you've parted company in your views. You're not far behind Nikolay Pavlovich, who also condemned me without even asking me whether I was really guilty.[2] If I could show you the answers that I wrote to the questions which were sent to me, you would surely be persuaded that without concealing anything, I not only didn't insult any of my friends, but didn't even think of renouncing them: I would consider that unworthy of myself. I confess that it is not without a certain amount of pride that I recall those answers, which in spite of the tone in which they were written, earned me the respect and trust of my judges.[3] As for the letter to the Emperor which you presented in such an ugly light, here it is:

Your Imperial Majesty!
Most Gracious Emperor!

I have already twice had the pleasure of addressing Your Highness in writing—and both times my requests were received favorably; please be so good as to grant me Your high attention this time, too, Your Majesty.

Today I received through our Embassy here an order to return to Russia immediately. I admit quite frankly that I cannot imagine how I have earned such a sign of distrust. I have never concealed my mode of thought, my activities have been known to everyone, and I am unaware of any reprehensible act on my part. I am a writer, Your Highness, and nothing more; all of my life has been expressed in my works—and I ought to be judged according to them. I dare to think that anyone who cares to take a look at them will have to note the moderation of my convictions, which are quite independent, but conscientious. It is difficult to understand that at the same time when You, Your Majesty, have made Your name immortal by carrying out a great deed of justice and philanthropy, it is difficult to understand, I say, how one could be suspicious of a writer who in his own modest sphere tried as much as possible to facilitate those lofty determinations.[4] The conditions of my health and affairs which cannot be put off do not allow me to return to Russia just now; therefore I beg Your Highness to deign to order that the questions be sent to me in writing; I give my word of honor to answer each of them immediately and with full candor. Please believe in the sincerity of my words, Your Majesty; to the faithful and loyal feelings which my duty requires that I have for Your Person may be added my personal gratitude.

Yes, the Emperor, who didn't know me at all—nonetheless realized that he was dealing with an honest person—and for that my gratitude to him has only increased; and old friends, who one would think knew me well, had no doubts about attributing baseness to me and trumpeting it in

19

print. If I were dealing with the former Herzen, I wouldn't ask you not to abuse my trust—and to immediately destroy this letter; but you yourself have confused my notions about you—and I ask you not to cause me any new unpleasantness: the ones in the past have been quite enough. Moreover, the very fact of this letter proves that my feelings for you have not entirely disappeared: I wouldn't have favored Bakunin with even so much as half a word. Be well.

Iv. Turgenev

Letter 176 (1493). To Ye. Ye. Lambert.
August 22/ September 3, 1864. Baden-Baden.

Baden-Baden.
Schillerstrasse, 277.
September 3, 1864.

Dear Countess, first of all I must tell you that for some incomprehensible reason the letter that you wrote August 18th didn't come into my hands until yesterday! That is doubly unpleasant for me: on the one hand, you might think that I was lazy in answering you—and on the other, my reply probably won't find you in Wiesbaden. But so be it—I don't want to lose another moment. I'm very grateful to you for your letter, although you both rebuke me and take leave of me...I see from it that you still remember me and even feel a certain friendship for me...Fortunately for me, there was never in you that haughty, though virtuous inability to understand—and sometimes even to forgive—the faults of others—which I have observed in many Christian men and women from society. You reproach me, it is true: but, in the first place, in the reproaches I sense your favorable disposition towards me, and in the second, they give me the chance to try to justify myself. From your point of view, I am guilty of two major faults: the first is the absence of Orthodoxy; the second is remoteness from my native land, which has occurred because of my desire for an epicurean life—in a word, out of egoism. I will not say much about the first point: I am not a Christian in your sense, and perhaps not in any—and therefore let us leave this to the side: it can only lead to unfortunate misunderstandings. As for the second point, first of all allow me to protest against the word "contempt," which you ascribe to me: only young, passionate people have contempt—and I wasn't guilty of that sin even in my youth. You say that one must serve the fatherland—fine; but you will agree that I cannot serve it as a soldier, a bureaucrat, an agronomist, or a factory manager; I can be of use only as a writer, an artist. I might remark in this regard that for every artist there comes a time of peace and even a right to it; I only want to draw your attention to the fact that there is no need for a writer to live in his native land and to try to catch the variations in its life— in any event, there's no need to do that constantly;[1] I have done rather enough work in that field—and now—how do you know?—perhaps I intend to begin a composition whose significance will not be specifically Russian, but broader? You'll respond that I only want to create a seemly excuse for my laziness...But you won't be absolutely correct.

In a word, I see no reason why I shouldn't settle in Baden: I'm doing that not out of a desire for enjoyment (that's also the lot of youth)—but simply in order to build myself a nest in which I shall await the inevitable end.

Well, look how much I've said and, of course, I've failed to persuade you. But for your part you didn't tell me anything about your health or your intentions. In spite of the *twenty-four-hour* time limit to which you unreasonably attached such significance, I would definitely visit you if I knew for certain where you were and for how long. Please write me a few words about that—and in general, let's continue our correspondence. In spite of all sorts of disagreements, we stand close to each other. In expectation of a letter, I clasp your hand firmly and remain your sincerely devoted

I.T.

Letter 177 (1501). To F.M. Dostoevsky.
October 3/15, 1864. Baden-Baden.

Baden-Baden.
Schillerstrasse, 277.
October 3/15, 1864.

Dear Fyodor Mikhailovich, I kept planning to answer your letter of August 24—but then the hunting season came around—and I forgot about it—for which I apologize to you: your letter of September 20 reminded me of my obligation, and I hasten to fulfill it. I'll begin by assuring you that my feelings for your journal have not changed in the least—that with all my heart I am ready to promote its success as best I can—and I *give you my promise* to send you the first thing that I write; but it's impossible for me to set a date for when that thing will be written—because I'm completely overcome by sloth—and I haven't taken a pen in hand for over a year.[1] Whether I'll be able finally to shake this off—God alone knows—but if that happens to me—my work will be exclusively at your service. I have often thought of you all this time, about all the blows that have struck you[2]—and I'm sincerely happy that you have not allowed them to break you completely. I just fear for your health, lest it suffer from overwork. I myself am very, very sorry that I don't see *The Epoch* here; I hope to make better arrangements for next year.

Give my friendly regards to all of your co-workers—and accept the assurance of my sincere sympathy for your activity and of my attachment to you.

Your devoted

Iv. Turgenev

Letter 178 (1506). To V.P. Botkin.
October 25/ November 6, 1864. Baden-Baden.

> Baden.
> Schillerstrasse, 277.
> November 6, 1864.

Dear Vasily Petrovich,

You can do me an important favor (not in regard to the edition—that's been taken care of completely)—but in another matter. I need a rather large sum of money in order to build my new house—and I was counting on 15,000 silver rubles—which I was due to receive for the redemption of my Tambov estate.[1] I had all the more right to count on it since I have lying before me a letter from the mediator of the second region of the Yelatomsky District, Tambov Province, Prince Kildishev, to my uncle,[2] in which he reports *(from May 27, 1864)* that the Tambov Province Executive Office *from May 13* "informed him, Kildishev, that the agreement about the redemption of I.S. Turgenev's short-term peasants in the villages of Pochkov and Istleyev has been approved by the Province Office and submitted to the Main Redemption Institution under No. 3113."

Since then the whole affair has gotten bogged down as if in Kama moss—the Main Redemption Institution seems to be keeping mum, doesn't answer my uncle's persistent wailing—and I'm sitting here without money. Please be so good as to find out through your many acquaintances (at the club and so on) through whom I can act and whom I need to ask to get the ball rolling. It's precisely for that reason that I have sent you all the data. By speeding up this scandalously slow process you'll perform a marvellous service for me—otherwise I might as well hang myself, since I can't even dream of an income, of selling land, and so on.

Please do me the additional favor of getting me Grigoriev's latest article about Grigorovich[3]—and sending it here in an envelope at my expense. Dostoevsky will give you a copy.

For the rest, I am well, I go hunting often, and am idle. Give my regards to all our good friends and accept my cordial handshake.

> Iv. Turgenev

P.S. Please fulfill my request *immediately*. The Annenkovs are leaving Paris for Petersburg tomorrow.

Letter 179 (1520). To Pauline Turgeneva.[1]
December 10/22, 1864. Baden-Baden.

Baden.
Schillerstrasse, 277.
Thursday, December 22, 1864.

Dear Paulinette, your letter made me very happy. It presages a development which I ought naturally to have expected, but which rarely presents itself under such favorable conditions and with such guarantees of happiness. If, as you say, this is the "right one" who has come, then one ought first of all to thank God—and then the dear and marvellous Mme Delessert,[2] who has had the solicitude of a mother for you. Let's hope that this all will be decided quickly and well.

Certainly, I'll come to Paris; I have a great desire to meet M. Gaston: I'll leave Baden on Friday, December 30— and, if it pleases God, I'll arrive at your place on Saturday, the 31st—at seven in the morning. I'll stay in Paris for the number of days necessary for arriving at a definitive agreement. And so, await me with complete assurance.

Mme Innis hasn't been writing to me—but I have no doubt that she will be just as happy as I am about the future that is opening before you. I have no need to tell that I will always consider her a member of the family and that the respect and gratitude that I feel toward her shall remain with me all my life.

I clasp your hand and kiss you hard.

I. Turgenev

Letter 180 (1533). To N.S. Turgenev.
December 31, 1864/ January 12, 1865. Baden-Baden.

Baden-Baden.
Schillerstrasse, 277.
Dec. 31/ Jan. 12, 1865. Thursday.

My dear brother, I hasten to calm you with the assurance that my "urgent" request will not require you to move from your place or be subjected to any constraints at all. Here is what it's all about: I am giving my daughter in marriage to Mr. Gaston Bruère, a young and well-educated man who is the head of a sizable glass factory; the wedding is to take place in Paris at the end of February, i.e., in slightly over a month. In submitting all the essential documents to the notary, I also presented him with your letter, in which, *in the event of my death,* you promise Paulinette twenty-five thousand francs; the question arose of whether, since I promise my daughter fifty-thousand francs within a few years, you wouldn't like to increase the sum promised by you to 50,000 francs.[1] I assume that you will agree, *since this puts you under an obligation only if you enter into the possession of my inheritance,* which undoubtedly exceeds this sum many times over. But in any event I wish to know your opinion and therefore I ask you to give me your written agreement *in French* so that I can show it to the necessary parties; but we won't compose the letter itself until immediately after the wedding, so that you can call my daughter Mme Bruère. I would be very happy if you could be present at the wedding; but we'll write to each other before then anyway. Please send me your reply as soon as possible, since I may have to make a trip to Paris in a few days.

The news of your illness upset me greatly; although I know that the tonsillectomy itself doesn't present any danger (many singers have the operation performed just to be done with it)—still, I feel very sorry for you—and I can imagine what torture you must be going through. I have only one "Universal Mittel"[universal remedy]—like Scribe's "prenez mon ours" [take my bear][2]—come to Baden; since I've been here, all my former "maladies" have disappeared.

Give my regards to Anna Yakovlevna;[3] I embrace you cordially and remain

Your loving brother

Iv. Turgenev.

P.S. My daughter's dowry consists of 100,000 francs, "une fois donnés" [once given]—and the promised 50,000, as well.

Letter 181 (1576). To Pauline Bruère.[1]
March 15/27, 1865. Baden-Baden.

Baden.
Schillerstrasse, 277.
March 27, 1865.

Dear Paulinette,

And so you're back at Rougement—I'm very happy for you and I hope that you're going to set up your nest in order to begin the calm and serious life of a *woman*. I'm also happy to see that all the little misunderstandings have disappeared—and I have no doubt that you'll make every effort to be always on good terms with your father-in-law and mother-in-law. My intention now is to leave Baden between the 15th and 20th of next month and come take a look at your household. For the rest, my health is good, in spite of the abominable weather here and which isn't any better where you are, if one can believe the newspapers.

Did you receive a letter of mine that I addressed to the Hotel Byron?

I received a letter from Mme Innis: the poor woman feels quite lonely and isolated. Don't forget to write her.

Embrace Gaston for me—and accept a cordial kiss

from your old papa

I. Turgenev.

Letter 182 (1583). To Ludwig Pietsch.[1]
April 7/19, 1865. Baden-Baden.

Baden-Baden.
Schillerstrasse, 277.
April 19, 1865.

My dear Pietsch, you were right not to believe that I allegedly had passed through town. As if I wouldn't have let you know! I haven't been out of Baden-Baden this whole time (I don't count short, one-day trips to Stuttgart or Carlsruhe) and won't leave for Russia until May 8th—too soon, par paranthèse [by the way]! I'll head straight for Berlin and spend at least 24 hours there: but will I meet you there in the springtime and in view of your disposition toward journeys? In any event, I'll knock on the door at Bendlerstrasse. I won't stay long in Russia, six weeks at the most, and I'll return directly to Baden-Baden. And so we'll be expecting you from *July* 1st on—both the good Frau Anstett[2] and I.

We celebrated the Viardots' silver wedding anniversary yesterday at the Thiergarten. Mme Viardot looks quite young; in Stuttgart she performed the role of Rosina in *The Barber of Seville* with enormous success—and really, there are twenty-year-old girls who do not possess such freshness and liveliness.

May that last for a long time yet!

That your Berlin acquaintance doesn't like her music is no great misfortune. In my presence she sang for Mörike his poems which she has set to music, and the old eccentric was quite beside himself; he ran back and forth like one possessed.[3] I hope that you'll like the Mörike cycle too.

You've really told me too many good and nice things—and I must thank those nice ladies for their kind words.[4] A photograph follows.

I'm very glad that your family's health has improved—just don't make any gloomy suggestions for yourselves. I can tell you that at least as far as I'm concerned, the following dictum has always turned out to be true: "Anything that you have a presentiment of never happens." Life consists of a succession of flowers ... or cobblestones falling on you from above. Let's hope that the latter will pass us by for a long time yet.

I clasp your hand cordially.

Your Turgenev

P.S. The second volume of Bodenstedt's translation is being printed ... But it's still uncertain when it will appear.[5]

Letter 183 (1601). To I.I. Maslov.
June 18/30, 1865. Spasskoye.

Village of Spasskoye.
Friday, June 18, 1865.

Dear Ivan Ilich,

Today I don't want to talk to you about sales and money, but about quite another matter. Listen.

In 1851, 1852, and 1853 I had a liaison with a girl named Feoktista, who lived with me in Petersburg and here. You may have heard about her. Later I helped her marry a minor civil servant from the Maritime Ministry—and she's now prospering in Petersburg. When she left me in 1853 she was pregnant and in Moscow she gave birth to a son, Ivan, whom she gave up to a foundling hospital. I have sufficient reason to believe that this son was not by me, but I can't vouch for that with certainty. He may perhaps be my offspring. That son, by the name of Ivan, ended up in a village at a muzhik's to whom he was given for maintenance. Feoktista, who went to see him last year, on the sly from her husband, couldn't tell me where that village is located and in which department: she only knows that it was 50 versts to the village and that it's called Prudishche. She also has reason to believe that some woman took the child in—he was having a hard time of it in the village—and that this woman has landed in the hospital. On the basis of all of this you can conclude that Feoktista's head is weak. Now she's on her way to Moscow again (she dropped by here to have a look at me—her husband was given a month's leave to the Bogoroditsky District)—and I've directed her to you for help in the search. If this Ivan is alive and is found, I'd be ready to place him in a craft school and to pay for him.[1] I'm leaving here on St. Peter's Day and on the 30th I'll be in Moscow—at your place. I hope that you won't have flown off to Petersburg already. In any event, please be so good as to render your lofty patronage to Feoktista Petrovna Volkova, who will present you with a letter from me in person. It may be that "Prudishche" is a crown estate, and then everything will be easy as pie. The husband doesn't know about a thing; but he's a mild and decent person. N.B. Don't give Feoktista any money—she already received some from me.

In conclusion, I embrace you and say "until we see each other soon"— in Moscow or in Petersburg.

Your devoted

Iv. Turgenev

Letter 184 (1619). To Pauline Bruère.[1]
October 7/19, 1865. Baden-Baden.

Baden.
Schillerstrasse, 277.
Thursday, October 19, 1865.

Dear Paulinette, you can imagine how greatly saddened I was by the letter that I just received from the kind Gaston—I, who was so rejoicing at the idea of soon becoming a grandfather. But now one must resign oneself and think that this has merely been delayed. The important thing now is to take care of yourself and to stay calm. For the rest, as for taking care of yourself, I'm certain that your excellent husband isn't letting you want for anything. And so, have courage, my poor dear; you must realize that these accidents frequently occur to women in the first year of marriage—I could cite many examples for you, but I'll content myself with that of the Empress. I rely on Gaston to keep me informed of what happens; I embrace him with tenderness, just as I do you, and I hope that your convalescence won't be a long one. Once again—courage and patience!

Iv. Turgenev

Letter 185 (1647). To P.V. Annenkov.[1]
February 24/ March 8, 1866. Baden-Baden.

March 8/ February 22

...since then I've also received the first three issues of *Notes of the Fatherland*—thank you. Your prediction about *The Russian Word*[2] didn't take long to come true, and for the ukase of February 19th liberating the state serfs I cry "Hurrah!"

I don't know whether I told you that for the last six weeks now I've been suffering from an inflammation of the muscles in my left arm: I had a hard time of it, but I'm gradually recovering. The expenses involved in building my house are staggering—but I don't regret my idea: in general, there's only one thing in my whole life that I regret, namely—having asked V.P. Botkin for money. Prince Trubetskoy[3] told me that Botkin had told him about it—and added: "I won't give it to him, I won't, I won't"—in addition to it which he even jumped up and down. What's he doing, that respected warrior? A strange thing happened to me a few days ago. For Mme Viardot's Russian reading (together with me) I recommended Tolstoy's *Childhood* as a classic work of its kind. I started reading—and was immediately convinced that this notorious *Childhood* is simply bad, boring, petty, strained—and incredibly outdated.[4] This discovery upset me—does that mean that this too is a mirage? And when will there be an end to the mirages? Or perhaps I've grown old and stupid?

I congratulate you on your being elected vice-president of our committee.[5] Tell me who the members are now—and at the first meeting give them all my cordial regards...

Letter 186 (1650). To M.N. Katkov.
March 8/20, 1866. Baden-Baden.

Baden-Baden.
Schillerstrasse, 277.
March 8/20, 1866.

Dear Mikhail Nikiforovich, when we saw each other in Moscow I told you that I intended to cease, or in any event suspend my literary activities for a time;[1] I haven't altered my intention, but I remain in debt to you,[2] and I feel obligated to settle accounts—but not with money. And therefore, here's what I propose: I have almost finished a translation of *Lazarillo de Tormes,* the well-known 16th-century Spanish satirical novel (the proto-type of all the subsequent Gil Blases and so on).[3] If you would like to publish this remarkable piece in your journal, along with a short historical introduction written by me, let me know. *Lazarillo* survived only as a fragment, unfortunately, and will take up 3 and 1/2 signature pages in your *Messenger;* it goes without saying that you may assume a moderate price per page. If, on the other hand, for some reason you should not wish to publish this translation, let me know just the same, and I'll immediately undertake to have the sum I owe sent to you.

In a few days, probably, a short story of mine, "The Dog," will be printed in *The St. Petersburg News;* but, in the first place, it was written a long while ago, and secondly, it wouldn't be at all appropriate for a serious journal, of which fact you will be convinced just by the first few lines; it is altogether insignificant.

The first issue of *The Russian Messenger,* which I received here, is remarkably well put together. Dostoevsky's povest is striking.[4] I hope that you're well and in good spirits, and I beg you to accept the assurance of my absolute devotion.

Iv. Turgenev

Letter 187 (1658). To P.V. Annenkov.
April 6/18, 1866. Baden-Baden.

Baden-Baden. Schillerstrasse, 277.
April 6/18, 1866.

You can easily imagine, dear Pavel Vasilievich, the feelings aroused in me by the news of the monstrous event in Petersburg.[1] Moreover, at first there was a rumor spread here that the Emperor was dangerously wounded. Fortunately, I soon found out the actual content of the telegram. All the Russians here were present at a service of thanksgiving—and I can tell you that this time there was no disagreement: everyone's feelings merged. One can't help but tremble at the thought of what would have happened to Russia if this villainous deed had been successful. But now I have an urgent request to make of you: you must tell me everything that you find out about Petrov;[2] you understand that this isn't a matter of simple curiosity: it's extraordinarily important to know what his past is and what could have impelled him to such a crime; I don't suppose that the journals will be quick to publish any precise information. I'll be greatly obliged if you fulfill my request.

It's impossible to write of anything else: my thoughts are too exclusively struck by this single fact. I read my piece in issue No. 85 of *The St. Petersburg News*[3] and I thank you for your troubles. I'm expecting some offprints for myself too. In conclusion, good-bye, be well...

Letter 188 (1703). To William Ralston.[1]
October 7/19, 1866. Baden-Baden.

Baden.
Schillerstrasse, 277.
Friday, October 19, 1866.

Monsieur,

I received the letter that you were so kind as to write me along with the copy of *The Fortnightly Review* that accompanied it. (I would ask your permission to write in French: I know the literature of your country well, I speak English fluently enough, but it would be difficult for me to write in that language.) I read your article on Koltsov[2] with the greatest interest; I personally hardly knew him, having met him only once or twice in Petersburg; but I was intimately involved with many of his friends, especially Belinsky, who also deserves to be better known and to have the influence that he had and the social role that he played appreciated. Koltsov was a true national poet,[3] as much as that is possible in this century—and if it does him too much honor to compare him to Burns, whose character and gifts are much richer and stronger—all the same he does not lack certain points of resemblance to him—and there are two dozen of his poems that will survive as long as the Russian language itself does.

I can't help but be happy to see that you intend to expand your compatriots' acquaintance with our literature. Besides mentioning Gogol, I think that the works of Count Leo Tolstoy, Ostrovsky, Pisemsky, and Goncharov could be of interest, since they present a new manner of understanding and rendering the poetic element; one cannot deny that since the time of Gogol our literature has acquired an original character; it remains but to find out whether that character is sufficiently distinct to arrest the attention of other nations. Yours is one whose approbation and sympathy would be the most precious—you are aware of how powerful the English influence is among us—and how much your writers are appreciated—and I repeat, I can't but applaud your intention and be happy for my country.

It would be very pleasant for me to establish personal ties with you—and I would be most happy to place myself at your disposal for any information that you might require. In any event, I beg you to rely on me.

I plan to spend the months of February, March, and April in Russia; but I'm afraid that I'll no longer be there when you arrive. I have no doubts about the cordial reception that awaits you there—and I would be happy to facilitate it.

It is with pleasure that I learn that the Mr. Lewes,[4] with whom I studied in Berlin in 1838, is the same person as the eminent biographer of Goethe. I beg you to give him my regards and to accept for yourself the expression of my sincere respect.

I. Turgenev

P.S. If you wish to reply, feel free to do so in English.

Letter 189 (1708). To N.N. Rashet.
October 29/ November 10, 1866. Baden-Baden.

Baden-Baden.
Schillerstrasse, 277.
Saturday, October 29/ November 10,
1866.

I must thank you sincerely, dear Natalya Nikolayevna, for your telegram—of all my absent friends you alone remembered my birthday.[1] That was very kind of you, and I was touched by your consideration. Thank you!

Yes, ma'am—I'm forty-eight! A large enough number—and the ominous fiftieth year is just around the corner. There's no helping it—all I can do is be happy that my spirits are to a certain extent good, my health decent—blindness, deafness, and other such abominations are still only distant threats—and most importantly, there are still a few souls on earth for whom the person bearing the name I.S. Turgenev hasn't yet completely become the equivalent of an old shoe.

I'm in debt to you for your kind letter. The reasons for my lack of punctuality are frequent hunting outings as well as work. I can't tell you exactly when I'll be in Stuttgart, but I'll definitely come and read you a few chapters.[2] Give my regards to the Hartmanns—I still haven't gotten around to writing them—and since at the conclusion of your letter you offer to do even the *impossible* for me (for which I thank you heartily)—then please be so good as to purchase a copy of the two volumes of Bodenstedt's translations *(Erzählungen von I.T.)*[3] at my expense and present it in my name via the Hartmanns to their writer friend Karl Mayer[4] (he visited me here in Baden). For that favor I'll kiss your hands in absentia now and in person when we meet.

Be well, good-bye, and accept my best wishes for you and Manya.[5]

Your devoted

Iv. Turgenev

Letter 190 (1709). To Pauline Bruère.[1]
October 30/ November 11, 1866. Baden-Baden.

Baden.
Schillerstrasse, 277.
November 11, 1866.

Dear Paulinette,

Mme Innis must have told you how much this second accident has saddened me; then I received a letter from her which reassured me about your health—and I take pen in hand to tell you in a couple of words that I embrace you very tenderly—and to recommend calm and resignation for you. It's apparent that you need to take some exceptional measures—I know women who stayed in bed for the entire second half of their pregnancy, and this helped them greatly. You have someone to take care of you—I rely completely on Gaston, whose hand I clasp cordially, by the way—the important thing for the moment is to recover your health completely. I can't yet give you the exact date of my trip to France—but in any case it will be before Christmas! Until then I embrace the two of you, and I beg you to give my regards to M. and Mme Bruère, Mme Innis, and young Paul.[3]

J. Tourguéneff

P.S. Everyone here is well.

Letter 191 (1719). To M.N. Katkov.
December 13/25, 1866. Baden-Baden.

Baden.
Schillerstrasse, 277.
December 13/25, 1866.

Dear Mikhail Nikiforovich, I just received your letter with the enclosed notes of exchange for 1200 rubles and I offer you my sincere thanks. As for your wish to publish my novel[1] in the first issue of *The Russian Messenger,* allow me to say the following: I really could send you the recopied first half of the novel, but the problem is that up until now I have never published a single one of my works without subjecting it to the scrutiny of my literary friends—and without subsequently making significant changes and corrections in it. This is more essential than ever now: I've been silent rather a long while, and the public—as always happens in such cases—regards me with a certain distrust; moreover, this novel touches on many questions and has altogether greater significance—for me, at least; and therefore I would be very obliged to you if you would allow me not to depart from my original plan, which consists of coming to Petersburg at the end of January, having a reading of it there,[2] and bringing it to Moscow early in February, so that it could appear in the February issue of *The Russian Messenger* (*Fathers and Sons* also came out in February). I can't come to Petersburg before the end of January. You could announce the novel in the January issue of *The Russian Messenger* or in *The Moscow News*—and you can do that with absolute assurance—for I give you my word of honor that the manuscript—with all the corrections—will be in your hands at the beginning of February.[3]

I would be very pleased if my arguments convinced you—and I beg you to accept the expression of my complete respect and devotion, along with my gratitude.

Iv. Turgenev

Letter 192 (1733). To Pauline Viardot.[1]
January 30/ February 11, 1867. Baden-Baden.

Monday morning. (February 11, 1867)

Oh theurste Freundin, welche Freude hat mir heute Ihr grosser schöner Brief gemacht; Ich küsse Ihnen dafür tausend mal die lieben guten Hände. [Oh dearest friend, how happy your lovely long letter has made me today; I kiss your dear, good hands a thousand times for it.] That consolation was essential for me: I'm nailed to my divan again—I can't walk at all any more—even with the help of a cane.[2] I won't say anything more about my illness or a trip. I see that you have to let events take their own course. And so I haven't the slightest idea when we'll see each other again.

I'm extraordinarily happy about what you say about my last book: you know that you're the supreme judge and ordainer; I sense, of course, that you read me with benevolent eyes, or, more accurately, with eyes that fill in what I have only outlined, and all the same I know that with your subtle and assured sensitivity you won't give me a good "grade" for what only deserves an average one. I don't know whether my work will be a success in Russia, but I already have a success—the only one in which I take pride—your approval. Of course I'm not so stupid as to take everything that Begas[3] says literally, but I'm satisfied enough that you apparently liked it. And so, take advantage of your stay in Berlin, may it be useful for you, and bring happiness to those who will see you and be near you.

Here's my opinion of Levirey's proposal: I'd prefer another opera, in spite of the marvellous third act, but if there's no other choice—take it. In the final analysis I'm certain that it will amuse you, and the good Berliners will be happy. But take steps to make certain that *i cani* [dogs] don't perform with you. Viardot would also prefer an opera other than *Otello*.[4]

My uncle[5] has been writing insane letters, he's been mortally offended by me, considers himself "a captive," has locked himself in his room and refuses to see anyone. You understand how much my finances are suffering because of this and how essential my presence in Spasskoye is. But my foot?!!

Letter 193 (1770). To N.A. Kishinsky.[1]
March 14/26, 1867. Moscow.

Moscow.
Crown Office Building on
Preschistenky Boulevard.
Tuesday, March 14, 1867.

Dear Nikita Alexeyevich, I'm still in bed, but I'm better; the fever has passed, and in a week I'll be quite recovered. I wrote my uncle[2] a long letter in which I ask him not to wait for my arrival but immediately to transfer the management to you and to turn over to you all documents, books, bills, in a word—the entire operation. I don't consider it necessary to repeat that you need not demand any accounting; just accept what is handed over to you and draw up an inventory. I wrote my uncle that he can stay at Spasskoye as long as he sees fit, and that the people who personally serve him and his household will remain on my account for the time being. As far as other people, that will depend on your directions. I ask you, besides the inventory, to draw up a list for me of the old house serfs who remain my dependents. I also wish you and my uncle to determine immediately which horses, cows, and so on remain and which ones leave; also direct your attention to the wheat now in the storehouses and don't let anyone take advantage of the change in power to dispose of it on the side; I also ask my uncle to help you in this. I also wrote my uncle about sending the money from the office here, since I need it. Write immediately about how my uncle received you and what's happening in Spasskoye.[3] I assume that you have settled in the wing. Did you find the papers about which I spoke to you, and have you sent them to me?
I send you my cordial regards and remain

Your devoted

Iv. Turgenev.

37

Letter 194 (1782). To Pauline Viardot.[1]
March 22/ April 3, 1867. Moscow.

Moscow.
Prechistenky Boulevard.
Crown Office Building.
Wednesday (March 22), April 3, 1867.

Alea jacta est [the die is cast], dear Mme Viardot. I'm not going to
Spasskoye. I couldn't do that any sooner than in two weeks, and by then the
roads here will be impassable, and I don't wish to stay in Russia so long;
and besides which, I'm finally beginning to receive sensible letters from my
uncle: he's made his peace with the necessity of transferring the reins of
power into other hands. My manager also informs me that he is finally
beginning to feel like the master: he apparently found unspeakable chaos
there. My presence wouldn't be of any great use—my uncle would like to
see me, and I myself would be sincerely happy to fulfill his wish, but it's
impossible. I write him very long letters every day and I hope that he'll be
satisfied that way. I see that I'll have to work a great deal—my uncle has run
the ship so firmly aground that it will take a long time to move it... For the
first two years I'll have to urge my Muse on quite a bit; it's a good thing that
literature still provides an income. I think that in my manager I've hit upon
a sensible and energetic person.

And so, here are my plans: if nothing prevents me, I'll stay here until
Monday, April 8. I'll finish correcting the proofs,[2] take ten copies under my
arm, and collect the money from Katkov; I'm giving *two* public readings—I
couldn't avoid it—*on Saturday,* in aid of the Galician Ruthenians, whom
our society supports against the attacks and intrigues of Austrians and
Poles; *on Sunday* at the "Society of Friends of Russian Literature"—I've
belonged for ten years and haven't yet read a thing for them; in a word,
there was no way out. I'll leave for Petersburg on Monday and arrive there
Tuesday. *On Thursday*—another reading, and once again public, for our
Society for the Assistance of Writers in Need—Annenkov made me
promise; *on Friday* I'll be on the road again—headed for Berlin. Sunday
morning I'll go from the train station to the hotel "England," in the evening
back to the train station, and on *Monday,* April 15, if the Lord allows me to
live until then, at 3:30 PM I'll be on the narrow-gauge to Baden... Silence!
Silence! Don't wake the bad-luck cat—after all, he sleeps with one eye
open.

Speaking of bad luck, I should tell you that my leg, which tortured me
again for two days, now seems to be returning to the same rather
unsatisfactory status quo in which it was a week ago. If only I can get back

to Baden one way or another!.. I'm certain that I'll soon recover, and if not, I'll easily take comfort in that.

You're as good as an angel, dear Mme Viardot—you spoil me with your enchanting little letters, which light up everything around for me. Your letters are a great boon, since if you feel sad about the tremolo of which you write, consider that I'm not at all happy here either. We'll have to take some sort of measures, however, in the event that E.[3] comes in *June;* the more I think about it, the more I'm persuaded of the impossibility of Louise's[4] staying in Baden, where nothing could soften the blow.

Long live Gérard[5] the Laggard! Thanks to him the music world will have the chance to enjoy those little masterpieces (I insist on that word) for viola and piano. I think that the poem by Lenau[6] that you transcribed is practically the only one of his poems that I like, and I'm very curious to hear what music those words evoked in you. Write something else, too, so that when I return I'll have new things to listen to... When I return!.. I won't believe it until at least two days after I arrive at Schillerstrasse, 277.

A thousand cordial regards to everyone, beginning with Viardot. I kiss your hands tenderly. *Until we meet on April 15!* Der Ihrige [your]

I.T.

Letter 195 (1803). To A.A. Fet.
March 31/ April 12, 1867. Moscow.

Moscow.
Crown Office Building,
Prechistensky Boulevard.
Friday, March 31, 1867.

So, dear Afanasy Afanasievich, we didn't get to see each other after all! Tell me now that there's no such thing as fate. If I hadn't been seized by a cold in Serpukhov—from which I haven't yet recovered—I would definitely have come to Spasskoye—if I didn't break my neck on the road! And how much I wanted to see you—to argue with you, with wheezing, yelling, squealing, and asphyxiation—properly—and with a constant feeling of friendship and good will toward the arguing party. What can be done! Perhaps we'll see each other next year—either in the country—but only in the summer—I won't be a winter traveller to Russia anymore—or in

Baden, if a lucky star should whirl you there! Since arriving in Russia I've been unleashing (this is a Gallicism, like the Gallicisms in *my* translations of Perrault, which I saw *for the first time* only when it was already in print—and learned that there are grey horses *with dapples*—tsk . . . tsk! this is a secret!),[1] I've been unleashing a horrifying amount of activity:[2] I'm being published (we'll see what you have to say about my povest in the March issue of *The Russian Messenger*—you'll probably criticize it),[3] I'm selling my new edition,[4] I've been giving public and private readings, I've been ill (my leg has abdicated completely),[5] I'm introducing a new estate manager . . . [6] By the way, so as to be done with this topic once and for all—so that there be no further discussion of this between us, and so that you won't have occasion to call me rabid, as you did in your letter to Botkin—here are the decisive figures that forced me to make the aforesaid decision—in Lapidarschrift [concise form]:

In 11 1/2 years I received	122,000 silver rubles!
Of which the capital sum was	62,000 silver rubles!!
The income was	60,000 silver rubles!!!
Which makes per annum	5,500 silver rubles!!!!

I find that for an estate of 5500 desyatinas, of which 3500 are absolutely free, that income is too small!!!! Since, in addition, the estate is falling apart, and there are no cattle, and my brother[8] receives up to 20,000!!!!!

My uncle is 75!!!!!!

I made up my mind to hire a different manager!!!! Let's assume, for the sake of argument, that I'm a horrible criminal—but all the same, it doesn't follow that I should immediately be cursed, the more so as I've made my uncle's future secure and am not demanding any accounting from him at all.

Sapienti sat [a word to the wise is sufficient]!

Well, and in closing, what can I tell you? I saw Polonsky in Petersburg: he's as nice as ever and sends you his regards—he's married to an attractive, quiet girl with dark eyes.[9] I won't mention literary squabbles—you don't like them. But what weather! Lord have mercy! And they write me that in Baden everything is in full bloom.

I'm leaving today for Petersburg (where I'm staying at Botkin's)—and on Monday for Baden . . . When can I expect you? Give my regards to your dear wife. I clasp your hand firmly.

Your Iv. T.

Baden-Baden.
Schillerstrasse, 1867.[1]
Saturday, May 11/ April 29, 1867.

Dear Countess,

I was in St. Petersburg for such a short time on my way back from Moscow that—to my great regret—I didn't have a chance to see you. I very much wanted to have a chat with you so as to strengthen the impression that our single meeting made on me—one of quiet, calm, and health—besides which, the renewal of our relations gave me pleasure. I don't know whether this letter will catch you while you're still in Russia—or in St. Petersburg. I don't know anything at all of your plans; but I'm writing you in any case, since to my desire to keep in touch with you is added the opportunity to direct you toward a good deed. What can I do? Of all the doors at which I—a poor Christian, following the Gospel rule, have knocked, yours always opened more easily and often than anyone else's.[2] This is what the matter involves:

It may be that soon after you receive this letter a young acquaintance of mine, Karl Karlovich Akhenbakh, will present himself to you. He was a teacher at a military school in Tambov for 16 years; when the military school was closed, he lost his position and didn't even receive the year's salary to which he had a right; he has gone blind, and to top everything off, on the way from Tambov to Moscow his travelling bag with all his possessions was stolen. I'm enclosing his letter to me: you'll learn all of this in detail from it. He's a thoroughly worthy and honest person who is on the brink of perishing. As you'll see from the letter, he requests that I afford him the opportunity to do translations: but besides the fact that such work is very poorly renumerated, how could he, with his poor eyesight, possibly work with a pen in hand? I don't know how to help him—and therefore I'm turning to you, dear Countess! Can't you think of something or find something for him? The female mind is inventive when it comes to charity—and yours especially so. Give him some advice. Akhenbakh belongs to that group of people who struggle with misfortune to the end: but misfortune knows very well how to defeat such people as well. Help him if you can: he deserves your sympathy.[3]

Write me a word or two: as you know, I have no intention of leaving here for a while.

I won't ask your opinion of my novel:[4] you probably haven't read it, and if you have, you didn't like it—I'm sure of that. Write me of yourself,

your husband, and your plans for the summer. All of that interests me—
because I'm sincerely attached to you—about which fact I hope you have
no doubt.

I clasp your hand cordially and remain

Your devoted

Iv. Turgenev.

Letter 197 (1838). To D.I. Pisarev.[1]
May 10/22, 1867. Baden-Baden.

Baden-Baden.
Schillerstrasse, 7.
Wednesday, May 10/22, 1867.

Dear Dmitry Ivanovich,

I spent such a short time in Petersburg on my way back from Moscow
that I didn't have a chance to see you. I regret that, because I'm certain that
after breaking what the French call the first ice, we would have spoken
frankly, if not actually agreed with each other. I think highly of your talent,
I respect your character, and since I don't share certain of your convictions,
I would have explained to you the reasons for my disagreement—not in the
hope of persuading you—but with the aim of directing your attention to
certain consequences of your activity. I don't know when I'll be in
Petersburg again; if you should have occasion to take a trip abroad and get
as far as Baden, it would truly be a pleasure for me to see you.

A few days ago I wondered to myself about what sort of impression
Smoke must have made on you and your circle—whether you were angered
by the scene at Gubaryov's and whether those scenes had thrown a veil over
the whole povest's meaning for you.[2] According to all the news reaching
me, *Smoke* arouses near-hatred and contempt for me in the majority of
readers; two or three articles that I had the chance to read were in the same
spirit. I can give myself credit that

"Mit keiner Arbeit hab' ich geprahlt—
Und was ich gemalt hab'—hab' ich gemalt—"
[I've never boasted of any work—
and what I've depicted—I've depicted][3]—

42

and for that reason I am not put out; I know in advance that I won't be upset if you were to speak disapprovingly, but I will take that fact into consideration—since although on the one hand I know that any talent, just as any tree, brings forth only that which is appropriate for it, on the other hand, I don't have any illusions as to my talent—my tree—and I see in it a quite ordinary, barely engrafted Russian apple tree. In any case, your opinion—if it is stated and motivated—will be of interest to me.

I would like to receive *The Cause*[4] here—and therefore I ask you to do me a favor and arrange for that journal to be sent to me at the above-stated address; you'll receive the money from Pavel Vasilievich Annenkov after you send him the attached note.

In closing, I wish you all the best and beg you to accept the assurance of my absolute devotion.

Your most humble servant,

Iv. Turgenev

Letter 198 (1851). To A.F. Pisemsky.
May 31/June 12, 1867. Baden-Baden.

Baden-Baden.
Schillerstrasse, 7
(no longer 277).[1]
Wednesday, June 12/ May 31, 1867.

Dear Alexey Feofilaktovich, you can easily take my word for it when I tell you that your letter made me very happy, the more so as up until now I've heard nothing but censure of my novel,[2] even from my friends, and the thought that perhaps I'd hatched a freak was arising involuntarily in my mind. People who have always been well-disposed toward me up until now have heaped abuse on me; F.T. Tyutchev composed a poem apropos of this . . .[3] Your approval was all the more pleasant for me: you're not the sort of person who thinks one thing and says something else; and if there is vitality in my work, the work will weather all these manifold attacks and contribute its bit of usefulness.

Everything that you say about the exhibit and about the "fraternal Slavs" seems quite accurate to me, but it's difficult to swim against the current—and when everyone's yelling you can't make out anything.[4] Let's watch what happens when it's time to move on to business. *The Voice* didn't find anything more practical to do than to recommend that the Slavs immediately adopt a common literary language, probably Russian.[5] Otherwise it really is a shame: the brothers are brothers, and they criticize the Germans, but they're forced to speak German among themselves.

My leg is almost completely back to normal, and I've already been hunting once and killed a wild goat. The weather here is marvellous, and after all sorts of calamities, my house finally is being put in order—just like my leg. I hope that next year—if you keep your promise and visit Baden— I'll be able to offer you lodging under my own roof.

The Emperor passed through here today and we all went to meet him at the railway. He seems to me to have lost weight. What a hideous outrage, that Parisian-Polish shot![6]

Send your plays to me here as soon as it's possible from the point of view of censorship.[7] I haven't been writing anything yet, but I'm thinking of a short preface to the separate edition of *Smoke,* in which I'll say a few words about the Slavophiles.[8]

Please give my regards to your dear wife[9] and lovely children; I embrace you cordially and wish you all the best.

Your sincerely loving

Iv. Turgenev

Letter 199 (1864). To Jules Hetzel.[1]
June 17/29, 1867. Baden-Baden.

Baden.
Schillerstrasse, 7.
Saturday, June 29, 1867.

My dear friend,

I was going to send you as my *note* on Paris that it's a beautiful city located on the Seine, when I discovered the following passage in an old letter of mine: "What attracts foreigners to Paris, especially young people (whether they realize it or not) is the secret desire to discover at last the true answer to the human enigma. Paris doesn't provide it more than any other city; but not having found it there, one no longer looks for it anywhere, and one gives oneself over to skepticism, indifference, and resignation. Every Parisian, the most flighty as well as the most important, carries that resignation, mute and as if ashamed of itself, concealed in the depths of his being, and this resignation, to those who are capable of understanding, speaks more than can the sorrowful or violent declamations of misanthropes."

I don't know what I caught there—a fish or a toad, but I'm sending it to you. If the phrasing seems a little lame to you, put it back on its feet and voilà. It's possible that this "observation" that I've made isn't correct, but it will be only one of the notes in the recital.

Viardot and I are going to set to work on the translation of the short story "The Brigadier " of which I spoke to you and which I'll send you as soon as it's finished. Until then I clasp your hand cordially.

I. Turgenev

Letter 200 (1875). To A.P. Golitsyn.[1]
July 14/26, 1867. Baden-Baden.

Baden.
Schillerstrasse, 7.
July 26, 1867.

Monsieur,

I've just looked through the first chapters of *Smoke* in *The Correspondent*[2]—and I'll tell you frankly that I haven't been able to free myself of a painful feeling created by seeing my name placed beneath a work that abounds—I must say—in mistakes and absurdities. You did not take into account the corrections that I hastened to send you through the agency of M. Mérimée:[3] therefore it was useless for you to send me the proofs. I don't object to the omissions, softened expressions, and so on, that you considered necessary, but I cannot allow myself to be made to say black where I say white. How can you want me to accept such absolute nonsense

45

as this—p. 691, line 3—instead of "Cure me—I'm dying of disease and weakness" one finds "I'm dying . . . of an abundance of goods!!" On another one—p. 693, line 11 from the bottom—instead of saying "a good pupil sees his teacher's errors, but maintains a respectful silence, for those errors themselves provide a salutary lesson," it reads "a good *professor* sees his *pupil*'s errors, etc.," so that it's Russia who is the professor and Europe the pupil!.. And that in the mouth of Potugin! I'd never finish if I were to list all the mistakes in this translation. But you need only to take a look at the proofs that I sent to M. Mérimée. I also confess that in view of the doubts of which you inform me in your latest letter as to the effect which might be produced on mothers of families by a certain page concerning the relations between Potugin and Irene, I don't understand what moved you to translate my novel: the relations between Litvinov and Irene are much more explicit—and I don't see any way to tone them down unless I were to make changes so complete as to distort the entire narrative. I'm sorry to say it, Monsieur, but if I had been able to foresee all of this, I believe that I would have asked you to abandon your idea. If it's possible, it would perhaps be best to limit it to the published fragment. In any case, Monsieur, I ask you most insistently from now on to send me the proofs in time and to take into consideration my corrections, which never concerned anything but the meaning of words and phrases.

Please accept, Monsieur, the assurance of my respect.

I. Turgenev

Letter 201 (1887). To P.V. Annenkov.
August 28/ September 9, 1867. Baden-Baden.

Baden-Baden.
September 9 / August 28, 1867.

Dear Annenkov! Not without secret trepidation, I've been expecting news from you all this time, and I was doubly glad for the letter that has now come. It was a difficult and serious business, but now, thank God, all of that is over, and from the bottom of my heart I congratulate you and your wife, to whom I ask you please to convey the expression of my most cordial affection. I hope that the battle is won completely, and that all that's left is to make good use of the victory. So now you're a father, the father of a child[1] given to you by your beloved wife. I never experienced such good fortune and I'm happy that it's been granted to a person whom I love . . . A new life is starting for you rather late; but in the very lateness of this appearance I see the promise of its long duration . . . Once more I congratulate you sincerely.

I'm healthy, I go hunting, and write French librettos for operettas that Mme Viardot sets to music—it's wonderful![2] One of them, bearing the title *Trop de femmes,* had such a success that even the Queen of Prussia wished to see it. The performance is taking place in my new house, in which I'm not living—thanks to my uncle, who is fleecing me not only of the original sum, but of the interest as well on a *moneyless* promissory note that I gave him (in the event of my death)—how can I even think of setting up a new household![3] A small stage has been set up in the main room, and the dramatis personae are Mme Viardot's children, her pupils, and so on. It's fun both for her and for me, and other people apparently don't find it boring either. That's the extent of my literature for now. I must tell you an enchanting fact. In issue No. 34 of *Revue et Gazette musicale,* from August 25th, are the following lines: "Ce type vivant de la critique éclectique parlée, ce *prodigieux* symphoniste de la causerie *Botkine,* qui enseignait, au grand enthousiasme de ses amis, les relations de plaisir existant entre le danse des vagues et celles des jeunes Espagnoles aux puissant mollets . . . " [That living model of eclectic verbal criticism, that *prodigious* symphonist of colloquy, *Botkin,* who, to the great enthusiasm of his friends, informed them of the relations of pleasure existing between the dance of the waves and that of young Spanish girls with powerful calves . . .] and so on. Well, what do you think of that?[4] That "prodigieux symphoniste" is now in Paris. In closing, I embrace you and your family and await further news.

Your Iv. Turgenev

47

Letter 202 (1898). To V.F. Odoyevsky.[1]
September 17/ 29, 1867. Baden-Baden.

Baden.
September 29, 1867.

My dear Prince,

The bearer of this letter, Mr. Eugene Schuyler[2] of New York, recently named to the American Consulate in Moscow, is very interested in everything Russian, knows our language, and recently translated my *Fathers and Sons.* I am happy to be able to grant him the good fortune of knowing you, and I count on our long-standing friendship as a guarantee of your cordial reception of him. I thank you in advance and beg you to accept the assurance of my feelings of affection and devotion.

I. Turgenev

Letter 203 (1912). To P.V. Annenkov.
October 7/19, 1867. Baden-Baden.

Baden-Baden.
October 7/ 19, 1867.

Dear Pavel Vasilievich! The French writer, M. Du Camp,[1] with whom I am on terms of friendship and to whom I am obliged to a certain extent, lives here. He wrote a novel, *Les Forces Perdues,* and when he learned that I liked it, he asked me to facilitate its translation into Russian, which I promised to do (all of this took place last winter). In March I saw Ye. M. Akhmatova,[2] the publisher of *Anthology of Translations* and so on, and agreed to write a preface to the translation, which was to appear in her publication and which, as far as I know, has been ready for a long time. But because of my habitual laziness I only just finished the preface (secretly blushing, I told Du Camp that I'd sent it off a long time ago), and now I'm forwarding it to you. Read this piece and after making corrections, if you need to, take it to Miss Akhmatova and present it to her with the greatest apologies on my part. I'm writing her about this preface and about the fact that I give you the right to make changes if the need arises. Please don't lose any time and ask Miss Akhmatova to hasten the printing, since I'm dying for shame before Du Camp. I'll be very, very obliged if you do this.

The enclosed poster will give you an idea of my activity. The eleventh performance was graced by the presence of the King and Queen of Prussia, the Crown Prince and Crown Princess of the same, the Grand Duke and Duchess of Baden, the Duke and Duchess of Darmstadt, the Prince and Princess Wilhelm of Baden (Maria Nikolayevna's daughter), and other extraordinary personages, ministers, generals, and so on. Well, what do you think of that, sir? This whole group, of course, was attracted by the enchanting Mme Viardot's music; I hasten to add that I didn't *sing,* but only acted, and not as horribly as one might have expected. The guests were satisfied, and Craquamiche's speech,[3] in which His Majesty Napoleon III's speeches are lightly parodied, even produced a hearty laugh on the august lips of King Wilhelm. Go ahead and make fun of us after this!

All in all, everything is fine; only the weather continues to be awful, and hunting is almost impossible. Send me Reshetnikov's *People of Podlipov*[4] and *The Notes of a Hunter from Eastern Siberia*[5] if you can. I'm still not receiving *The Cause.* Give my regards to your dear wife and all our friends. I clasp your hand firmly.

Your Iv. Turgenev

Letter 204 (1943). To Ludwig Pietsch.[1]
November 29/ December 11, 1867. Baden-Baden.

Baden-Baden, Schillerstrasse, No. 7,
December 11, 1867.

My dear friend,

I just learned that Stuhr's Publishers and Booksellers in Berlin is planning to publish a number of my novels in Russian. Formally, it has the right to do so. But I can't at all understand why it is doing this. Many a Russian book has been published abroad, but then it was always a forbidden book that was suppressed within Russia itself.[2] Here that is not the case, however; my novel, in a more complete form, just came out in Moscow.[3] Consequently, this edition will not be advantageous for Stuhr's publishing house; and it could harm me, because my Moscow publisher has already spoken of a second edition, since the first is already sold out. Couldn't you please be so kind as to see those gentlemen and explain all of this to them? You could present this letter as your credentials.

Pardon me for the inconvenience, but you're a good friend.

My regards,

I. Turgenev

P.S. Please respond in any case.

Letter 205 (1944). To A.I. Herzen.
November 30/ December 12, 1867. Baden-Baden.

Baden-Baden.
Schillerstrasse, 7.
December 12, 1867.

Dear Alexander Ivanovich, I received and read through your French *Bell*. Thank you for remembering me. As for your article—this is an old argument between us; as I see it, Europe is neither so old, nor Russia so young as you imagine: we're all in the same bag and I can't foresee any "special new word" for us. But God grant that you live a hundred years— and die the last Slavophile—and write intelligent, amusing, paradoxical, and profound articles that one won't be able to help reading to the end. I only regret that you've found it necessary to clothe yourself in garb that doesn't suit you at all.[1] Believe me—or don't—just as you like—but articles are useless when it comes to any so-called *influence* on the European public...[2] Hic Rhodus, hic salta [Here Rhodus, jump here]...[3] If a great Russian painter were to appear, for instance, his picture would be better propaganda than thousands of discourses on the artistic capabilities of our tribe. People are altogether a coarse breed and they have absolutely no need for justice or impartiality: but if you hit them in the eye or the pocket...that's another matter. But perhaps I'm mistaken and you're

50

right: we'll see. In any event, the moment has scarcely been well chosen: right now the real question is which is going to win out—science or religion, and what has Russia to do with this?

Since the first copy of *Smoke* didn't reach you, I want to try again, and I'm sending you a copy of the separate Moscow edition in which all the omissions due to Katkov's censorship are reinstated.[4] You won't like the book itself, of course, but on page 97 there's the biography of General Ratmirov, which may cause you to smile.

Farewell; let me know about yourself and your family. I'm living here like an anchorite, and unfortunately, I can't go hunting. My knee hurts as the result of a clumsy movement. Be well.

Iv. Turgenev

Letter 206 (1968). To Ya. P. Polonsky. January 13/25, 1868. Baden-Baden.

Baden-Baden.
Schillerstrasse, 7.
January 13/25, 1868. Saturday.

Well, dear Yakov Petrovich, this time you've distinguished yourself— all three poems are marvellous—and, as they say, without a single false note—with the exception of one line in the third one, "The Whirlwind"— which I like almost best of all, even it it is written, as you say, to order, namely, the line "I'll give you my *little* mouth to kiss" stuck in my throat— please do me a favor and change it—it's awfully saccharine and inadequate.

There's no reason for you to thank me for my frankness: how could I not be frank with you, when you're the only one in our time in whom the flame of divine poetry still burns. I don't count Count A. Tolstoy or Maykov; Fet has completely exhausted his talent; and there's no point even in mentioning the Messrs. Minayev[1] and the like, since their teacher, Mr. Nekrasov, is himself a poet only if you stretch things and use trickery; a few days ago I tried to read through his collected poems . . . No! Poetry never so much as spent the night there—and I threw that crumpled papier-mâché made with spiced vodka into the corner. You alone can and should write verses; of course, your position is all the more difficult in that since you don't possess a colossal talent, you can't step on the throat of our muddle-headed public—and therefore you have to spend your time in the dark and cold, rarely encountering sympathy—doubting yourself and losing heart; but you can console yourself with the thought that the good things that you've written and will write will not die, and that if you're "a poet for the few," those few will never disappear.

We won't come back to "the hill" again; as for "The Snake," I nonetheless repeat: you must *maintain* the comparison; otherwise it would be better to speak without beating around the bush and portray the human figure itself.[2] (By the way, I can't help protesting against one of your examples: I didn't know Zmeyeva—but you made quite a choice with the *genius,* Alexander Bakunin, whom not everyone recognized as a remarkable idiot only because he was an odd and confused idiot—and in such cases we always suspect profundity: a person hems and haws because his tongue doesn't work very well, and we think, "Oh! How many thoughts he has! So many that he can't even express them all!")

The idea in "A Pagan's Dream" is fine, but the form...the form... everything is unravelled in all directions, like a bast bag (sorry, but I don't give Strakhov's[3] opinions any credence—and not because he criticizes me, but because he's a Slavophile—and those gentlemen may be eagles when it comes to politics, but in esthetics they're first-class dullards). I'm not about to demand of you Goethe's objectivity and calm, but what you can do, you should.

Please send me a line to replace the "little mouth." As for literary activity in general, everyone ought to follow his own path steadfastly and unswervingly, while quietly keeping his eyes open around him as much as possible. The results will show you whether you're right—but for the meanwhile keep rereading Pushkin's "The Poet": "Poet, don't treasure the people's love," and so on.

Regards to your wife. I embrace you.

Iv. Turgenev

Letter 207 (1993). To N.S. Turgenev.
February 6/18, 1868. Baden-Baden.

Baden-Baden.
Schillerstrasse, 7.
February 6/18, 1868.

Dear brother, I imagine that you were surprised by the telegram that I sent you today, but read this letter through and you'll find out what the problem is. Uncle[1] is continuing to behave villainously towards me (I can't think of any other words for it) and has apparently sworn to ruin me. You are aware of all the sacrifices that I've made in order to satisfy him, the sale of my home here, and so on. I sent him a Rothschild note of exchange c/o Akhenbakh in the amount of 13,000 silver rubles, and my estate manager was supposed to deliver an additional 3500 rubles to him. That would seem to be a decent sum of money from a person to whom he, of course, never loaned so much as a kopeck. And despite all of that, Nikolay Nikolayevich, as far as I can tell from a telegram that I received, refused to take Rothschild's note of exchange, since he obviously wants to fleece me of the interest as well as those promissory notes that I, like a fool, gave him out of the kindness of my heart—and of which one has even been declared *disputable* (i.e., on which he's already received the money in full). Can you imagine my position? The telegram asks me what to do with the note of exchange. After long thoughts and at the advice of my local bank, I've decided to send a *second copy of the note,* here appended, care of you, since you're in Moscow and know Akhenbakh, and to destroy the *original* that has Uncle's name on it and which is now in the hands of my manager, Nikita Alexeyevich Kishinsky—i.e., to erase everything written on it and return it to me, which I've already asked him to do. (Just now it occurred to me that it would be better to send that *original* to you, so that you could show Akhenbakh that it's been invalidated—and receive the 13,000 rubles from him which are written, as you can see, à vue [to be paid upon demand].) After you've received the 13,000 rubles, the following commissions will begin for you. You'll need to write immediately to (a) Ivan Petrovich Borisov (his address is Mtsensk) and (b) my estate manager, N.A. Kishinsky. Borisov is a wonderful person and a genuine friend, and he's been a real help in this whole business. Notify them both that you have the 13,000 and that it's waiting to be picked up. I can't ask you to go to Mtsensk, the more so as the railroad only goes as far as Tula, but you'll find a safe way to deliver that important sum into the hands of Borisov and Kishinsky. In case of need, I'm certain that Borisov, out of friendship for me, will be willing to make a trip to Moscow with Kishinsky. Then I'll have to enter into a lawsuit in which after declaring that the promissory notes which I gave to Nikolay Nikolayevich did not have any monetary value, I'll add that I am willing to pay them off, with compensation even, since I'm proposing 16,500 rubles instead of 14,000—but that I refuse to pay the interest. I'll probably lose—but at least I'll try to defend my property to the very end and publicly expose my malefactor's greed and lack of principle. Who would think that I could expect this from a person who . . . But what's the point of talking about it? *That* uncle is dead as far as I'm concerned, and this new one is an alien, avaricious plunderer, and that's all.

And so, with a low bow I beg you to extend your fraternal hand in this painful matter! (Note that by bringing proceedings against me for the recovery of the promissory note and putting a distrain on Spasskoye, N.N. is aiming to purchase my best estate at auction!!!) Notify me immediately, *in the first place,* of the receipt of this letter, (b) of the receipt of the *original* from Kishinsky, (c) of the receipt of the money from Akhenbakh, and (d) of your further determinations. In doing this you'll oblige me to the very grave in this, my bitter distress.

I embrace you and send my fond regards to Anna Yakovlevna.

Your brother,

Iv. Turgenev

P.S. When you receive the money it might be safer to keep it with the banker until it's sent off.

Letter 208 (2001). To P.V. Annenkov.
February 14/26, 1868. Baden-Baden.

Baden-Baden.
Wednesday, February 14/26, 1868.

Your letter found me still here, dear Pavel Vasilievich! I was detained in Baden by Viardot's very serious illness, which only two days ago took a decisive turn for the better . . . On Sunday, if everything works out, I'll leave for Paris for about eight days. But before that I want to have a chat with you. First of all, please give Korsh the enclosed letter—and ask him to publish it in *The St. Petersburg News*. I began to feel sorry for that poor unfortunate fellow whom they're kicking even after his death.[1] Secondly, I read both Tolstoy's novel and your article about it.[2] I'm not trying to flatter you when I tell you that it's been a long time since you wrote anything more intelligent or sensible; the whole piece testifies to its author's true and subtle critical perception, and only in two or three phrases is there any vagueness or any sort of awkwardness of expression. The novel itself aroused my lively interest: there are dozens of pages that are entirely remarkable, first-class—all the scenes of everyday life and the descriptive ones (hunting, sleighing at night, and so on); but the historical passages, which are the real reason for our readers' delight, are a puppet theater and charlatanism. Just as Voroshilov in *Smoke* throws dust in people's eyes by citing the latest words of science (without knowing either the first or second ones, which the conscientious Germans can't even imagine), so Tolstoy strikes the reader with the tip of Alexander's boot[3] or Speransky's[4] laugh, making him think that if he's even gotten down to these minor details, then he knows *everything* about it—when in fact he knows only the minor details. It's a trick, nothing more—but that's just what the public has fallen for. And one could say a great deal in regard to Tolstoy's so-called "psychology": there's no real development in a single character (which you noted very well), but there's the old habit of conveying the vacillations and vibrations of one and the same emotion or state, which he places so mercilessly in the mouths and consciousnesses of each of his heroes: I love, but really I hate, and so on and so forth. Oh, how tired and fed up I am with these quasi-subtle reflections and thoughts, these observations of one's feelings! Tolstoy either doesn't seem to know any other psychology or he purposely ignores it. And how painful are these premeditated, obstinate repetitions of one and the same trait—the little moustache on Princess Bolkonskaya's upper lip and so on. But along with all that there are things in the novel that no one in all of Europe but Tolstoy could write and which aroused the chill and fever of delight in me.

I've already written you that I've received all the journals safely, but the copies of the translation of Du Camp's novel still haven't turned up!![5]

Two articles by Mérimée about Pushkin were published in two issues of *Moniteur* around January 15th, New Style, definitely between the 10th and the 20th.[6] I clasp your hand cordially and remain

Your devoted

Iv. Turgenev.

Letter 209 (2016). To Pauline Bruère.[1]
March 1/13, 1868. Baden-Baden.

Baden.
Schillerstrasse, 7.
March 13, 1868.

Dear Paulinette,

Your letter isn't cheerful; but I had a certain presentiment of what you tell me. What is most important in such circumstances is to be able to persevere to the very end and at the same time to make a resolute decision when it's necessary. I don't doubt the courage of the two of you; but you must not build any more illusions.[2] We'll see what I can do.

I'll begin by telling you that I'll catch up on all my back payments to you by the end of the month; you may rely on that—as well as on my arrival around *March 20,* since Viardot is feeling better and better and his convalescence is under way. If my uncle had not acted so unworthily toward me, I would be able to pay your 50,000 francs; but I've just spent around 75,000 in order to redeem the promissory notes that I'd given him eleven years ago (without having received a sou from him) to be presented in the event of my death; and he not only presented them while I'm still alive, but made me pay the interest on the interest on the interest!!—that is, more than double. This blow was quite painful for me—and with the present state of affairs in Russia, my fortune has been rather shaken. I hope to put myself afloat again in a little while: but you can see for yourself that I can't even dream of making any outlays—and the delay in paying you had no other cause.

As for *fixing up* Gaston somewhere, I wish nothing better than to do everything in my power—and I'll take advantage of my stay in Paris to knock on all doors: unfortunately, I no longer live in France—and of course it's in France that we must find something. You can see that none of this is easy. In any event, be assured that I take the well being of the two of you in heart and that I'll do everything possible to contribute to it.

And so—au revoir within *ten days:* I'll write you as soon as I arrive in Paris. Take care of yourself and be prudent. I embrace both of you.

J. Tourguéneff

Letter 210 (2023). To Moritz Hartmann.[1]
March 9/21, 1868. Baden-Baden.

Dear friend, what you write about my book[2] made me very happy. You're right: this work has earned me more than a few enemies; but a single friend such as you outweighs a thousand of those enemies. And in the last analysis, every honest person is obliged to state what he considers to be the truth, even if it comes flying back and strikes him. It was with *Fathers and Sons* that I began to bring harm to my own cause; it may be that I am now the most unpopular person in all Russia: I've wounded national vanity— and *it* is even less forgiving than anything else. But no matter! Things will work themselves out! I haven't lost any weight over it.

But I don't think that *Smoke* is suitable for a German translation; the work is just too Russian. You can judge better about this, of course: but I still have great doubts.

I'm very pleased that you translated "The Diary of a Superfluous Man." A bit of real life is captured in that work. When you have the time, read "Anchar" in *Scènes de la Vie Russe* and let me know your opinion of it.

I'm going to Paris for a week, then I'll return to Baden, and at the end of May I leave for Russia. Will we by any chance see you here before that? That would be really wonderful! The entire Viardot family sends you fond regards; I clasp your hand and send my greetings to your dear wife.

Your I. Turgéneff

Letter 211 (2031). To Pauline Viardot.[1]
March 15/27, 1868. Paris.

Friday, midnight (March 27, 1868).

Theurste Freundin [dearest friend], this evening I was at the Théâtre Lyrique and heard the first three acts of *Rigoletto* with Schröder.[2] Before talking about it, I can't restrain myself from exclaiming: "Oh, how that theater has come down in the world—the theater where the noble strains of *Orfeo* used to resound!"[3] Now it's only a tertiary provincial theater (all the people sitting around me, both men and women, had dirty hands and black nails, and the most refined of them were cleaning their nails with toothbrushes). The tenor Puget[4] would be hissed off the stage and beaten in Carpentras. And what costumes! What choristers! The twenty-year-old director waved his baton out of time with the music, and the musicians all went their own way. The auditorium was half empty. As for Mme Schröder, she's not bad on the stage: her acting is nothing much, her gestures are awkward and monotonous, her face lacks expression, her pronunciation is inexact, and the voice seems very, very small, especially at first, but she sings very well, very accurately, with refinement and great taste. That was too subtle for the audience and the singers bawling around her. Since all of M. Carvalho's[5] serious artists have moved over to the "Renaissance,"[6] she's been forced to sing literally every day. They say that she's in despair, preserves herself as much as she can, and only thinks about how to make it to the end. In order to tell you everything—she omitted her aria in the third act.

I wasn't able to stay to the end: I had promised to visit Mme Mohl,[7] that dear, strange hundred-year-old woman who nurses such tender feelings for me. She receives on Fridays. I saw Laugel, Lanfrey, Scherer, Dupont, White, and Renan.[8] I didn't want to be introduced to Renan. I don't care for that "refined" seminarian. His wife was also there; she's grown terribly fat. It turns out that my book is definitely a success, and they told me many nice things in this regard.[9] I made the acquaintance of Liebreich,[10] the well-known oculist, who is one of the most cultivated people I've ever met. He spoke to me of his teacher, Helmholtz,[11] with enthusiasm.

I had dinner at Pomey's[12] and told him the plot of your opera; he's anxious to receive his role as soon as possible and sing through it.[13] But what an impression Verdi's music made on me after Thomas'![14] I thought that I'd been carried out into the bright rays of the sun after wandering in a thick, damp fog. Here at least you have before you a musician rather than a gentleman who has managed not to give anything while using quite a bit of dubious material. Oh, the art of incompetent people! There's nothing more irritating or unbearable!..

Letter 212 (2057). To Ambroise Thomas.[1]
April 13/25, 1868. Baden-Baden.

Baden-Baden.
Thiergartenstrasse, 3.
April 25, 1868

My dear friend,

I'm writing you from my home in Baden, where I've been installed for several days—and where, by the way, I would be happy to offer you my hospitality if a favorable wind should carry you to our parts this year. I was only passing through Paris at the end of March and it was physically impossible for me to see my friends there: but for that, your door would have been one of the first at which I would have knocked. However, it's not only the desire to send my regards to you that has made me take pen in hand today; I have something to tell you that may interest you. While rummaging through his old papers, Viardot recently discovered a plan for a five-act opera libretto (provisionally entitled "The Scourge of Orchomène") which he tells me he showed you at one time and which, to judge by the letter that you inserted in the pages of the manuscript, you found very beautiful. The same libretto seems to have made the same impression on Augier,[2] who offered to set it to verse. That was in 1850; then everyone separated and everything was forgotten. Viardot read me his scenario after having made a few minor changes—and I must say that I was struck by it. It's certainly a magnificent subject for an opera. The third act (it takes place in the forest of Dodon) seemed to be especially admirable: it's *living antiquity;* and there is a variety of tones and colors in the whole work that ought to seduce a musician with imagination. I have no need to tell you that you now are the only maître in Europe who is equal to such a task, the only one not to shrink before antiquity. You must be overwhelmed by offers of libretti; however, the good ones are rare, and there has been no more talk of "Francesca da Rimini"[3] (fortunately, I think, since the subject, reduced to stage proportions, is nothing but a rather vulgar melodrama). Would you like Viardot to send you his scenario? Read it again and see whether something can't be done with it.[4]

Messrs. Barbier and Carré would be more than sufficient for the versification. As for Viardot, he would be enchanted to provide the chance for a new masterpiece to be created, and that would be quite sufficient for him.

Send me a word of answer and please believe in the sincerity of my long-standing friendship.

Iv. Turgenev

P.S. Are you still living at your old place?

Letter 213 (2063). To M.V. Avdeyev.[1]
April 18/30, 1868. Baden-Baden.

Baden-Baden.
Thiergartenstrasse, 3.
April 18/30, 1868.

I just received your letter, dear Avdeyev, and I'm answering you immediately, since the matter is obviously urgent. First of all, about your translations.[2]

In Paris translations are published stingily and unwillingly, because they sell poorly. Dickens is no match for us, and not a single one of his novels has come out in a second edition, while G. Droz's *Monsieur, Madame et Bébé* has already gone through 20 editions.[3] My books have been translated, but I personally have never received a single kopeck for them—and the translators—as an act of great kindness—were paid, and even then not always, 300 or 400 francs. As you can see, it's not a sparkling business venture. I don't even need to tell you that not one of my books has ever sold out in the first edition, i.e., 2400 copies. I've been asked to try to persuade the publisher Hetzel to publish an excellent translation of *Prince Serebrany*[4] *gratis,* and I doubt that he'll accept. There is an additional difficulty: your translation was done by a Russian and probably written (I know Mme Chekuanova[5]) in that Muscovite French that simply horrifies Frenchmen: absolutely everything will have to be redone, because we Russians don't even suspect what purists they are. Two of my books were translated that way, and the translators were told that in the future such work would not be accepted. For all of that, if you want me to try, send me the manuscript, and I'll do everything that depends on me: but I forewarn you that it will be a great indulgence on the part of the publisher if he prints it *gratis* (N.B. I didn't receive anything for *Smoke,* either, which is without doubt my most successful novel *from the point of view of sales in Paris);* if they give 300 francs—ce sera le bout du monde [that will be amazing]... Russian ladies who want to earn money ought to think up some other means. I repeat—send the manuscript: I'll do everything that I can.

Everyone in Russia is displeased with my "Story"[6]—yes, everyone, without exception. In such cases I always agree with the criticism willingly—but this time it seems to me that that little piece didn't deserve such indignation. And as if I'd even think of putting an *idea* in it! But I imagined that there was something in it besides an idea: apparently I was mistaken.

I'm setting out for Russia in a month—but I'll only stay in Petersburg two or three days: I have to spend about six weeks in Moscow and the country. It would be fine if we had the chance to see each other. Then I'm coming back here and I'll be here until the winter.

I like your novel less than your previous works.[7] It's well-written and intelligent—but it's too drawn out and one senses a sort of constant tension—and there are a few too many love scenes.

I share your opinion of *War and Peace* completely—but there are some first-class scenes in it.[8]

And so, send me your manuscript—be quick about it—and I clasp your hand cordially.

Your devoted

Iv. Turgenev

Letter 214 (2068). To P.V Annenkov.
May 7/19, 1868. Baden-Baden.

Baden-Baden.
May 7/19, 1868.

Dear Pavel Vasilievich! Let your imagination summon up the following picture: my whole house is flooded with girls, Mme Viardot's pupils, who are singing, dancing, and donning costumes. Today is the *first* rehearsal in costume for our third operetta.[1] I play the role of the *ogre* (!) in it—I don't sing, of course—I'm dressed all in red, with a huge red wig! The last few days there's been an incredible commotion: rehearsals every day, the maître de ballet from Carlsruhe is staging the pas—sets, the clatter of hammers. The Queen of Prussia keeps sending people to find out when we'll finally be ready. Noise, din, terrible sweating in twenty-five-degree heat,[2] laughter, gaiety—tra-ta-ta, tru-tu-tu!

Notwithstanding all this, I'm dashing headlong to Petersburg in three weeks and on the day after my arrival, God willing, I'll be sitting at your place in Lesnoye over a cup of tea.

The good-for-nothing Stromilov looked for you in Moscow![3] You did well in sending him 35 rubles—at least those five were left, because it's really the same as throwing them down the drain. How many such arch-empty, arch-unnecessary and arch-unfortunate creatures there are in Russia! You can't even count them all. Au revoir, my dear fellow. I embrace you and your wife. Give my regards to the Tyutchevs and to Kartashevskaya.

Your devoted

Iv. Turgenev

Letter 215 (2119). To N.S. Turgenev.
July 16/28, 1868. Baden-Baden.

Baden-Baden.
Thiergartenstrasse, 3.
Monday, July 16/28, 1868.

Dear Brother,

Your letter from Carlsbad found me at Maslov's in Moscow, in bed, seized by a malevolent attack of gout which, according to the doctors' assurances, I couldn't have expected so soon after last year's assault. This time, though, it was rather bearable and allowed me to reach here—with difficulty—three days ago—and as soon as I arrived I was again felled, which now bothers me less, since I'm home. I'll definitely have to take some waters next year. I spent two weeks at Spasskoye—and I can tell you, like

Marius, that I sat on the ruins of Carthage.[1] For this year alone "the unfortunate old man,"[2] the brigand, squeezed out of me 36,500 silver rubles in cash, cattle, carriages, furniture, and things (I had to pay a debt of almost 5,000 rubles for him)—not to mention the fact that the estate was left by him in chaotic, abominable disorder, that he didn't release anyone, deceived everyone, and so on. He was no longer at Katushishchi when I got there, and I'm very glad for that. The whole time that I was at Spasskoye I resembled a rabbit on the run: I couldn't show my nose in the garden without being rushed at and attacked from behind trees, under bushes, and practically from the earth—by household serfs, peasants, petit-bourgeois, retired soldiers, girls, women, the blind, the lame, neighboring landlords and their wives, priests, sextons, my own and others'—all of them shaggy from hunger, with mouths wide open, like baby jackdaws, tumbling down at my feet, crying with hoarse voices: "Little father, Ivan Sergeyevich! Save us ... save us, we're dying!" I finally had to save myself by fleeing so as not to remain without anything myself. Moreover, a terrible year is under way: the spring crops are a loss, the rye is as large as straw, but there's no grain in the ears. And what a view Russia now presents—that land which according to everyone's assurances is so rich! The roofs are *all* open, the fences have fallen down, there's not a single new building in sight except for taverns— the horses and cows are dead—the people emaciated—three coachmen could hardly lift my suitcase! There are clouds of dust everywhere—around Petersburg everything is on fire—the forests, homes, *the earth itself* ... All you see are people sleeping stretched out on their stomachs—there is debility, sluggishness, deep mud and poverty everywhere. This is a sad picture, but an *accurate* one.

I wish you and your wife a speedy and complete recovery. Will you by any chance drop in to Baden? Mr. Zhikharyov's[3] package (I don't know him, by the way) contains a photograph of Chaadaev's study: *8* such photographs have already been delivered to me, and I'm beginning to think that this is a mystification.

Write me here—I'll be here for a long time now. I embrace you and send my regards to your wife.

Your loving brother

Iv. Turgenev

Letter 216 (2144). To Ludwig Pietsch.[1]
September 26/ October 8, 1868. Baden-Baden.

Baden-Baden.
Thiergartenstrasse, 3.
Thursday, October 8, 1868.

What the devil has gotten into you, my dear friend? Allow me to scold you like that! Why on earth did you send me the 45 thalers? I could easily have waited a very, very long time. I'll keep them in a special pull-out drawer in case I need to make a return trip to Berlin.

Great events are taking place in Baden-Baden! First of all, Mr. Anstett[2] died four days ago and was buried the day before yesterday—Mrs. Minna Anstett is wearing black dresses and is a widow. She gave me a very vivid description of *how* her husband gave up his soul to the Lord (at this point came an amazing imitation of wheezing, gurgling, and stretching out of hand and foot)—and *how* the sound of the saw that penetrated Anstett's skull at the autopsy pierced her to the very marrow of her bones and so on. Now, of course, she's thinking about how to defend her will—that is, her husband's will, and I too, of course, will support her as a helper and Chevalier d'honneur [knight of honor]—even in court. But what onomatopeia! The bed creaking under her dying husband was not forgotten—and the fact was even pointed out that where the doctors were looking for water they found lard! The word *Speck* [lard] leapt from her mouth like a pistol shot: Ss-pe-ckkk! But all of this is just between the two of us, all right?

The other great event is Auerbach's[3] presence in Baden-Baden. I had to translate *my* preface to him—and to hear his witty and profound comments about it—it will appear in *print* (I really *just copied the German original*). There were remarks such as: "There, you see, you sensed *that* profoundly—and only you could have done that!" I sat there with a foolish look and just thought: "Oh, if you only knew!!" But silentium about this too.[4]

In general, everything is fine here. The libretto for my new operetta is almost worked out—one chorus has already been written. Viardot and I often go hunting—my gout has disappeared. The King and Queen of Prussia are here—they're very kind. At one of the matinees Mme Viardot sang a scene from *Alceste* divinely.[3]

I send regards to your family and friends. I clasp your hand warmly.

Your I. Turgéneff

Letter 217 (2153). To N.A. Kishinsky.
October 12/24, 1868. Baden-Baden.

Baden-Baden.
Thiergartenstrasse, 3.
Saturday, October 12/24, 1868.

Dear Nikita Alexeyevich,

Yesterday I received an anonymous letter full of accusation against you. Following my constant rule always to act directly and openly and to avoid misunderstandings, I'm enclosing an exact copy of the letter.[1] I hasten to add that I'm not sending you this letter so that you can acquit yourself—the majority of the accusations are too obviously absurd—but for your information. As for me, I'm not in the habit of changing my opinion of people on the basis of unfounded denunciations and gossip; only facts, clear and undeniable, could cause my trust to waiver, and I don't see so much as a trace of such facts.

Therefore I beg you to be absolutely calm and be as little worried as I am; this is all in the nature of things—and there's no reason to be surprised.

I send you my cordial regards and hope that things will move ahead as they should.

Your well-wisher,

Iv. Turgenev

Letter 218 (2167). To Charles Sainte-Beuve.[1]
November 12/24, 1868. Paris.

Paris. Hotel Byron, rue Laffitte.
Tuesday, November 24, 1868.

Monsieur,

Letters that I have received from Baden oblige me to leave this very evening and deprive me of the pleasure of having dinner with you. I need not tell you how much I regret this: such a lost opportunity is not one of those which one finds again or for which one is soon consoled.

I allowed myself—a while ago—to offer you some of my works: I cannot recall whether the two volumes here enclosed were among them. As you can see—just in case, I am not restraining myself; I am too honored by your reading me not to run the risk of seeming importunate.

Please believe the sentiments of sincere admiration

Of your devoted

J. Tourguéneff.

P.S. Please allow me to give you my winter address: Carlsruhe, Grand-duché de Bade, poste restante.

Letter 219 (2168). To Gustave Flaubert.[1]
November 12/24, 1868. Paris.

Paris. Rue Laffitte.
Hotel Byron. Tuesday, November
24, 1868.

My dear friend,

The cheese just arrived; I'm taking it to Baden, and with every bite we'll think of Croisset and of the lovely day that I spent there. I definitely feel that *we* have grown close to one another.

If all of your novel is as good as the excerpts that you read me—you will have created a masterpiece—mark my words.[2]

I don't know whether you've read the *little volume*[3] that I'm sending you; in any case, put it on one of the shelves in your library.

Give my regards to your mother[4] and allow me to embrace you.

Your J. Tourguéneff

P.S. My address is Carlsruhe, poste restante. Please be so kind as to send me a photograph of yourself. Here's one of me where I look rather unfriendly.

P.P.S. Choose another title. "A Sentimental Education" is bad.

Letter 220 (2174). To Ludwig Pietsch.[1]
November 19/December 1, 1868. Carlsruhe.

Carlsruhe.
Hotel Crown Prince.
Tuesday, December 1, 1868.

My dear friend,

A million thanks for the really marvellous photograph! I'll have it framed and from now on it will adorn my room.

Yes, my friend, I'm 50 years old—or, as you express it so euphemistically—I've lived the first half of my century, but I have no hope of seeing the end of the coming quarter. By the way, I know the year of my death quite accurately: 1881. My mother predicted it to me—in a dream—the same numerals as the year of my birth—1818—but reversed—oh, yes: I'll definitely die in 1881—if it doesn't happen sooner—or later. But 50 is a foul number! One must resign oneself.

Madame Viardot has taken a beautiful apartment—Lange Strasse, 235—with a large salon where music sounds marvellous. She has already sung once at a soirée at our *friend* Pohl's[2]—songs by Schubert and *Schumann* (One of them especially, "Longing," you have to hear!)—Lessing[3] was there—he looked like a retired Austrian major. Such a severe, robust, upright figure—and such a flabby, limp, wan talent! There was a painter there—Mr. von Breuer[4]—who spoke a great deal of Riefstahl and other Berlin artists—but who seems himself to be rather superficial and a not very genuine Hurluberlu. Do you know him? I haven't yet met Woltmann[6]—but I'll receive him with open arms, of course—just as I will Riefstahl. Didie[7] is working very zealously; for my birthday she made me a "Removal from the Cross"—an absolute miracle! That child has more imagination in her head than ten Lessings! All in all, everything is fine, but poor Viardot is aging greatly. Fortunately, Berthe[8] stayed in Baden!

I'm going to translate my gloomy and ugly story; my friends in Petersburg liked it.[9]

I'm very happy for your Weimar success; watch out—or you'll earn a noble title and the White Eagle, First Class.

I was upset by the sad news of your wife's poor health; let's hope that she'll soon improve!

Aglaya[10] will be on tour here in December—she is living in Berlin now, you know—if they stage *The Huguenots,* be sure to go see it!

Write me here poste restante and give my regards to all my good friends—Menzel,[11] especially Jul. Schmidt and his wife,[12] the Eckerts[13] (I

67

hope that you see them often, although you don't mention them), Begas, and the others.

I thank you once again and clasp your hand most intimately.

Your I. Turgéneff

Letter 221 (2207). To N.N. Rashet.
January 3/15, 1869. Carslruhe.

Carlsruhe.
Hotel Prince Max.
Friday, January 15, 1869.

Dear Natalya Nikolayevna—what can I say to you in answer to your letter? I'm very sorry for you—and my heart is filled with surprise: how is it possible to continue nursing the feelings of which you write? Can it really be that you don't see—and that I have to tell you—that for about ten years at least I've been a man who has finished with agitation and who lives—calmly and peacefully—on recollections alone—and the tranquil participation in the current of everyday events? How could buds blossom on a barren tree? You'll respond that you know all of this, that you don't ask for anything; and that things are fine for you even as they are: but in that case—whence the mournful note that sounds in everything that you say? I'm beginning to think that our meetings are harmful for you and that they undo you. I'm very, very sorry that your life has unfolded so sadly and become empty so soon—and that for filling it up you happened to find at hand such a dead lump as myself. I think it would be best not to indulge in these anxieties which, in actuality, leave nothing behind but grief.

I've ordered tickets for *The Minnesingers*[1] and will let you and Zhemchuzhnikov[2] know about the day of the performance.

I clasp your hand firmly and wish you all the best. Regards to Manya[3] and a kiss for Lenochka.[4]

Your devoted

Iv. Turgenev

Letter 222 (2230). To P.V. Annenkov.
February 9/21, 1869. Carlsruhe.

Carlsruhe.
February 9/21, 1869.

My dear friend Pavel Vasilievich, here at last is the piece on Belinsky.
You were probably beginning to think that I'd been crying wolf. I don't
know how it turned out, but I wrote diligently, rewrote everything twice,
and was moved more than a little ... Recollections came and remained ...
Whether I caught our deceased friend's image is a matter about which
you'll be better able to judge than I. And now begins a number of requests:
(1) The piece must be published without fail in the March issue (it's not too
late, I don't think)[1] in accordance with my agreement with Salayev.[2] (2)
You do the proofreading, and carefully, old boy! (3) I give you the full right
to throw out anything that you think necessary. (4) Be certain that the word
"Mr." stands before Nekrasov's name. (5) Notify me of the arrival of these
two packages and your opinion of their contents as well. Perceptive readers
will surely guess that the subject of discussion in the excerpts from
Belinsky's letters is Nekrasov; but I took only the most seemly passages,
and that was most of all in order to characterize Belinsky himself. If you
know the date of Belinsky's death, put it in; I wrote "May, 1848."[3]

Well, my dear fellow, I'm reading the continuation of *The Precipice*[4]
and my hair is falling out from boredom. I can't recall such hellishly
insufferable conversations in any literature. And all the characters—
Marfinka (I just got to Vera, but she's already rattled off about eight pages
of dialogue), and Mark, and everyone seem clichéd, and Goncharov—a
sort of god and tsar and poet of the cliché, deus loci communis [a god of the
commonplace]. Only two women are captured in a lively and original
way—Marina and the impossibly boring Leonty Kozlov's wife. Ivan
Alexandrovich[5] has grown out of date, out of date, and his philosophy—
fusty. And what an unfortunate figure Raysky is! Could there be anything
more hideous than his speechless ecstasy when Marfinka sits on his knees?
Oh, how fabricated all of that is!!

Your Iv. Turgenev

P.S. And so, Leontiev is still writing novels! About three years ago he
sent Mérimée, from his consulate, two of his novels to be translated, and
when the latter declined, Leontiev wrote him that he wasn't able to
appreciate him and that his things would outlive all of contemporary

literature! Qui a bu boira [he who has drunk will drink, i.e., one cannot change people].

P.P.S. Please retain the mention of the English Club[6] in conjunction with Mr. Nekrasov's name.

Letter 223 (2290). To Pauline Bruère.[1]
April 11/23, 1869. Baden-Baden.

> Baden.
> Thiergartenstrasse, 3.
> Thursday, 23 April 69.

My dear daughter,

I really am a terrible lazybones, and that's all the more inexcusable as the performance at Weimar was very lovely—a considerable success—and *The Last Sorcerer* made a most agreeable impression on us as well.[2] The Queen of Prussia and the Grand Duke and Grand Duchess of Weimar congratulated Mme Viardot—and for the next season the Grand Duke himself has ordered a real opera in three acts whose text I am to write.[3]

I'm enclosing an excerpt from the stagebill; you can't have so forgotten German that you can't read it and understand it. I'm also enclosing two photographs of Claudie and Marianne; I don't have one of Paul handy.[4]

I've been back here five days and right now I'm putting up the entire Viardot family: their house is being cleaned from top to bottom; this will go on for another three or four days. I won't be leaving Baden again until the winter.

I would be happy to see you in Baden, but *only* on one *condition:* that you not renew your past caprices and that you go to visit Mme Viardot. If you don't intend to do that, you would do better not to come to Baden—because that would be an offense that I could not tolerate. I repeat: *this condition is indispensable:* you yourself wouldn't want to put me in an impossible situation.[5]

In the meantime I wish you and Gaston all the best and I embrace both of you cordially.

> J. Tourguéneff

Letter 224 (2319). To Ludwig Pietsch.[1]
May 22/ June 3, 1869. Baden-Baden.

Baden-Baden.
Thiergartenstrasse, 3.
Thursday, June 3, 1869.

Dear Pietsch,

I want to stand on a par with the 19th century and I beg for an advertisement "misérablement" [pathetically]. Lend me a willing ear!

You write me that you're supposed to write reviews of *Fathers and Sons*. Good! Make one of them restrained and stern—but express in it your bewilderment and surprise at the fact that the Russian young generation took the figure of Bazarov as an offensive caricature, a libelous lampoon. And what is more, point out that I even conceived that rogue in a too heroically idealized manner (which is also *true)* and that Russian youth has a skin that's too sensitive. It's precisely because of Bazarov that I've been attacked with so much mud and filth (and continue to be so). So many insults and curses have fallen on my head (Vidocq, a Judas bought for gold, fool, ass, reptile, *spittoon*—those are the mildest things that have been said of me) that it would be a pleasure for me to show that other nations see this matter quite differently. I dare to ask you for such an advertisement because it corresponds completely to the truth and doesn't contradict your opinion in the least. If the opposite were the case, I wouldn't trouble you. If you wish to fulfill my request, do so quickly so that I may add a translation of the most important parts of the review to my literary memoirs, which are to be published soon.[2]

Dixi et animam meam salvavi [I spoke and saved my soul]!

Mme Viardot has been in bed since yesterday; she's caught a cold, but—thank God—it's nothing dangerous.

Greetings to all our friends—and take care.

Your I. Turgéneff

P.S. And what about the "Feuilletons"?[3]

71

Letter 225 (2334). To I.P. Borisov.
June 18/30, 1869. Baden-Baden.

Yesterday I travelled to Heidelberg, dear Ivan Petrovich, to see the renowned Doctor Friedreich[1]—and returned with disquieting news: he confirmed my local doctor's opinion—I have a heart disease—and I must avoid any tiring activity—and therefore give up hunting *forever!*[2] You can imagine how these words affected me... Hunting was the only thing I loved. Otherwise Friedreich threatens me with Panayev's fate—i.e., sudden removal *to the beyond.* With Panayev the disease revealed itself just as unexpectedly and late. All that I can do is take care of myself; it's a useful business, but not a cheerful one. So this is how the quadrille of my life has resolved itself. It could have been worse, though: I could have gone blind. Well, I'll take care of myself and won't speak of this.

I've been forced definitely to renounce the trip to Russia—and that's also the source of more than a little woe for me. Seeing you and chatting with you is just like candy for me. I sense that you love me—and though I have other good friends in Russia as well—they all have a shade of egoism, of which there isn't even a trace in you. Even Annenkov couldn't restrain himself and scolded me for my disease on the one hand, while on the other he showed signs of not believing it. As though inventing things of that sort could bring anyone pleasure! You write and tell me not to be despondent— and I'm trying to keep my spirits up, but I feel enveloped in a fog—the kind that we have in the summer, at the bottom of ravines just after the sun has gone down; you remember—a milky-white gelatine settles over everything—and how one wants to rush out of it as quickly as possible!

What literary plans were fermenting in me—true, they weren't robust—have come to a standstill, too. I haven't yet managed all my *Literary Memoirs.* Did you read my excerpt on Belinsky in *The Messenger of Europe*[3] and did you like it? I was very careful—and even at that I've been attacked for it.

I'm happy for Fet at his not having been rejected by his fellow district landowners.[4] Give him my regards and tell him how sorry I am that I won't get to see him and argue with him. Anyone who wants to see me now is welcome to come to my house in Baden—and he oughtn't to be too slow about it—otherwise I might not be in Baden, but on Mercury Hill, where the tired find rest from earthly tribulations.

I haven't yet been able to get through the last part of *The Precipice,*[5] and I'm rereading *War and Peace* with the same mixture of contrary emotions. What's good in the novel is remarkable, and what's bad or weak or pretentious still isn't boring—in a certain sense it's even interesting—like the clowning and grimacing of a man of genius.

Please be so good as to keep an eye out on Spasskoye and Kishinsky from time to time. I've had no reason to complain so far, but it wouldn't be bad to have a certain degree of checking going on.

Kiss Petya[6] for me and tell him that tribulations at school—even getting beaten up—develop a heroic spirit and independence. Look at the English.

Farewell, my good friend—and write me. I need some support. I embrace you cordially.

Your devoted

Iv. Turgenev

Letter 226 (2337). To P.P. Vasiliev.[1]
June 23/ July 5, 1869. Baden-Baden.

Baden-Baden.
Thiergartenstrasse, 3.
Monday, June 5/ July 22, 1869.

My dear sir, Pyotr Petrovich! I'm very grateful for your leaflet[2] and letter; I'm happy to see that I haven't been completely forgotten in Russia.

Your information about the translations of my works into foreign languages is not quite accurate or complete: allow me to pass on to you some details—not for the sake of my own vanity—but in order to satisfy your bibliographical curiosity.

Almost everything that I have written has been translated into *French*, under various titles. Besides *Notes of a Hunter, A Nest of Gentlefolk*, about ten stories, as well as *Smoke*, have been translated into *German;* the bookseller Behre[3] in Riga has begun an edition of selected works of mine—the first volume includes *Fathers and Sons*, the second—"The Unfortunate One" and three other stories. *Notes of a Hunter, Smoke, Fathers and Sons*, and *A Nest of Gentlefolk* have been translated into *English*. The last novel, only recently published, was especially well translated by Mr. Ralston.[4] (The rumored translation of "The Brigadier" turned out to be false.) *Smoke* and *Fathers and Sons* have been translated into *Dutch; Smoke, A Nest of Gentlefolk*, and several stories—into *Swedish;* a few stories were translated into *Czech, Serbian*, and *Hungarian*. I have also been informed that *Notes of a Hunter* has been translated into Spanish and will soon be published . . .

Letter 227 (2365). To I.P. Borisov.
August 24/ September 5, 1869. Baden-Baden.

> Baden-Baden.
> Thiergartenstrasse, 3.
> Sunday, August 24/ September 5,
> 1869.

Dear Ivan Petrovich, I just received your letter along with Fet's—what does his announcing his arrival here—in Baden—on September 20th our style mean? It's surely just a fantasy, because you don't say anything about it—and he himself doesn't mention it again.[1] There's no need for me to tell you that we'd be very happy to see him and would give him the chance to do some hunting. I hope that the stomach bruise didn't have any nasty consequences.

I imagine that you've already returned from Moscow—where you dropped Petya[2] off... The end of vacation is bitter—I remember that well—the root of learning is bitter—but its fruits are sweet. If only his health remains satisfactory!

Your remarks about building a house at Spasskoye are quite true—and I'm writing Kishinsky to that effect.[3]

I'll also ask you to do me a favor and talk to him about whether he ought to send me the money that he received for my little village *Kholodovo* now. If the rate of exchange isn't too low (the last time it was 207 francs per 100 rubles!), I suppose that he ought to send it, since the sum is rather large—11,500 rubles—and it's inconvenient for him to keep it.

I went to Munich a few days ago to see the first performance of Wagner's opera *Das Rheingold* and a few other things too.[4] Munich is an interesting city. The King of Bavaria, as you may know, is a close and even *strange* friend of Wagner's,[5] and his music is an affair of state in Bavaria; but, as the result of various amusing and tangled intrigues, out of which Aristophanes could have extracted a very interesting moral-satirical-political comedy, the opera wasn't given—but the dress rehearsal, at which I was present, took place. The music and text are equally tedious, but you know that among the Germans there are those for whom Wagner is practically Christ. I was greatly amused by this whole muddle. Sometime I'll tell about it—perhaps even in print.[6]

I can't do any work, and I haven't even finished my *Memoirs*—the devil take them! My literary screws have been stripped.

I don't yet now where I'll spend the winter—but it won't be here. You will be informed in good time.

Be well; I clasp your hand firmly.

Your Iv. Turgenev

**Letter 228 (2388). To A.A. Fet.
October 3/15, 1869. Baden-Baden.**

Baden-Baden.
Thiergartenstrasse, 3.
Friday, October 3/15, 1869.

There's no "culpa [guilt]" on your part, dear Afanasy Afanasievich—just my rashness.[1] I couldn't really imagine that it would be possible for you to tear yourself away from your *peace-keeping* activities[2] this year and turn up here, on the *peaceful,* but remote banks of the Ooss! But if not this year, then for next year I'm very much counting on you—and already see you in my mind's eye, alternately with a rifle, or simply chatting about the fact that Shakespeare was a fool, or that, to use L.N. Tolstoy's words, only that activity which is unconscious bears fruit.[3] Do you think that the North Americans laid a railroad from New York to San Francisco in their sleep, without any consciousness? Or is that not *fruit?* But let's leave philoso-phizing aside—we'll have time to succumb to it when we see each other. It's bad that you can't do any hunting; you'll have to put off such thoughts until your arrival in our heathenish parts. My doctor rather disconcerted me by forbidding me to go hunting, on the grounds that I have a "Verdichtung der rechten Herzklappe" [thickening of the right heart valve], but things seem to be improving—and besides, the heat has let up. I've been working very little, of course; take a look at the *Literary Memoirs* that serve as a preface to the new edition (Salayev will send you a copy in my name). Maybe one or two things will bring a smile to your lips.

My letter probably won't reach you at Stepanovka; you'll be in Petersburg, marvelling at the vicissitudes of time when you gaze at the ruins of Botkin. Give me a description of that meeting—though there probably won't be anything very joyous in it.[4]

"O armes Menschengeschlecht, dem Laube des Waldes vergleichbar!" [O poor human tribe, that resembles the leaves of the forest!], as Homer already exclaimed long ago.[5]

The Viardot family is hale and hearty and sends you greetings. We're continuing to make music, busy ourselves with operettas, and so on. Today, for example, we're giving a performance in the newly-built theater in the presence of the King and Queen of Prussia, etc., etc. That's the sort of gonorrheas, I mean—honors that surround us, old chap![5]

I'm planning to spend the winter here, or perhaps in Weimar. In any event I won't leave here any earlier than the end of December. Give my regards to your charming wife; and what of your muse—has it fallen completely silent?

I clasp your hand firmly and wish you all the best.

Your Iv. Turgenev

Letter 229 (2398). To P.V. Annenkov.
October 24/ November 5, 1869. Baden-Baden.

Baden-Baden.
November 5/ October 24, 1869.

Dear Pavel Vasilievich! Botkin's death[1] brought on philosophical reflections which I won't relate to you, because I'm certain that you too gave yourself up to such thoughts. The French say "Au bout du fossé la culbute!" [Riding for a fall], and none of us can know when he'll have to go flying head over heels. It has been a long time since there disappeared from life's scene a person so capable of enjoying life; he was a gifted person of sorts; but inexorable fate doesn't spare even the talented. One comrade fewer! He was good to his brothers and others; but in his eyes our poor Society remained an unworthy bunch of black sheep.[2] Amazingly retrograde instincts and prejudices sat in that Muscovite merchants' son. On a par with an Prussian Junker or general of Nikolay's time . . .[3] All the same, literature for him gave off a taste of something like rebellion. Peace to his ashes!

My fragment on Pletnyov produced just the impression on you that one should have expected.[4] I wrote it sluggishly and unwillingly (like

76

almost all of my *Memoirs)*, at Bartenyev's request. I was hoping to kill two birds with one stone, but all that I killed was time. In closing, I embrace you cordially.

Your Iv. Turgenev

Letter 230 (2400). To A.V. Pletnyova.[1]
October 25/ November 6, 1869. Baden-Baden.

Baden-Baden.
Thiergartenstrasse, 3.
Saturday, October 25/ November 6,
1869.

Madame,

If my piece on your late spouse[2] wounded you—then I can say the same thing of your letter to me—and surely with greater right. I console myself with the thought that except for you, surely no one in all of Russia saw anything in my evaluation of Pyotr Alexandrovich other than a tribute of sympathetic respect for a person who was quite worthy of it. Your spouse belonged to that group of people who have no reason to fear the truth either during their life or after death; and in speaking the truth about him as best I was able, I hoped in that way to prove my respect for him. His own sincere humility surely would have itself protested against my words if I had taken it into my head to represent him as a scholar or a warrior. As for your sons, they have as little need to be offended by my remarks about their parent's learning as if I had denied him the title of a great poet, in spite of the fact that he wrote poetry. Pyotr Alexandrovich's image—even in the absence of great learning—a lack that he had in common with many of the best men of that time—remains in all its attractiveness and clarity. If, in remarking on the happiness[3] that continuously accompanied his life, I had even remotely hinted that it was undeserved—I would understand your irritation; but surely it cannot be that to call a person happy in his relations, in his family life, and in all his surrounding means to destroy him?

The words that apparently upset you, "that everything floated right into his hands," were used by him himself several times in conversation

77

with me. Can you really imagine a reader who, having run over my article, would not experience a warm feeling for the kindhearted personality that I summoned up before him?

I am certain, Madam, that after the first impression which was so unexpectedly aroused in you has passed, and the time for calm reflection comes, you yourself will be persuaded that there was no reason to reproach me—and that in publishing my article I have not betrayed so much as by a hair those feelings of unhypocritical respect and, I dare to add, friendship, which I always held for your late spouse and you—and with whom I have the honor to remain,

Madame,

Your humble servant,

Iv. Turgenev.

Letter 231 (2410). To Ya. P. Polonsky.
November 9/21, 1869. Baden-Baden.

Baden-Baden.
Thiergartenstrasse, 3.
Sunday, November 9/21, 1869.

Your letter upset me greatly, my dear Yakov Petrovich; there is something like despair expressed in it. Poetry really is hard pressed in our time, especially if it doesn't mock you in an indecent manner.[1] I've thought up the following plan: in a day or two I'll write a feuilleton about you and send it (with my signature) to *The St. Petersburg News;* I'm certain that it will be accepted—though I doubt that it will be of much use to you—since my authority, too, has been shaken strongly—but just the same it's worth a try; besides which, it will be a pleasure for me finally to express my thoughts about you—and about poetic activity in general, which is being trampled so cruelly by the feet of pigs and other swine.[2] I intend to get to work on the feuilleton immediately—and before that, to read *Chalygin's Confessions,* about which I'll also express my opinion if I like it.[3]

And you, my dear boy, I advise you not to lose your presence of spirit. How many times in my life have I had occasion to recall the words that a certain old peasant told me: "If man didn't destroy himself—who could?" And don't you destroy yourself either. Continue doing what you do, without haste or agitation; if your work is taken, hand it in; if not—keep it in your portfolio for a more suitable time. After all, there isn't anything *else* that you will or can do; besides, who knows how and when talent finally makes itself felt. Cervantes was a mediocre, tenth-rate writer up until the age of 63, and then he suddenly up and wrote *Don Quixote* and became No. 1. We have another such example before our eyes: S.T. Aksakov. Your literary activity, nonetheless, is not ignominious; you haven't served as a laughingstock, like S.T. Aksakov,[4] or a disgraceful name, like Orlov[5] or Askochensky.[6] And therefore—take heart and, gritting your teeth, move on ahead, always ahead!

And so, expect the feuilleton—and be well and don't weep openly or privately. That doesn't lead anywhere.

I send you my cordial regards to your wife and clasp your hand.

Your devoted

Iv. Turgenev

Letter 232 (2452). To P.V. Annenkov.
January 10/22, 1870. Baden-Baden.

Baden-Baden.
Thiergartenstrasse, 3.
January 10/22, 1870.

I'm writing you while still under the influence of sad news, dear Annenkov: about an hour ago I learned that Herzen is dead.[1] I couldn't restrain myself from tears.

No matter what the differences were in our opinions, no matter what conflicts occurred between us, still and all, an old comrade, an old friend has disappeared: our ranks are thinning, thinning! Moreover, as ill luck would have it, I saw him in Paris no more than a week ago, had breakfast with him (after a seven-year separation), and never was he more merry, talkative, even noisy. That was last *Friday*; he fell ill that evening, and the next day I saw him in bed with a high fever and pneumonia; up until my departure, last Wednesday, I visited his family every day, but I couldn't see him anymore—the doctor wouldn't allow it; and when I left I already knew that his case was hopeless. His illness consumed him horribly quickly. I couldn't stay in Paris any longer; but it is almost with horror that I think of what will become of his family. His son[2] hasn't yet had time to arrive from Florence. His elder daughter Natalya[3]—a wonderful, charming creature—was out of her head for six weeks as a result of some strange misunderstandings and has just barely recovered now . . . This death may again jolt her sanity. Everyone in Russia will probably say that Herzen ought to have died earlier, that he outlived himself; but what do those words mean, what does our so-called activity mean in the face of that mute abyss that swallows us all? As though to live and continue living weren't the most important thing for a person? Death especially nauseates me inasmuch as a few days ago I had the quite unexpected chance to smell my fill of it, specifically, via a friend[4] I received an invitation (in Paris) to be present not only at Traupmann's[5] execution, but at the announcement of the death sentence to him, at his "toilette," and so on. There were eight of us in all. I won't ever forget that terrible night during which "I have supp'd my full of horrors"[6] and conceived a decisive loathing for capital punishment in general and the way that it is carried out in France in particular. I've already begun a letter to you in which I relate all of this in detail and which, if you want, you may then publish in *The St. Petersburg News*.[7] I'll just say one thing for now—that I couldn't even imagine such courage, such contempt for death, as there was in Traupmann. But the whole thing is horrible . . . horrible.

By the way, did you receive my letter about Polonsky and did you have it placed in the journal? He is wailing *like a gull* about this and assures me in his letters that he is so unfortunate and unlucky that he is certain of the article's non-appearance.[8] Please prove to him that the opposite is the case, although my article, alas, cannot grant him any special *good fortune*.[9]

So long, my friend. Be well. I send my regards to your wife and clasp your hand.

Your Iv. Turgenev

P.S. I'm not moving to Weimar until February 7, New Style.

Letter 233 (2460). To A.A. Fet.
January 23/February 4, 1870. Baden-Baden.

Baden-Baden.
Thiergartenstrasse, 3.
Friday, February 4 N.S., 1870.

Dear Fet, your letter found me still here—but on the very eve of my departure for Weimar, where we're all moving together for two months (my address is now Weimar, Hôtel de Russie).

I have a couple of things to tell you about Louise Héritte, Mme Viardot's eldest daughter. That unfortunate and foolish woman has caused her family a great deal of grief and will end by destroying herself. After getting married—at her own insistent wish, to M. Héritte (just a few days before her decision I travelled to see her to deliver a proposal from another Frenchman, a marvellous person whom she seemed to have loved up until then), she suddenly conceived a hatred for her husband—although there was nothing that she could reproach him for other than a certain limitedness; she fled from the Cape of Good Hope, where he was the Consul—and turned up in Baden; then she abandoned her parental home—and after various wanderings wound up in Petersburg, where she became a professor of singing at the Conservatory (she's a good musician). Up until then she had been receiving punctually from her husband (who didn't hinder her at all and didn't take advantage of the frightening rights granted by the French law code to spouses of the male sex) the interest from her dowry and a pension; all of that together came to 10,000 francs; but now she suddenly declared that she would make do with her salary and didn't want so much as a kopeck from him. Meanwhile her health couldn't bear the Petersburg climate and, forced to resign from her position, she galloped off to some acquaintances in the Yekaterinoslav Province, where she'll live on their benevolence, since her pride doesn't allow her to appeal again to her husband, who has been appointed Consul-General to Denmark and lives there (in Copenhagen) with his (and her) son. One has to give him his due—he has behaved impeccably in this whole affair: up until now he has neither refused to pay her her pension nor to take her into the house again; he allows her to live wherever she sees fit—with only one condition: that she not take up the theater, towards which she has no disposition anyway. That's the *true* story of this unfortunate woman, who, though not of Russian descent, is a nihilist vom reinsten Wasser [of the purest water]. How will this all end? Perhaps with suicide... I'm just amazed that Mme Artôt[1] could have spoken of this matter so vaguely and flippantly.

81

And now allow me to grumble a little. I readily tolerate any exaggeration, any so-called "comic ire"—especially when it concerns people or things that are essentially *dear* to us; but your comments about your confrères, about our poor Society, are beginning to be—I'll not mince words—revolting.[2] It would be most fortunate if *you* really were the poorest Russian writer! I repeat: the impression produced by your constant complaints becomes linked unpleasantly in my head with your name, with that essentially warm remembrance that I have of you. Enough, Afanasy Afanasievich! Enough!.. Stop flinging mud! Otherwise you may slide down to Katkov's level or fall to Bulgarin's! Don't be angry with me . . . I'm only telling you this because I love you sincerely. I was going to tell you lots of things, about my trip to Paris . . . and so on. But there's no room—I'll leave it for another time! I clasp your hand cordially. Your Iv. Turgenev

Letter 234 (2468). To Ludwig Pietsch.[1]
February 5/17, 1870. Weimar.

Weimar.
Hôtel de Russie.
Thursday, February 17, 1870.

My dear friend, here's the absolute truth about the Carlsruhe story, as you call it. Our operetta's[2] lack of success (it was no "fiasco," nor did I hear any hissing—it's just that no one was called back and applause was sparse) was the result—to use the new Bismarckian language—of the following contributing *factors*: the hostility of old Devrient,[3] about whose qualities as a director Mme Viardot and I do not consider it necessary to remain silent—the feelings of envy on the part of the remaining theater personnel, especially Hauser,[4] as a singing teacher—the displeasure arising from the fact that all last winter Mme Viardot held herself at a distance from them, envy of the Court's favorable disposition toward us, the usual opposition to the Grand Duke, who actually pushed the whole business through—and especially the profound disdain of *foreigners* and their arrogant presumptuousness—these are the main reasons for the "Carlsruhe story," as you call it. Fortunately, the wrath was directed primarily at my unfortunate libretto—the *Badische Landeszeitung* even maintained that one could say many good things about the music, but that the text was gross swinishness. In the *Badischer Beobachter* I was branded straight out as "a nonsense-scribbling barbarian."[5] Add to that can-can a small, tight-fisted town: the rumor was spread that Mme Viardot received *400* gulden for each evening, I—*200*—and Richard Pohl—her friend—*100*! Just imagine the outrage!!! One art-loving officer yelled in the open street: "For that much money we could have had the best tenor—and really, there's no reason to shove such a sum of money, one that undoubtedly exceeds his entire royalties for a year, in the hungry maw of a scribbler who was thrown out of his own country and literature with a kick in the hindquarters . . . " *Verbatim.* Yes, my dear friend, in Baden-Baden I now stand on the same rung as in my native land. There's no need for me to tell you that of course we neither requested nor received so much as a single kreutzer. But I repeat: fortunately, the main blow fell on me, and I can bear a great deal.

We're very sorry that you can't come here to see us—I can't as yet say anything about the trip to Berlin: in ten days (on Sunday) *Orfeo* will be given.[6] And besides, we're so shamefully frozen that all we can think about is warming our bodies. N.B. Since the weather has grown milder the cold in our rooms has *increased* considerably.

Claudie[7] has found a teacher in the person of the painter Verlat.[8]

Give my regards to your friends in Berlin and retain your favorable disposition toward the "nonsense-scribbling barbarian."

I. Turgéneff

P.S. If you see Auerbach, tell him that I fulfilled his request and sent my *autograph* (!!!risum teneatis, amici!) [restrain your laughter, friends]to Herr Lewald.[9]

Letter 235 (2483). To A. A. Fet.
March 21/April 2, 1870. Weimar.

Weimar.
Hôtel de Russie.
Saturday, March 21/April 2, 1870.

Dearest Fet—you begin your letter with the exclamation "Fatum!" [Fate!] And I repeat that word after you. Our written conversations are of an amusing and strange character. I, for instance, begin like this: "This horse is white." "What?" you exclaim with indignation. "You dare to assert

83

that this piglet is green!?" "But birds sometimes have noses," I remark in a persuasive voice. "Never!" you join in. "On the $<$———$>$—yes, but in the air—never ever!" and so on and so on. And therefore I think it would be better to put off our arguments until we meet, which will occur—"God granting"—by St. Nikolay's Day, May 9th.

I have extracted two convictions, two facts, however, out of all the foam and squish of your remarks, namely:

1) That for you—the poet Fet—to publish such verses as those which you composed apropos of V.P. Botkin's death is unforgivable.[1]

2) That in your eyes M.N. Katkov deserves a bronze statue. "Well, go ahead, I don't give a hoot!" as one of Ostrovsky's heroes says.

But how far talent can decline! Did you read his latest comedy, *Easy Come, Easy Go?* That—and the *philosophy* in the sixth volume of *War and Peace*—I think Satan himself, after gorging on rotten eggs, couldn't pluck such crap from his own ass!

But the greatest fact of recent time is P. Bonaparte's pronouncement in regard to the 200,000 citizens accompanying the coffin of V. Noir, who was *murdered by him*: "C'est une curiosité *malsaine,* que *je blâme!*" [It's an unhealthy curiosity that I censure].[2]

That's worthy of Shakespeare; Richard III never said anything better. Après cela—il faut tirer l'échelle [after that—one has to draw in the ladder, i.e., that's beyond comparison].

And in closing, I send you cordial greetings and ask you to convey my respects to Maria Petrovna.[3]

Your devoted,

Iv. Turgenev

Letter 236 (2542). To N.S. Turgenev.
July 28/August 9, 1870. Baden-Baden.

Baden-Baden.
Thiergartenstrasse, 3.
Tuesday, July 28/August 9, 1870.

Dear brother, I received your letter yesterday and today I sent your package by registered mail to your wife in Berlin, since the mail service is now guaranteeing letters again. That your package will reach Berlin is beyond doubt; let's hope that it finds your wife still there.

Don't waste your time worrying about me;[1] from the papers you can see what an unexpected turn the war is taking; it's not the French who are beating the Germans, but the Germans beating the French—and it's not the French Army that has invaded Germany, but the German Army that has invaded France. For the time being there is no danger here in Baden— because on the other side of the Rhein all of Alsace has been occupied by the German Army. Nor is there anything to be heard of disease yet—and comestibles have even become less expensive. In any event, I'm remaining here.

I embrace you and remain

Your loving brother

Iv. Turgenev.

Letter 237 (2546). To I.P. Borisov.
August 12/24, 1870. Baden-Baden.

Baden-Baden.
Thiergartenstrasse, 3.
Wednesday, August 24, 1870.

You could already demand the bottle that you won from L.N. Tolstoy now, dear Ivan Petrovich—since the latest blows delivered by the Prussians seem essentially to have already settled the matter. One can't help marvelling at the artistry with which they first held back the stupid Bazaine[1] in Metz, then blocked his way to Verdun—and finally routed him utterly and hurled him back to Metz, where he must either starve to death or surrender. Those three battles (on the 14th, 16th, and 18th of August) cost them terrible sacrifices—but the results are great. Now nothing hinders the Crown Prince's army from reaching Paris. MacMahon[2] will surely abandon the Chalon encampment. It's impossible as yet to foresee the war's ultimate outcome, but all the chances are on the Germans' side.

I understand very well why Tolstoy takes the French side. French phrase-mongering is repugnant to him—but even more he hates calculation, systems, science, in a word—Germans. All his last novel is built on that hostility toward intellect, knowledge, and consciousness—and suddenly the learned Germans are beating the French ignoramuses!! (By the way—can it really be that the holy fool who published some sort of absurd prophecies with *plans* in *The Moscow News* is the same *Prince* Urusov with whom Tolstoy is so friendly?)[3] For my part, without sophistry, I rejoice at France's defeat—for along with it the Napoleonic Empire is mortally defeated—an Empire whose existence is incompatible with the development of freedom in Europe. I expressed that view in letters to Annenkov, excerpts from which correspondence appeared in issue No. 216 of *The St. Petersburg News* (August 8). By the way, I cited several superb little examples of French phrase-mongering there.

What you write me of Tolstoy and Fet makes me very happy; I'm only sorry that the latter still refuses to part with his muse. Ye. D. Shenshina[4] is described by you superbly, as is her son.

I've already been hunting three times. I was a disgusting shot the first two times, and the third time the hunt was not a success. However, I've already bagged 23 partridges and 8 hares. My hound is as superb as ever.

At night here one can hear the bombardment of Strasbourg, which has already been half burned down. Even while lying in bed with the windows closed one's ear still catches a dull rumbling and shuddering. One gives over involuntarily to philosophico-historico-social reflections of a quite gloomy nature. The iron age hasn't yet passed—and we're still barbarians! And we'll probably remain so until the end of our days.

Our weather has turned bad—they say that there will be an early winter.

Kiss Petya[5] for me; I clasp your hand firmly and remain

Your loving

Iv. Turgenev.

Letter 238 (2567). To P.V. Annenkov.
October 16/28, 1870. Baden-Baden.

Baden-Baden.
October 16/28, 1870.

One may really call your silence eloquent, dear Pavel Vasilievich; without any notification on your part I realize that my old man has followed the example of his elder brothers—"The Brigadier" and "Yergunov" and has been received by our readers as a complete fiasco.[1] It doesn't much matter; I just hope that these successive defeats haven't shaken the spirits of my editors, or more accurately, my editor (since I have nowhere to publish except with Stasyulevich[2]) and stripped him of the willingness to pay me 400 rubles per signature, and I won't accept any less, for how else am I to preserve myself from the fate of the Archbishop of Granada in *Gil Blas?*[3] And that's why from now on I'll write for my *friends,* as retired authors say: more likely, I won't write at all. But just the same, if you can, send me two separate offprints of the ill-fated "Lear." In about seven or eight days I'm leaving for London, where I'll stay until the New Year, i.e., until my trip to Russia. If it should occur to you to write me, your letter would still reach me here. When I get to London I'll send you my address there. The whole Viardot family is already there: the war has ruined them, and Mme Viardot must try to earn some money for herself in England, the only country where that commodity is still to be found. It would be a little too bitter staying on alone in Baden for the winter.

The news arrived today that Metz has been surrendered with its entire army of 150,000 and with notre glorieux [our glorious] Bazaine. Notre glorieux Bazaine probably reckoned like this: "You, MacMahon, thought to surprise me, I suppose, by surrendering with an army of 100,000 and a trashy little fortress? Well, just wait a bit: I'll surrender an army of 150,000 and a first-class fortress!" It's incomprehensible how France will continue to show resistance after this blow. Her entire army has been captured—has anyone ever seen the like?!

The day before yesterday we had a horrible storm that felled almost half the Schwarzwald and among other things, toppled my ghastly chimney in the style of Louis XIII, which nearly crushed the entire roof when it fell and practically mangled my whole house. While it was being built I allowed myself to remark to the architect, a Frenchman named Olive, a great scoundrel and dolt, that in view of the local winds, such chimneys were dangerous: "Monsieur," he answered me, "ces chiminées sont aussi solides que la France" [these chimneys are as solid as France]. In the first place, that answer reminded me of the reply of another Frenchman, the Petersburg coiffeur Heloit, who asserted that his reputation was plus solide que la colonne Alexandre [more solid than the Alexander column], and later ended up in Toulon headed for the galleys because he'd poisoned his wife, and secondly, since the beginning of the present war guarantees of France's solidity have seemed doubtful to me. And that's just the way it turned out: my chimney really was just aussi solide que la France.

Can you by any chance tell me where N.A. Milyutin[4] and his family are—in Petersburg or in Moscow? Arapet probably knows. In closing, I kiss you on both your cheeks.

Your devoted

Iv. Turgenev

Letter 239 (2596). To P.V. Annenkov.
December 19/31, 1870. London.

4, Bentick Street.
Manchester Square.
Saturday, 31/19, 1870.

Dear Pavel Vasilievich, on this last day of the present ill-fated year I'm writing to you with numb fingers (we don't know how to withstand the cold here as well as we do in Russia)—and I have to write a great deal, i.e., there are many requests in store for you. Namely, *No. 1.* I've made the acquaintance here of two Galician Poles[1] who are starving to death; from the attached document you can see what they are asking for. They came to London in the hopes of receiving naturalization here, but that's only possible after a three-year residency. They seem to me to be good and honest fellows; moreover, the elder one's face reminds me of one of the people I sincerely loved—the late Count Nikolay Tolstoy, Lev Nikolayevich's brother. Please find out on the sly, but *for certain* whether they can risk returning to Russia, and whether they won't be delivered over to Austria, since their passports are Austrian and expired. They left a very good reputation in Warsaw—in the eyes of the government—and the local Consul, Berg (the Governor's brother)[2] has taken them under his wing. If it's possible, write me—and after I return to Petersburg I'll get them out of here. They don't know English—and there's nothing for them to do here nor can there be.

No. 2. Do me a favor and send me right away the latest and best map of railroads in Russia. Send it through the mail, like a letter. I promised it to an Englishman who needs it desperately for a lecture of Russia that he is planning.

No. 3. Please get the money for "Knock, Knock"[3] and keep it until my arrival. If none of my earlier money is left, then use this money for expenditures.

I still can't find a photograph of Gambetta—but that the portraits that I've sent are good is demonstrated by the resemblance that you noted—one which exists in my eyes too—with the exception of Pelletan-Leontiev, whom, i.e., Leontiev, I do not have the honor of knowing.[4]

Pypin's article in *The Messenger of Europe* is extraordinarily interesting and it gave great pleasure to the old man N.I. Turgenev, to whom I passed it on.[5]

The Professor Engelhardt who was arrested has a very nice, intelligent wife[6]—whom I saw twice in Baden. I hope that this whole incident blows over.

Mme Viardot found Rimsky-Korsakov's romances *remarkable* and indicative of an indubitable and original talent, though one that because of youth still poses and plays fancy tricks; Borodin's romance is pleasant, but weak and too drawn out; Musorgsky's piece is neither amusing nor clever—a zero. Rubets' transcriptions[6] are very interesting, but the accompaniment is heavy and monotonous. That's her unhypocritical opinion.

In closing, I embrace you and remain

Your Iv. Turgenev.

P.S. I'm *definitely* leaving here the 18th.

Letter 240 (2621). To Pauline Viardot.[1]
February 23/ March 7, 1871. Petersburg.

No. 12

St. Petersburg.
Hotel Demut, No. 7.
Tuesday morning. February 23/
March 7, 1871.

Dear and good Mme Viardot, here is a letter which I've been asked to pass on to you.[2] As you can see, these Moscow gentlemen have no doubts about anything and deny themselves nothing. I know very well how you'll answer them, but just the same, it's nice.

Nikolay Rubinstein[3] is here and will participate in one of his brother's concerts; I hope to see him (however, I have yet to see Anton). Do you know who's here and plans to give a concert? Little Servais,[5] whose head shakes. I haven't yet seen him, but, good Lord, how all of this is reminiscent of Weimar![6] I had dinner yesterday at Annenkov's, who was celebrating his wedding anniversary.

Both my portraits are moving ahead; they're in absolutely different modes, but I think that they're both good and lifelike.[7] The reading that I was supposed to give on Saturday has fallen through; evidently the authorities wouldn't allow it—rumors had started that a collection would be taken up for wounded followers of Garibaldi. I'm not the least bit irritated; these self-exhibitions aren't at all to my taste.

Patti[8] is creating a sensation in Moscow; they say that she earned 40,000 rubles there. And people claim that there's no money in Russia! She's singing here as well—the day after tomorrow; I know someone who won't be going to hear her...[9]

This is just a note—there will be a real letter tomorrow. A thousand regards to all und tausend Küsse Ihren lieben Händen [and a thousand kisses for your dear hands].

Der Ihrige I.T. [Your I.T.]

Letter 241 (2634). To Pauline Viardot.[1]
March 6, 7/ 18, 19, 1871. Petersburg.

> No. 18.
> St. Petersburg.
> Italian Street, Ovsyannikov's Building.
> Saturday evening, March 6/ 18, 1871.

Dear and adored Madame Viardot, I'm writing you from your friend Annenkov's apartment, and here's why. For about a week now cholera, that terrifying monster, has been devastating Petersburg; I fear it like a green devil, and the last three nights have been torture—ennui, insomnia, palpitations of the heart, cold sweats, and so on and so forth. It's shameful, of course, to be such a coward, but I think that the reason in this case is a purely physiological one, and it's stronger than I am—no other disease inspires me with such dread. Seeing that, and most importantly, in view of that fact that I'm leaving tomorrow, Annenkov suggested that I stay over at his place. Here there's a doctor handy who lives in the same building, and in case anything happens, they will calm me...

It's eleven-thirty now, and there's no sleep in sight, although I'm very tired. I'm telling you all these details so bluntly because (1) I promised always to write you the truth, and (2) this letter won't be sent off until tomorrow, a few hours before my own departure for Moscow. If only I can get there, and then I hope that everything will be all right again. And after all, if the situation in Petersburg doesn't improve, I can take the train abroad directly from Moscow and even from Oryol. Because I *must* be in London in 26 days. It would be such a shame if I were held up...

I looked through the text of the Russian translation of the romances[2] once more very carefully, in Louise's[3] presence and with her help. We made a few changes, and now everything will be fine. Iogansen has already turned them over to the printers.

The day before yesterday was the occasion of the founding of a literary and artistic circle about which I think I wrote you, and the idea for which belongs to Rubinstein.[4] A committee of 8 members was elected, who were given the assignment to work out something like a plan for weekly meetings. I've become very popular in Petersburg: the public's tastes are fickle. At that meeting a toast to my health was drunk, to the accompaniment of thunderous applause. On the same evening there was a public lecture at the city duma auditorium... about the characters portrayed in my works... There were many people at the lecture, but the lecture ultimately bored them to death. You realize that I didn't go to hear myself explained to me, and in general I find that one could have selected a more interesting and broader topic. Be that as it may, this is flattering nonetheless, but the gentleman who read the lecture apparently was a real bore.

1 A.M.

I still can't sleep, and I have the strangest sensations in my stomach, arms, and legs; it's all just nerves and doesn't mean a thing, but it prevents me from sleeping or even lying down...I wouldn't like for anything to happen to me far away from you...far away from you, no, that must not be. And that's why I shouldn't ever leave again.

What a misfortune that soon it will be an entire week without any letters! I hope that they'll be waiting for me in Moscow—how greedily I'll rush at them! It's horrible not to know where you are and what you're doing...

Today is Saturday...Perhaps you have guests and are making music, while I struggle with a vile phantom that has me in its claws...

Yesterday I was present at a public lecture by one of our best physiologists, Sechenov.[5] He explained the functions of the eye very clearly and scientifically. I was sitting quite close to him—he suggested that I, a confrère, participate in some experiments...

Sunday, 9 A.M.

I slept soundly for the first time in a week and I now feel fresh and vigorous, as one ought to for a trip. It would be impossible to be a better person than Annenkov is.

Hotel Demut, No. 7. 12 Noon.

I'm a little bit upset again, but I'm leaving in an hour, and once I'm on my way this will all pass—all I want to do is to get on the train. And so, I'll write you tomorrow from Moscow.

A thousand thousand regards to everyone—Viardot, the children. I kiss your hand tenderly and remain eternally

der Ihrige [your] I.T.

Letter 242 (2640). To Pauline Viardot.[1]
March 13/25, 1871. Moscow.

No. 23.

Moscow.
Prechistensky Boulevard.
Crown Building.
Saturday, March 13/20, 1871.

Dear, adored Mme Viardot. I can't help telling you that the horrible news from Paris has seized me up entirely and thrown me into despair.[2] It's just like Imperial Pretorian Rome, perishing from anarchy, and Horace's cry "Quo, quo, sclesti, ruitis? [Where, where are you rushing, criminals?]"[3] rings in my ears constantly.

The latest events are especially lamentable in that through force they are shattering the good feelings that Europe felt for France (at the moment that's all I see around me), and are playing marvellously well into the hands of the enemies of freedom. "There, you see," they're exclaiming, "there, you see what those famous principles of 1789 lead to" and so on and so forth. This is the triumph of the July '48 uprising—and what will happen to France? Can it really be that the fate of Poland or Mexico awaits a nation that we all loved so much and to which we're obliged for so much?.. I can't stop asking myself these question, and when I attempt to look into the future, I feel a certain obtuseness and bewilderment. To all that is added the constant worry—not about myself, of course, but about what will happen to you, to your house on rue Douai, to your stocks, and to that ill-fated farm... All the trade relations that we just started up with France again were immediately terminated... The bankers can only shrug their shoulders... "It's a sinking ship," Akhenbakh told me yesterday.

I have bought 17,500 francs' worth of Russian railway stock to add to Didie's[4] dowry. Now she has about 80,000 francs. Viardot wrote me and asked whether I didn't think that part of that money should be used to buy a new French bond; that, he says, would be "a sacrifice at the altar of the fatherland." In my opinion that would only be a sacrifice, plain and simple—and I answered him to that effect. If Claudie, when she is quite grown up and independent, wants to make use of her money in such a manner, that will be her business.

Today is Saturday, and I've already reckoned that in two weeks—that's more than likely—I'll be able to be present at your evening musicale on the eve of Easter Sunday.

And so, here's what you need to do: as soon as you receive this letter, write me as soon as possible, or better yet, send me a telegram in Berlin, "Hotel St. Petersburg, Unter den Linden," as to whether I should head for London directly and forthwith, as I plan, or whether for any reasons, business and so on and so forth, you find it essential for me to make a detour to Baden, which will hold up my arrival for two or three days. Viardot writes that he'll come to Baden just for a few days in the fall in order to gather up the pictures and so on and be on his way again; but perhaps you ought to make some provisions in the spring to have the houses sold or rented. Talk to him about this, and if he thinks that my presence in Baden in the spring is essential, I repeat that I'll make the detour. Not with any great pleasure... but I'll do it. But I'll have to know immediately upon my arrival in Berlin.

I'm including in this same envelope a note for Claudie and Marianne. I tell them a few details that might interest you as well.

Along with the telegram to Berlin send a letter to Baden with all the essential instructions if you think that I ought to drop in to Baden.

Perhaps four or five days after you receive this letter we'll see each other. My heart leaps from joy. A thousand friendly regards to everyone. I kiss your hands. Auf ewig [forever],

der Ihrige [your] I.T.

**Letter 243 (2651). To I.I. Maslov.
March 22/ April 3, 1871. Petersburg.**

St. Petersburg.
Monday, March 22, 1871.

Dear Ivan Ilich,

I'm writing to you from the Warsaw railway station a half hour before my departure. Annenkov sent me a letter from my daughter that consists of nothing but an extended *wail;* if she doesn't have 40,000 francs soon, she and her husband will be ruined.[1] And therefore I ask you *not to put too high a price* on the estate[2] and if need be to make a concession of two or three thousand rubles—all I care about is getting the money as quickly as possible. In case of success please let me know immediately at my London address—send a telegram even. I kiss you and thank you for all the past, present, and future.

Your Turgenev.

Letter 244 (2667). To M.A. Milyutina.[1]
April 15/27, 1871. London.

London.
16, Beaumont Street. Marylebone.
April 15/27, 1871.

Dear Marya Ageyevna, I received your letter of April 1st a few days ago—and yesterday Chaikovsky's romances came, which Mme Viardot played through at once and of which she especially likes the last three—and especially the very last one—to a poem by *Goethe* (not Heine, as the text states), "Nur wer die Sehnsucht kennt," in Mei's translation.[2] Mme Viardot is planning to sing that romance at one of her "Saturdays"—and she has now asked me to thank Mr. Chaikovsky; all her romances will be sent to him. And I for my part thank you for the speedy and kind fulfillment of my request. My friends—Russian ones—don't usually spoil me so.

I can appreciate what you tell me of Nikolay Alexeyevich's[3] attitude toward your—I won't yet say literary, but writing activity; and at the same time I'm absolutely certain that no one would be happier than he if you achieved undoubted success. But for that you need to make up your mind—and *begin;* unless you dive into the water, you'll never learn how to swim. And that's just what I advise you to do: you aren't about to sink.

I flatter myself with the hope that you have finally come to believe what I told you about those genuinely cordial feelings that I've always had for you—especially since the time of my last day in Moscow. The society there does me a great honor by occupying itself with me even after my departure: but they need not distort my words. I never said anything like the phrase which is attributed to me;[4] all I remember is that in answer to someone's remark that I despised something (I don't remember just what it was, but certainly not the Russian people) I said that I rarely experienced that feeling—and if I were to despise anything, then I would surely start

95

with myself. You can see what a distorted meaning was attached to my modest confession. But this is all nonsense. My "I" has ceased to interest me: could I possibly then be interested in what others say and think about that "I"? That doesn't prevent me, however, from being grateful to all those who see fit to be well disposed towards me. As Sollogub's song says: "Thank you—I didn't expect it."

Give my regards to all your family and my Moscow friends. I clasp your hand cordially.

Your devoted

Iv. Turgenev

Letter 245 (2669). To P.V. Annenkov.
April 19/ May 1, 1871. London.

London.
16, Beaumont Street. Marylebone.
Monday, April 19/ May 1, 1871.

Dear Pavel Vasilievich—yesterday's *Pall Mall Gazette* contained the following little item:

"A letter from Paris, in the *Temps,* announces the death of Madame Pauline Viardot, née García, sister of Malibran[1] and creatrix of the role of Fidès in Meyerbeer's *Prophète.* The celebrated artiste has just entered on her 54th year."

You can imagine what an effect that announcement would have had on me if I had read it anywhere else but in Mme Viardot's salon and in her presence.

But since news like this spreads with lightning speed—and all the newspapers reprint it immediately, I appeal to you with a request to forestall that or refute it, as you wish. Mme Viardot, thank God, is well— and she's 49, not 54.

I think that I already wrote you about sending me four copies of the last album of romances[2]—and to have *all* of Mme Viardot's romances delivered to the composer Chaikovsky in Moscow; just in case, I'm repeating that request.

I send you my regards and embrace you cordially.

Your devoted

Iv. Turgenev

Letter 246 (2674). To Ya. P. Polonsky.
April 24/ May 6, 1871. London.

London.
16, Beaumont Street, Marylebone.
April 24/ May 6, 1871.

My dear friend Yakov Petrovich, I received your letter this morning along with the article against Saltykov which you enclosed—and I'm answering immediately. Your reply to the criticism of your *Sheaves* is completely logical and irresistible; and yet you would do better not to print it. You know the old saying: "Don't touch it ... and it won't stink." He's replying ... that means he's justifying himself ... that means he's wrong— that's the inevitable syllogism that takes shape in the heads of the public in such cases. But if that won't satisfy you, it won't make any difference.

As a result of letters received from abroad I left Russia much sooner than I had planned. I'm staying here until July, then I'm off to Baden, and God knows where in October—perhaps to Russia.

I've been told that Dostoevsky has caricatured me ... [2]Well, so what? Let him have his fun. He came to see me in Baden about five years ago—not to repay the money that he had borrowed from me—but to abuse me roundly for *Smoke,* which in his opinion ought to have been burned by the hand of an executioner. I listened to that whole philippic in silence—and what do I find out? That I allegedly expressed to him all sorts of criminal opinions, which he hastened to pass on to Bartenyev! (Bartenyev actually wrote me about this.) This would simply be slander—if Dostoevsky weren't insane—which I don't doubt at all. Perhaps he imagined all of this. But my Lord, what petty squabbles!

97

I'm very vexed that Princess S.A. Gagarina considers me haughty. Please tell her that if I had left her kind letter without attention, I would have been an ignoramus, not haughty. The fact is that immediately upon receipt of it I reported to the Academy and asked that I be announced to the Princess; but a man came out to tell me that she was busy... Perhaps he garbled my name—or perhaps she really was busy—I was definitely planning to visit her the next day—but then I suddenly left, driven off by fear of cholera. Please don't neglect to explain all of this to her—and add that I beg her to forgive me for not having answered in writing, and that on the contrary, I have always held her in the highest regard.

In closing, be well and work without being put out of countenance by criticism. I give my regards to your wife and clasp your hand firmly.

Your devoted

Iv. Turgenev

Letter 247 (2770). To V.V. Stasov.
November 28/ December 10, 1871. Paris.

Paris.
48, rue de Douai.
Sunday, November 29/ December
10, 1871.

I ought to have answered your letter long ago, dear Vladimir Vasilievich—but what with literary work, gout, and the fuss and bother of moving, there wasn't any time. I've now settled in Paris for a couple of months—in the middle of our January I'll be in Petersburg, if I'm alive and well. I'm very glad that you found Antokolsky[1] (I'm returning your letter to him, by the way). I'm afraid of his getting married, more from the physical than the moral point of view: people with weak chests—all of them—are terribly lustful, and they exhaust themselves—and not on artistic works. I am in fundamental agreement with your view of marriage; I would even expand that view and apply it to any *continual* association with a woman; you know that there are such things as unofficial marriages: that form is sometimes even more poisonous than the generally accepted one. This question is quite well known to me and I have made a thorough study of it.

If I have not yet touched upon it in my literary endeavors, it is only because I've always avoided topics that were too subjective: they constrain me. When all of this is at a further remove from me I may think a bit and attempt something—if only my desire to write doesn't disappear... It's becoming very difficult to muck around with this painstaking business—moreover, with each day it becomes more difficult to satisfy myself. I've just finished a long povest[2] (for The *Messenger of Europe*) which I rewrote *three* times—that's a labor of Sisyphus of sorts! But the French say "qui a bu, boira" [he who has drunk will drink], and there's nothing that's impossible.

I read your article about the academy competition and Repin[3] in the *St. Petersburg News.* I was very glad to learn that that young boy is moving ahead so vigorously and quickly. There is a large talent in him—and the indisputable *temperament* of an artist, which is most important of all. One can't help but rejoice at the cessation of our revolting Bryullovism;[4] living waters will spring forth among us only when the carrion dries up and falls off, like a scab.

I haven't taken a look around here yet, haven't seen anyone or anything—and therefore I have nothing to report. The Republic is very sick—the whole nation is sick. God alone knows that will come of all of this; and I think even He doesn't know.

Give my regards to Antokolsky and accept the assurance of my absolute respect and devotion.

Iv. Turgenev

Letter 248 (2791). To P.V. Annenkov.
December 19/31, 1871. Paris.

Paris.
48, rue de Douai.
Sunday, January 19/31, 1871.

Oh, dear Pavel Vasilievich—you both gladdened me and killed me with your letter! Gladdened me with the praise that you lavish on my "Freshets"[1]—and killed me with the irrefutable accuracy of your reproach regarding the denouement! Can you imagine that in the first version *it was exactly* as you said—just as if you had read it.[2] My misfortune this time was that I didn't have time to read my povest—before its publication—to anyone; neither to Mme Viardot (which I've always done up until now, translating into French), nor to you. So, in spite of all the reworkings, it went to press raw. There's nothing that can be done about that misfortune now—but in a separate printing, of course, Sanin will be somewhat rehabilitated.[3] I think that I wrote Stasyulevich about printing ten offprints and sending them here—as well as the January issue; but please remind him. In addition, tell him that at the request of my estate manager, I would like to have one copy of *The Messenger of Europe* sent to the following address:

Nikita Alexeyevich Kishinsky.
Manager of the Estate of Turgenevo.
Oryol Province, City of *Mtsensk*.

Please subtract the money for the subscription from the sum that I'll receive for "Spring Freshets."

Hang on to "Pégas"[4] until I receive a reply from my hunting correspondent in Kazan. (The publisher of *The Hunting Journal* was Nikolayev, not Ivanov, and the name Gieroglifov frightens me.)

Mme Schneider[5] should have been hissed. For heaven's sake, what do we need that *cracked* chamber pot for?

I send regards to all and clasp your hand cordially.

Your Iv. Turgenev

P.S. Please be so good as to ask *The Messenger of Europe* for my manuscript of "Spring Freshets" and keep it until my arrival.

Letter 249 (2808). To P.V. Annenkov.
January 13/25, 1872. Paris.

Paris.
48, rue de Douai.
Thursday, January 13/25, 1872.

Dear Annenkov!

As you predicted, Burenin[1] was dissatisfied—and according to Stasyulevich, other critics are also reproaching me and asking why my povest lacks "a filling."[2] It's very difficult to answer that—you can't redo what's already been done!

Mais je ne vous tiens pas quitte [But I don't release you from] letters in which you inform me of the opinion of people who are interested in my works.

And now comes an important request! Mme Viardot's daughter, Mme Louise Héritte, has not written to her parents for over two months—and it's apparent from the theater posters that she is no longer performing at the Russian opera. Since she's terribly vain and had staked everything on *that* card, her parents are worried that she might have pulled some new prank. Perhaps she's ill? And in general, is she in Petersburg or not? She was living at Serova's, the composer's widow,[3] not far from Kavelin's, on the same line, in Vyazemsky's[4] building. Please find out what's going on and let us know right away. By the way, what is Antokolsky doing?

Just for fun I'm enclosing my *obituary,* which appeared in a London music journal.[5] They confused me with N.I. Turgenev. Several French journals have also buried me. They say that that's a good omen. Who is *Letnev,* the author of the povest in *Deed?*[6]

And where is *The Stone Guest?*[7] I'm asking Stasyulevich to send me the offprints of "Spring Freshets" here.

We'll see each other at the *end* of February! Regards to all.

Your Iv. Turgenev

Letter 250 (2810). To William Ralston.[1]
January 14/26, 1872. Paris.

Paris.
48, rue de Douai.
Friday, Jan. 26, 1872.

My dear friend,

I have received the *Orchestra* with the very flattering article.[2] Chorley must feel a very great "dépit" [resentment]; but I must nevertheless think that it is better so as it is. I am rather surprised to find myself a "somewhat *fatiguing* enthusiast"; I did not imagine my defaults laid in *that* any but nobody knows who he is.[3]

I sent you yesterday—no, the day before—a copy of my novel; I hope you will not be *too much* shocked by its rather lax morality.[4]

Believe me

yours very truly,

J. Tourguéneff

P.S. *Saturday morning.* I have just received the n° of the *Athenaeum*—many thanks.

Letter 251 (2822). To Ludwig Pietsch.[1]
February 5/17, 1872. Paris.

Paris.
48, rue de Douai.
Saturday, February 17, 1872.

My noble friend and benefactor Ludwig Pietsch!

There comes a moment, I have noticed, in the best relations between one friend and another, where one friend suddenly appears to the other as a dead dog and can no longer make any claims to high regard. On the basis of various symptoms and indications I can conclude that one may consider that dead dog moment to have set in in my life as concerns my German Phythiases.[2] If that is the case—oh, then it will be enough for you to pass over this in silence—and my heart, filled with premonitions, will understand everything. However, it will not break. If, however, I am mistaken—to err is human—then say but a word, and I'll be very gladdened.

Things here with France and Paris are very bad, with the Viardot family—fine. And at the end of March I'll be travelling to Petersburg via Berlin.

My novella that rings with the voices of skylarks has suffered a fiasco.[3] Regards to your family—and be well.

Your I. Turgéneff

Letter 252 (2848). To N.V. Khanykov.
March 22/ April 4, 1872. Paris.

Paris.
48, rue de Douai.
Thursday, April 3, 1872.

Dear Khanykov, this evening there is a large gathering hosted by J. Simon[1] at the Ministry of Enlightenment (rue Grenelle, St. Germain). If you are curious to hear Mme Viardot and see Thiers[2] and other such famous personalities—here's a ticket of invitation for you. I'll be there. It starts at 9:45.

Your Iv. Turgenev

Letter 253 (2851). To Edmond de Goncourt.[1]
March 25/April 6, 1872. Paris.

48, rue de Douai.
Saturday evening.
March 6.

Dear Monsieur,

If I didn't respond to your letter immediately, it's a little bit your fault: like the majority of your compatriots, you don't indicate your address—and I had completely forgotten it—the more so as it was Flaubert who brought me to your place. I wasn't able to find it in the directory of addresses; I finally had the bright idea of asking Mlle Mathilde's[2] concierge, who gave it to me. I'm very glad that you like my work; as for the books of yours that you've sent me—I started reading the story of de Mailly[3] immediately—and I take a great interest in that character whom you've studied and researched intriguingly. He is very much of our time and all countries—but he's also very French.

I would be very happy to meet you and have a good chat with you. Would Thursday suit you? Fix a time and place for me where we could meet in Paris in order to go dine somewhere. In the meantime accept my cordial regards.

J. Tourgéneff

Letter 254 (2856). To A.A. Fet.
March 29/April 10, 1872. Paris.

Paris.
48, rue de Douai.
Wednesday, March 29/April 10, 1872.

And so, dear Afanasy Afanasievich, the good-natured giant, V.A. Shenshin,[1] has passed away. Death really is buzzing all around us...it really is a "battle of life." I hope that you survive this crossfire as long as possible—and I rejoice at the strengthening of your intestinal tract. Drink water, water—in great quantities!

As for Afanasiev (A.N.),[2] allow me to remark that you are not well enough aware of the subdivisions of literature into so-called belles-lettres, journalism, and scholarship (and pedagogy)—or, to be more accurate, you recognize the subdivisions but value only belles-lettres—and of all things, poetry! But our Society was founded expressly for men of letters, whose worth you have difficulty admitting and without whom the business of enlightenment would be in a bad way. That is precisely why we trouble ourselves to safeguard those very men of letters from hunger, cold, and similar horrors.

Well, and now, since in your "Exegi monumentum" [I have erected a monument][3] you treated the poet Fet objectively—allow me to do the same. Fet really is a poet in the genuine sense of the word, but he lacks something very important, namely—the same subtle and accurate sensitivity to the *inner* man—his spiritual essence—which Fet possesses in regard to nature and the *external* forms of human life. On this point not only Schiller and Byron, but even Ya. Polonsky beats him to smithereens. To be touched or shaken by one of the products of Fet's muse is just as impossible as walking on the ceiling. And that is why, for all his gifts, he must be ranked with the dii minorum gentium [minor gods]. But it's no joke that in a hundred years some 20 of his beautiful poems will be remembered—what more could one want? But may he not repeat himself, as he has been doing for ten years now. An old nightingale is a contradictio in adjecto [contradiction in terms].

One can't but praise you for your campaign against syphilis—that is a very worthy cause—and God grant you success and help from all sides! I'm contributing 100 silver rubles to your hospital and *home*[4] right away; I'll have the pleasure of entrusting the money to you when we see each other at Spasskoye in May. Until then be well and prosperous. I send my cordial regards to Maria Petrovna and clasp your hand firmly.

Your Iv. Turgenev

Letter 255 (2892). To V.V. Stasov.
June 14/26, 1872. Moscow.

Moscow.
Prechistensky Boulevard,
Crown Office Building.
Wednesday, June 14/26, 1872.

I received your letter of May 17th only a few days ago and here, dear Vladimir Vasilievich. When you wrote it I personally was in Petersburg (at Demut's hotel)—but was told that you were out of town—and I didn't look for you, which I now regret greatly. But I was only in Petersburg a few days anyway. I'm leaving here on Thursday if the attack of gout to which I was suddenly subjected allows—but I'll only be in Petersburg 24 hours—and therefore it's unlikely that I'll see you—the more so as you may now be in Moscow, without my knowing of it. We'll have to argue on paper rather than in person.

Why do you imagine that I—not a musician and not a painter, and besides, already an old man fed up with any and all hypocrisy and who only obeys his own impressions—why do you imagine that I'm infected with fetishism and that I bow down before European authorities? The devil take them all! I'm delighted by Gluck's recitatives and arias not because authorities praise them, but because at the first sound of them tears leap to my eyes—and it's not authorities who force me to be thoroughly disdainful of *The Stone Guest*,[1] which I had the patience to listen to twice, and not in a *dubious* piano transcription, but a masterful one. You don't even list the authorities accurately. You imagine that Ary Scheffer[2] means something to the French (I'm talking about artistic nature, not philistines) or Kaulbach[3] to the Germans, when they've been turned over to the archives long since and *no one* speaks of them seriously; as for Delacroix,[4] I could only hope for such an irregular, uneven, but brilliant talent for our school! I saw Repin's picture[5]—and with true regret I recognized in that cold mish-mash of the living and the dead—forgive me—the sort of far-fetched nonsense that could only be born in the head of a Khlestakov-Porokhov-shchikov with his "Slavic Bazaar." And that opinion of mine is shared by the painter himself, who sat with me for a couple of hours and spoke with sincere distress about the theme imposed upon him and even regretted that I had gone to see his work, in which a remarkable talent is nevertheless evident, but which at this moment is suffering a well-deserved fiasco. God forbid that his other themes be as still-born as this one! No, my dear Vladimir Vasilievich, I'll be the first to rejoice over Russian art; but I don't want to be like Wagner,[6] of whom Goethe says that he

> "Mit gier'ger Hand nach Schätzen grubt—
> Und froh ist, wenn er Regenwürmer findet
> [With greedy hand he digs for treasures—
> And is happy if he finds worms].[7]

He found a home-grown talent—Glinka—so rejoice and be proud of him...but all those Dargomyzhskys, Balakirevs,[8] and Bryullovs will be washed away by the waves and carried away together with the sand and every sort of dust.

All of this may seem to you to be sacrilege, rubbish...But I also remember people who also considered me practically a criminal because I didn't recognize Kukolnik,[9] that *young genius*...But that's enough. Neither is Antokolsky here nor have I heard anything about his statue. *That's* something that I'd like to take a look at—and I believe in his things, because he has *temperament*—not just pangs of pseudo-inspiration.

But that really is enough—lest we just keeping digging the ground underneath us. Won't you take a trip to Europe and stop off in Paris? I'll be there from the early part of October on—and if you want, you can already write me at 48, rue de Douai.

Good-bye and be well.

Your devoted

Iv. Turgenev

Letter 256 (2912). To Gustave Flaubert.[1]
July 18/30, 1872. Saint-Valery-sur-Somme.

Saint-Valery-sur-Somme.
Maison Ruhaut.
Tuesday.

Where are you at this moment, my dear friend, and what are you planning to do until winter? Please write me a word or two. As for me—I've been in the backwater from where I'm writing you for fifteen days now—

and I would be just fine if it weren't for the cursed gout which has me by the paw more obstinately than ever. It seized me six weeks ago in Moscow—and won't let me go. I've had three or four relapses, walked with the aid of crutches—later with two canes—then one—and here I am again almost immobile. With all due deference to Mr. Cicero, old age is a vile thing.[2]

I'm here with the Viardot family—I have a very nice room where nothing prevents me from working... but nothing comes! There's rust in the spring.

And what is Antoine doing? Give me some news of him.

That loan of 9, 12, 15 billion had the effect of a huge artillery salvo on me.[3] You devilish Frenchmen are born to astonish the world in one manner or another.

I've been a grandfather since the 18th; my daughter was delivered of a girl whom they've named Jeanne[4]—and to whose christening I'm going toward the end of August. I'll have to pass through Paris on the way there and back. If you're at Croisset at that time, I'll push on to your place as well.

And so—be well and au revoir! I clasp your hand firmly.

Your J. Tourguéneff

Letter 257 (2948). To George Sand.[1]
September 28/ October 10, 1872. Paris.

Paris.
48, rue de Douai.
Wednesday, October 10, 1872.

The girls[2] are writing to you and I must add a word or two. I must tell you how happy I was to have seen Nohant, and to have seen you there along with it. You have the most charming nest that one could imagine, and the surroundings are lovely. You deserve that; but one is fiercely happy to see things that are deserved come true. The girls speak of nothing but Nohant, and I myself hope to return there during the winter, when I no longer have my gout. Tell our delightful Lolo[3] that I'll tell her some good stories! And it will be something different from that little fool Blaise.[4]

You'll be coming to Paris in a few days, won't you? I rejoice at the idea of seeing you here, and until then I kiss your hands affectionately and at the same time beg you to give my best regards to all of your loved ones.

Yours with all my heart,

Iv. Tourguéneff

Letter 258 (3026). To V.A. Tsurikova.[1]
December 16/28, 1872. Paris.

Paris. 48, rue de Douai.
Saturday, December 16/28, 1872.

If, in your words, you experienced agitation when writing to me—then I too must confess that it's not without a certain discomfiture that I take pen in hand to answer you. You shower me with praise that would be appropriate for Shakespeare or Goethe. Your youthful enthusiasm, reinforced by the isolation of rural life, elevates a rather ordinary phenomenon to the ideal and surrounds it with a halo. Believe me, dear Varvara Alexandrovna, I'm not at all a *genius,* as you put it—and I have no pretension to such a sonorous title; I'm already satisfied and happy that with my writings I have given a few pleasant moments to some of my fellow countrymen—and that perhaps I was not without influence on their moral and spiritual development. Thanks of the sort that you've expressed are my greatest reward. That's why I thank you sincerely for your letter.

I fully approve of your desire to do something not just for your close family circle, but for a wider circle of readers as well. The dissemination of free, honest thoughts and feelings is a useful cause, a good cause everywhere—and especially in Russia—and there's no reason for you to fear possible censure and retreat before it.

In closing, I wish you all the best in life, health, activity, and success— and I beg you to accept the assurance of my complete respect and devotion.

Iv. Turgenev

P.S. Your letter was addressed to Baden, but I've sold my house there—I now live in Paris.

Letter 259 (3060). To Gustave Flaubert.[1]
January O.S., 1873. Paris.

> 48, rue de Douai.
> Wednesday morning.

My dear friend,

I have spoken to Mme Viardot about the wish expressed by Mme E. Grisi.[2] Unfortunately, it's impossible. Mme Viardot has had to adopt a rule not to sing for private parties: she receives so many requests that if she were once to accept, there would be no grounds for refusing others. She greatly regrets not being able to do anything just at this time. When she was younger, she could manage it—but now she must save herself as much as possible. That, my good friend, is the honest truth.

I'll certainly come on Sunday, perhaps a little early—I'll probably be going to Princess Mathilde's that evening.

Cordial regards from your

> J. Tourguéneff.

Letter 260 (3066). To Julian Schmidt.[1]
February 11/23, 1873. Paris.

> Paris. 48, rue de Douai.
> Sunday, February 23, 1873.

My dear friend,

You can do me a great favor: this will demand a half hour of your time and five silver groschen of your money. Here's what the matter is: the second edition of *Fathers and Sons* is being published, and I just now read the book—the translation—for the first time. In spite of the fact that in the preface I praised the translation to the skies, there are quite unacceptable inaccuracies and omissions in it (see, for instance, pp. 358!!, 202, and others). I've corrected them, but I'm not absolutely certain that I expressed myself in German properly. Look through the book. There's no need, of course, to read it all; just pause at the corrections. After you've done that and fixed up everything that's essential, please send the book, with your approval, to Rudolstadt, "Fröbelsche Hofbuchdruckerei" (here's where the five silver groschen come in). Accept my heartfelt gratitude in advance.

My gout has left me, and I'm now working on an unfortunately rather long novel[2] with which I intend to close my literary career. On November 9th of this year I'll be 55, and my intellectual activity, just like any other sort, ought to cease.

I'll see you at the end of June, of course. Until then, be healthy and vigorous. Best regards to your dear wife, all our friends, and you, too.

Your Iv. Turgenev

P.S. I would be happy to have a few words in answer from you.

Letter 261 (3128). To P.L. Lavrov.[1]
May 20/ June 1, 1873. Paris.

Paris. 48, rue de Douai.
Sunday, June 1, 1873.

Dear Pyotr Lavrovich, I hasten to inform you that on Wednesday I'm leaving for Baden—and on Saturday or Sunday I'll turn up in Zurich, where, of course, I'll have the pleasure of seeing you. Vyrubov,[2] with whom I dined yesterday (he also seems to be planning to come to visit you) informed me that according to you, fierce passions have been kindled in Zurich, so that your secretary even suffered physical harm;[3] knowing my young compatriots' disposition towards me, I ought to ask myself whether I can subject myself to such a risk.[4] But why not give it a try? I'm going to Zurich, hoping for the best.

And so, I'll see you soon. Drop me a line in Baden at the following address: H-n I. T., Baden-Baden, per Adresse Frau Minna Anstett, Schillerstrasse, 7.

And accept the assurance of my respect and devotion.

Iv. Turgenev

Letter 262 (3177). To P.V. Annenkov.
August 16/28, 1873. Bougival.

> Bougival.
> (Seine-et-Oise). Maison Halgan.
> Thursday, August 28, 1873.

Dear Pavel Vasilievich, they say that Pushkin was quite sensitive in regard to what foreign newspapers printed about him; although I'm far from Pushkin—and I am not especially sensitive about criticism, nonetheless, the enclosed excerpt gave me a certain pleasure.[1] You'll see from it that the reviewer remarks with disdain and irritation on the "Russian school" in German literature that is allegedly following in my footsteps. I'd heard of this fact before—and the names of my "followers" were even conveyed to me—but this is the first time that I've seen it with my own eyes. So this is how things go: the Germans imitate me—and in my native land Mr. "Postny" in *The Deed* calls me a writer *covered with spittle*.[2] Le système des compensations [the system of compensations]!

What are you up to in Baden—and how is your health and your family's? I'm getting ready for the hunting season, which begins Sunday, if only my gout will allow me. But right now everything is fine.

But not in Russia, where poor Tyutchev (F.I.) is dying and where *The Messenger of Europe* has received a second warning for an article that could serve as a model of moderation![3]

Drop me a line. I embrace all of you and remain

> Your devoted Iv. Turgenev.

P.S. Tear off the attached note and give it to Madame Anstett.

Letter 263 (3200). To A.A. Fet.
September 13/25, 1873. Nohant.

Château de Nohant. Près La Châtre
(Indre).
Thursday, September 13/25, 1873.

Dear Fet, I'm here as a guest of Mme George Sand's—I arrived here from Paris the day before yesterday and brought with me your letter with the epigraph from Goethe—I can't tell whether it refers to you or to me. (You forgot the fourth line: "In jeden Quark begräbt er seine Nase"[He sticks his nose into all sorts of rubbish].)[1] I'll begin with the fact that you're mistaken in accusing me of turning to you with the lining side out. Life's lining is a coarse and stinking cloth—it surrounds me from all sides; what can you expect of me! When you have occasion to think of me, please don't forget that I've now become a creature who is constantly fluctuating, like a clock pendulum, between two similarly disgusting feelings: revulsion for life and fear of death—and therefore don't be angry with me. I now have rare occasion to meet with the esthetic things and similar subtleties that you valued in me ... I haven't become more serious, but certainly more boring. That can't be changed—take me as I am.

You're right: the line that I attributed to Aksakov belongs to Khomyakov[2]—but it called to mind K.S. Aksakov, in the first place, because it very much suits him—and in the second, because I often heard it from the lips of K.S., accompanied by the usual tolling of bells.[3] As for my antipathy toward Slavophilism, I'm ashamed to say that I have to quote myself: "It's all a matter of sensations," says Bazarov.[4] You dislike the principles of '92 (but do you really care so much for those of '89?),[5] the International, Spain,[6] priests' sons[7]—all of that sickens you; and Katkov, *Baden,* generals,[8] militarism, and so on, make me sick. Just as with smells and tastes, you can't argue about these things. You, for example, accusing me of being wrong, write that you spoke of all this with M.N. Longinov[9] with *laughter;* but I would sooner admit to thievery than to a merry conversation with such an exceptional scoundrel. But it can't be helped.

You're wrong to be so critical of Virgil. The composition, characters, and so on of his *Aeneid* have no significance; but in individual phrases epithets, and coloration he's not only a poet, but a bold innovator and Romantic. I'll remind you of "per *amica silentia* lunae" [in the moon's friendly silence] (that's worthy of Tyutchev)—or "futura jam pallida morte" [pale from on-coming death] (of Dido, when in a fury, she mounts the pyre to commit suicide), and so on. I read Ovid so as to etwas Latein

113

treiben [study a little Latin] with the young Viardot.[10] And he's not as bad as you say, either.

Our hostess here is impossibly nice and intelligent; she's now a quite good-hearted old woman—and any unpleasant agitation has long been alien to her. She's very kind to me—and I'm sincerely attached to her.

I'm glad that Lev Tolstoy doesn't hate me—and even gladder at the rumors that he's finishing a long novel.[11] But please God, let there be no philosophy in it!

Give my regards to Maria Petrovna, kiss smart little Petya[12] for me— and be healthy, happy, and prosperous.

Your Iv. Turgenev

P.S. I went hunting a few days ago and killed a *fox* (the third in my life). I'll be in Paris again from the 15th N.S. on.

Letter 264 (3215). To P.N. Polevoy.[1]
October 17/29, 1873. Paris.

Paris. 48, rue de Douai.
Wednesday, October 17/19, 1873.

Dear Pyotr Nikolayevich,

I must apologize to you for taking so long to fulfill my promise, but I fell rather seriously ill as soon as I arrived here; I was in bed for several days and still haven't gone out, but I don't want to put this off any longer, and I take pen in hand.

The enclosed biographical sketch was published in *The Field* and is rather accurate in its overall features. I'll add a few details—and you can do with all of this whatever you want. (I'll speak in the third person.)

Of the historical personages belonging to his family, Turgenev especially esteems two of them: the Pyotr Turgenev who *exposed* the False Dmitry[2] and who was executed for that *exposé* the very same day in

114

Moscow on Red Square—and Peter the Great's jester, Yakov Turgenev, who on New Year's Day 1700, had to cut the boyars' beard with scissors;[3] in his own way he, too, served the cause of enlightenment.

In 1838 Turgenev often saw Stankevich and T. Granovsky in Berlin; and in 1840 he shared a room for an entire semester with Mikhail Bakunin, who was later to become so well-known. The two of them didn't even think of politics back then—they were studying Hegel assiduously.

In 1841, instead of returning directly to Petersburg, Turgenev went first to Moscow, where his mother lived—and where he became acquainted with the Slavophiles: the Aksakovs, Khomyakovs, and Kireyevskys. Slavophilism was just coming into being then, but Turgenev already had a negative attitude toward it.

In the first part of his *Literary Memoirs* (see Vol. I of his works) the course of his intellectual development is described rather faithfully and accurately.

In 1848 he had practically made up his mind to leave Russia and remain abroad. The melancholy feeling that involuntarily overcame him at the thought of this decision was reflected in *The Notes of a Hunter*, which he was then writing—it's especially noticeable in the descriptions and pictures of the woods and countryside which Turgenev did not imagine that he would ever see again.

In 1870 Turgenev left Baden-Baden for good, sold the house that he had built there—and for the time being has settled in Paris. He visits Russia annually.

That's everything that I had to say, dear Pyotr Nikolayevich. My life has been primarily literary—and therefore offers few external events and very little factual interest. I think that the data herein related will be quite sufficient for the public.

I hope to have the pleasure of seeing you in Petersburg—and in the meantime I beg you to accept the assurance of the complete admiration of

your devoted Iv. Turgenev.

Letter 265 (3224). To N.S. Turgenev.
October 30/November 11, 1873.

Paris. 48, rue de Douai.
Tuesday, Oct. 30/ Nov. 11, 1873.

My dear brother,

I was planning to answer your letter of September 27/October 9—but kept delaying—and a second letter of October 24/November 5 has arrived—and I don't want to put off replying any longer. As you correctly assume, I'm in Paris now—and I'll be staying here until New Year's, since I won't be able to leave any earlier. But at the beginning of January, if I'm alive, I'll definitely go to Petersburg—and from there to Moscow. It would be very good if we could then leave for abroad together.

My health is quite satisfactory: I attribute that to the Carlsbad waters—I intend to take them next year as well.

The duel about which you express curiosity took place between Prince Dolgoruky,[1] the brother de la grande demoiselle,[2] and Heeckeren,[3] the son of the villain who killed Pushkin.[4] The quarrel was not over Heeckeren's wife, but simply over the well-known<--->Mlle Leteyssier, whom they are both courting. Prince Dolgoruky, by the way, is a brazen, impudent bit of trash—and Heeckeren is no better. This is definitely a case of trash fighting trash over trash. Prince Dolgoruky's wound is very dangerous. They say that his arm will have to be amputated. I'm very glad that you managed to sell Dolgoye and Alexeyevka for a handsome profit. In our time there couldn't be anything better than ready money—or stocks that are as good as money.

I wish you all the best and embrace you.

Your loving brother Iv. Turgenev

P.S. I hope that you've finished building your house.

Letter 266 (3255). To M.M. Stasyulevich.
December 20, 1873/ January 1, 1874. Paris.

Paris. 48, rue de Douai.
Thursday, Dec. 20, 1873/ Jan. 1, 1874.

Dear Mikhail Matveyevich, I have some nice news for you: my friend Flaubert (the author of *Madame Bovary,* etc.) has finally made up his mind to publish his novel *La Tentation de St. Antoine,* which everyone who has heard (including me, by the way) considers one of the most remarkable works of recent literature. He is willing to give it to me in galley proofs so that the Russian translation could be done without delay. This novel will appear in Paris at the end of February—it could appear in Russia in the April issue of *The Messenger of Europe*—and since I'll be spending the month of March in Petersburg (if I'm still alive), I could look over the translation—and will do that with pleasure—both for Flaubert and for the honor of our language, which will have to do battle with a dangerous rival. Flaubert has asked me to find out whether you agree to this and how much you'll give him per signature page. There will be no more than 10 of them (of *The Messenger of Europe's* format). Write me your reply, which I'll relay to the author immediately.[1]

For my part, on this European New Year's Day I wish you all the best for our Asiatic one—and clasp your hand cordially.

Your devoted Iv. Turgenev.

Letter 267 (3261). To Pauline Bruère.[1]
January 1/13, 1874. Paris.

To Pauline.

Paris. 48, rue de Douai.
Tuesday, January 13, 1874.

My dear Pauline,

I'm just writing you a short note to tell you about a letter that I've written to your husband and which he'll doubtless show you. Since it's likely that you've already talked both about your affairs and about the conversation that I had with Gaston and his father—you won't find anything new in the letter. I'm simply anxious to confirm to you the decision that I've made to re-establish your pension[2] and to send it to you directly for as long as the affairs at the glass factory are in the mess that they are. I cannot allow the idea that the two of you—you and Jeannette, might not have anything with which to provide for your needs.

Meanwhile, I embrace the two of you. Au revoir.

Iv. Tourguéneff

Letter 268 (3268). To Ya. P. Polonsky.
January 25/ February 6, 1874. Paris.

Paris. January 25, 1874.

Dear Yakov Petrovich,

Since I want to contribute my bit to *The Pool*[1] and don't have anything ready, or even begun, I started to dig around in my old papers and found the enclosed piece from *The Notes of a Hunter,*[2] which I ask you to forward to the proper quarters. In all, twenty-two of the pieces have been published; but about thirty of them were prepared originally. Some of the sketches were left unfinished because of fear that the censorship would not pass them; others—because they didn't seem interesting enough or suitable. The latter group includes the sketch entitled "Living Relics." Of course, I would have been happier sending you something more significant; but this is all that I have. Besides, an indication of our people's "mighty endurance" may not be completely inappropriate in a publication such as *The Pool*.

By the way, allow me to tell you an anecdote that is likewise related to a hungry time in Russia. In 1841, as you know,[3] Tula and its adjoining provinces were nearly depopulated. A few years afterwards, a friend and I, passing through Tula Province, stopped at a country tavern and began drinking tea. My friend started to relate an incident (I don't remember which one) from his life and mentioned a person who had starved to death and was as "thin as a skeleton." "Allow me to point out, sir," intervened the old tavern-owner, who had been present at our conversation, "that people don't get thin from starvation—they swell up." "What do you mean?" "Just that, sir, a man swells up like a jar—you, know, the ones that look like an apple. In 1841 we all walked around puffed up." "Ah, in 1841!" I joined in. "Was it an awful time?" "Yes, my friend, terrible." "Well, and how was it," I asked, "were there disorders or plundering?" "What disorders, my friend?" the old man objected with amazement. "You're already being punished by God as it is; why would you add to your troubles by sinning?"

It seems to me that helping such a people when it is struck by misfortune is the sacred duty of each of us.

Ivan Turgenev

Letter 269 (3271). To P.V. Annenkov.
January 26/ February 7, 1874. Paris.

Dear Pavel Vasilievich, first of all I want to express to you my joy that nothing sorrowful has happened in your family—and the hope that your little sick one will get well and become a fine young fellow.[1] The manuscript that you returned has already been sent off to Petersburg.[2] As soon as I read that part of your letter in which you express doubts about a certain passage, I immediately thought: "He's talking about la tartine sur l'émancipation" [the tirade on the emancipation]—and that's just what it turned out to be—and the result was that I immediately removed the above-mentioned passage.[3] I have never yet regretted taking your literary advice—and I thank you sincerely and entrust myself to your attention in the future as well.

An unusual thing happened yesterday that I can't resist telling you about. There exists a certain American publisher, Henry Holt, who has been publishing translations of my things for five years now. Since there is no copyright convention between America and Europe, Holt didn't even think of asking for my authorization—especially since other publishers were also printing my things. Imagine my amazement when I received a letter from this Holt yesterday in which after a number of compliments (he even uses the word "enthusiasm"!) he informs me that at first the sales of my things were slow, but that now the profits are such that he can send me 1,000 francs by way of compensation—in fact, enclosed with the letter was a note of exchange à vue [payable on demand] for 1,000 francs. This genuinely American grandiosity touched me; I confess frankly that in the course of my literary career I have rarely been so flattered. I had been told before that, if I may venture to say so, I enjoy a certain popularity in America; but this first-hand evidence nonetheless made me happy.

In closing, I send my regards to all your loved ones and clasp your hand firmly.

Your devoted Iv. Turgenev

P.S. The wedding is set for the 8th of March;[4] everything is going well so far.

Letter 270 (3324). To A.V. Sorneva.[1]
Between November 13/25, 1871 and April 6/18, 1874. Paris.

48, rue de Douai.
Saturday.

My dear madame, Alexandra Vladimirovna,

You wish to know my opinion regarding your povest: allow me to take advantage of the fact that I don't have the honor of knowing you personally, so that I may be absolutely frank with you. I've read only the first two notebooks, but they were quite sufficient to convince me that the author is still inexperienced and ought not to think of publishing his work. He is even rather poorly acquainted with the Russian language, proof of which are the numerous grammatical errors which I permitted myself to correct. Continuing to speak to you in the third person, I consider it my duty to advise the author first to master the language and only then to ponder characters and situations; in particular, I beg him to avoid like the plague descriptions of the beauties of nature, for they are unbearable if they aren't superior—and in any case they must be as short and concise as possible. The business of literature is quite a painstaking and difficult one; it's a hundred times better not to write anything at all than to write in a mediocre, flabby manner.

I hope, madame, that you won't be too upset with me for my frankness; but I repeat that I considered it my duty to speak the unadulterated truth.[2]

In closing, I beg you to accept the expression of the complete respect and devotion

of your humble servant Iv. Turgenev.

Letter 271 (3421). To A.S. Suvorin.[1]
August 24/ September 5, 1874. Bougival.

Bougival. (Près Paris.).
Maison Halgan. Seine-et-Oise.
Saturday, August 24/ September 5, 1874.

I always read your witty feuilletons with special pleasure, dear Alexey Sergeyevich, but I beg permission to thank you for the last one (from August 18/30).[2] I was touched not so much by the compliments that you saw fit to lavish on my eloquence,[3] as by the fillips that you delivered to the reporter for *The Russian World*. That young, sugary little Tartuffe (a new type among us, by the way) turned up at my place with the suggestion that I take part in some charitable undertaking in which—according to him—he had already managed to interest General Trepov[4] and Her Imperial Highness the Crown Princess. I pointed out to him that having secured such authorities, there was no reason to seek any others—and refused.

Then he began to pester me with all sorts of "intimate" questions. (Among other things, he began assuring me that if my leg was better, it was because he had *prayed* for it! I replied that in such instances henbane ointment was preferable even to his prayers.) I confess that while conversing with that gentleman, all I thought about was how to get away as quickly as possible from having to contemplate his saccharine physiognomy; I don't recall a single one of the words that he put in my mouth; in general, as far as I am aware, I do not pronounce such banalities. This is a new attempt to introduce to Russia the American manner of interviewing a man! Thanks once again for the lesson that you gave that most unpleasant fellow.

I still haven't gotten rid of my gout, in spite of Mr. B.'s prayers. And this vile illness, by the way, is all the more unpleasant in that it prevents me from working. If, however, a decent hour or two turn up, I'll give you several more characteristics of eloquent Russians which you could include in one of your feuilletons, if you'd like.

I doubt that I'll be in Petersburg soon—I'll be here another month— and then I move on to Paris, rue de Douai, 50, where you visited me, as I recall. I was very glad to learn that you're beginning to recover from the terrible blow that befell you.[5]

Accept the assurance of my absolute respect and devotion.

Ivan Turgenev

Letter 272 (3446). To M.M. Stasyulevich.
September 24/ October 6, 1874. Bougival.

> Bougival. Maison Halgan.
> Tuesday, September 24/ October 6, 1874.

Dear Mikhail Matveyevich, since, to my sincere regret and thanks to M.N. Longinov,[1] you couldn't come to Paris, as you had planned, for negotiations with E. Zola, I decided to conduct them myself—and after a meeting with him and with his publisher, *Charpentier,*[2] I reached the following quite favorable results. Zola's novel, the title of which will be *La faute de l'abbé Mouret,* will appear in Paris *around January 20th* N.S.— but will be sent to you in the form of galley proofs, *beginning* on October

8/20: it will be divided into three parts, which can be published in the *November, December,* and *January* issues of *The Messenger of Europe*—so that it will be completely finished in your journal before it appears in Paris—an entire week before it is published (from January 13th to the 20th).[3] The novel, as far as I can judge by the contents and the first chapters, will be excellent—and it won't have anything that might be censored—in point of fact, it's aimed against celibacy for the priesthood. The conditions are the following: *30 silver rubles* per signature page—and if you wish to do a separate edition, settle that by letter—for *500* francs. I think that Charpentier surely will cede that to you. I hope that you won't find these conditions burdensome. In any case, please send a letter, as soon as possible, in which the above-mentioned conditions are laid out (and accepted by you), to Charpentier (M. Charpentier, librairie, quai de Louvre, 28, Paris)—since by contract Zola's works belong to *him*. On his part he'll then send you a letter—and by October 20th the first signatures will be on their way to Petersburg.

In your letter you express a slight hope of being in Paris at the beginning of October—but it doesn't seem likely—the most important thing for you is to see that *The Messenger of Europe* isn't closed down in your absence. If I knew where your wife will be staying in Paris, I'd definitely seek her out—I'm moving there in five days.

I still haven't rid myself of my illness—and haven't begun to work.

N.B. If you have *other* conditions for a *separate* edition, tell Charpentier—that perhaps he'll be satisfied with payment by the signature page. I hope that you are happy with my negotiations and I clasp your hand cordially.

Your devoted Iv. Turgenev

P.S. Send me the Czech translation of *Notes of a Hunter.*[4] I regularly receive books from Russia through the mail—and there are no problems.

Letter 273 (3497). To A.A. Fet.
November 28/ December 10, 1874. Paris.

Paris. 50, rue de Douai.
Thursday, Nov. 29/ Dec. 10, 1874.

Dear Shenshin, I received your letter today—and three days ago I had a letter from Polonsky, from which I quote the following passage:

"Fet (Shenshin) has set a rumor afloat that during your last visit you spoke to some youths (I heard that it was Milyutin's grandsons, Fet-Shenshin's wards)—and tried to infect them with the desire to go to Siberia...

I first heard this from Markevich[1] at Prince Meshchersky's[2] five or six weeks ago... A few days ago I heard the same rumor repeated, with the same reference to Fet-Shenshin."

Recalling my conversation at Mulyutina's with her son and Petya,[3] and knowing your love of exaggeration and other such habits, I'll tell you straight out that I quite believe that you really said the words that are attributed to you—and therefore I think it best to break off our relations, which, as it is, because of our differing views, have no "raison d'être" [reason for being].[4] I fail to see what there can be in common between me and a *justice of the peace* who in all seriousness reproaches *big, hearty* peasants for not having taken *the end of a shaftbow and beaten the living daylights out of a thief whom they had caught*— and even boasts of it, as if he didn't understand the ghastliness of his words.[5]

I take my leave of you not without a certain sense of sadness that is related exclusively to the past, however—I wish you all the best in the company of the Markeviches, Katkovs, and others ejusdem farinae [of the same dough].

Give my farewell regards to your kind wife, whom I probably will not have occasion to see again.[6]

Iv. Turgenev

Letter 274 (3550). To Julian Schmidt.[1]
February 1/13, 1875. Paris.

Rue de Douai. 50. Paris.
Saturday, February 13, 1875.

My dear friend,

I'm very glad that you liked the photographs. I'd send you Flaubert's and Zola's pictures, but that's not so easy. Flaubert hasn't allowed anyone to photograph him for 15 years, and Zola has never allowed it. He's what the French call "un sanglier" [a wild boar]: he stays at home with his wife all the time, doesn't wear gloves, doesn't own a dress coat, and won't even hear about any of life's vain trifles—including photographs. Nonetheless, don't consider it a lost cause yet. I'll use the force of my persuasiveness.

I received the four issues of *Wiener Zeitung* and I'll show them to Zola tomorrow; you give it to him a little bit in places, but all in all, you treat him as a major figure, and that's the main thing.[2]

Do you by any chance know Flaubert's *Education Sentimentale* (a terribly stupid title)? I doubt that you do. It is perhaps his most significant work, though not a very winning one. It was a failure in France—for the French it was too bitter a truth. It came out shortly before the war and turned out to be prophetic (do you say "Prophezei" or "Profezeihung"?). Wouldn't you like me to send you the book?

There was a word in your letter that I couldn't read—where you talk about Tatyana B-a. "Faithful..." What is it?[3]

Cordial regards to your dear wife and all our good friends, and my best wishes to you.

Your Iv. Turgenev

Letter 275 (3569). To M. A. Milyutina.
February 22/ March 6, 1875. Paris.

Paris. 50, Rue de Douai.
Sunday, February 22/ March 6, 1875.

What a task you've set me, dear Maria Ageyevna! I doubt that any other writer has ever received such an assignment. To define my personal worldview... what's more, in concise form, in a letter?! It would be easy and even natural to treat such a question either negatively or humorously... and would be no less natural or accurate to say "the Lord only knows!" But since I don't want to cause your son[1] any trouble (though I confess frankly that I can't help but be amazed at the strange assignment that the students of the Katkov Lycée are given), I'll say, in brief, that I am predominantly a realist—and that more than anything else I'm interested in the living truth of the human physiognomy; I'm indifferent to the supernatural, I don't believe in any absolutes or systems, more than anything else I love freedom—and, as far as I can tell, I'm receptive to poetry. Everything human is dear to me. Slavophilism is alien, just as is any orthodoxy. I think that I've said enough—and in essence, this is all just words. I don't know how to tell you anything more about myself.

I'll be very interested to read your son's composition on this topic.

Thank you for the news of yourself. We had our own share of alarms and troubles, too, but apparently everything is back to normal now, *which is the best thing of all.* Oh, the blessed charm of uniformity and the similarity of today and yesterday! I thoroughly enjoy that charm. My gout is leaving me alone—for the time being; all my loved ones here are well, including the newly-arrived little girl (my dear Claudie's daughter, Mme Viardot's granddaughter)—so there's nothing more that one could wish for; to my great pleasure, I'm not working either.

I'm glad that Antokolsky has undertaken a statue of Pushkin, and I'm not surprised that the bust of your husband wasn't a success: portraits aren't in his line.

Apropos of portraits: the painter Kharlamov[2] has done remarkable portraits of M. and Mme Viardot—and now he's doing mine.

Give my cordial regards to all your loved ones and accept the assurance of the sincere attachment of

Your devoted Iv. Turgenev.

Letter 276 (3596). To A.V. Toporov.[1]
March 20/ April 1, 1875. Paris.

Paris, 50, Rue de Douai.
Thursday, March 20/ April 1, 1875.

Dear Alexander Vasilievich, I'm a little guilty before you for not having answered your letter right away. And although I'd like to use the excuse that I've been working hard, it's not so! I've been lazy, as usual. And my health is as usual—i.e., not bad, in spite of the fact that from time to time gout knocks at my door, i.e., at my legs. I'm going to Carlsbad in six weeks—and I'll somehow make it until then.

Miss Arnholt[2] receives *The Citizen* regularly—and I read it.[3] If *The Deed* really is so empty, then forget about it.[4] The Christmas gift was long since received and eaten with gratitude. As soon as I found out that it came from the Ragozins, I wrote him[5] a letter. That was very kind and nice of them.

I have informed my estate manager that he is to send you a *hundred* rubles to cover the debt and forthcoming expenses.

And now I'll tell you something that I beg you to keep a deep secret. Iogansen isn't paying me anything for Mme Viardot's romances,[6] but so as to spare her self-respect, I've been telling her that he's been giving me 25 silver rubles for each one. Write me a letter in which you tell me that you've received 125 silver rubles for the last 5 romances—and I'll show her the letter (she reads Russian), since she's beginning to suspect my amiable craftiness—and I'll pay her that money here, and you'll allegedly keep it for me in Petersburg to apply to my expenses according to my instruction. Do all of this just as I've laid it out for you, dear Alexander Vasilievich, and I'll be profoundly grateful. And keep all of this a secret!

We received *The Demon*[7] here (in a piano arrangement)—read through it attentively—and came to the conclusion that although it's respectable, it's boring and unoriginal. L.N. Tolstoy's novel[8] brought us a much greater disappointment (because our expectations were greater). With his talent, to wander into the swamp of high society and stomp and shove in place—and treat all that rubbish not with humor—but, on the contrary, with pathos, seriously—what nonsense!!![9] Moscow has done him in—and he's neither the first nor the last to be so done in. But I feel sorrier for him than for all the others.

My dear friend, you're bored . . . What can one do?! In general, it's a boring time in Russia, and for you particularly . . . The 40s are making themselves felt. I can only repeat along with I.S. Aksakov:

"When will you finally pass,
O youth, o burdensome time!"

There's no sensible activity—that's the tragedy.

If I manage to shake off my sloth and finish my long novel,[10] we'll see each other at the end of the year—I'll bring it to Petersburg . . . If not . . . perhaps you'll visit Paris?

I wish you all the best and clasp your hand cordially.

Your devoted Iv. Turgenev

Letter 277 (3657). To S.A. Vengerov.[1]
May 25/ June 6, 1875. Carlsbad.

Carlsbad (Bohemia).
May 24/ June 6, 1875.

My dear Semyon Afanasievich!

I received your book just before my departure for Paris, read it carefully, and, in accordance with your wishes, I am relating to you the impressions that it produced on me. As far as I am able to judge in a matter that concerns me so closely, there are many accurate and good things in the book—and the very idea underlying it is correct and useful;[2] I can't help regretting that you saw fit to devote such attention to my poetry— moreover, you occasionally attribute the censor's distortions to me—for instance, I had "had his fill of sweet *lordly* food"—and the censor changed it to *proprietor's*—which resulted in nonsense and a lame verse. But this is a minor point. My dislike of my own poetry can be explained by the ancient

"Mediocribus esse poëtis
Non di, non homines"
[Neither gods nor men (allow) poets to be mediocre] and so on.[3]

128

What really upset me—and, I admit, surprised me—was your supposition that "certain of my povests (which ones?) were written by me in German": "he has original povests in French" (!) and so on. This is not the first time that this supposition has appeared in print; but I always saw in it the intent to wound me. That intention is unthinkable in you—but that makes your words all the more incomprehensible. *Never in my life have I ever published so much as a single line in a language other than Russian;* otherwise I would be simply trash, not an artist. How could one possibly write in an alien language when even in one's own native tongue one can hardly cope with the images, ideas, and so on! Frankly speaking, that supposition is at odds with the esthetic understanding and critical tact displayed on more than one occasion by you in your work.

As long as we're speaking of censure, allow me to say a few words about your language. To me, an old philologist, it seems too careless. Sentences such as the one to be found on p. 32 and which begins with the words "For the bourgeois spirit of our time"—pardon me for the sharpness of my expression—are unforgivable. "The intelligentsia's varnish of idealism, which is a reaction of materialism" can only drive away your reader's interest, the more so as the idea which you intended to express is a quite common one and did not need such garnishing.

I'm certain that you won't be angry at me for my frankness and will only see in it a sign of my sincere sympathy.

I await the continuation of your brochure and hope that censorship difficulties will not prevent its publication.

I'm staying here until July 3/15—and then I'll go back to Paris again.

Accept the assurance of my absolute respect and devotion.

Iv. Turgenev

P.S. My address in Paris in 50, rue de Douai.

Letter 278 (3724). To Jules Hetzel.[1]
September 11/23, 1875. Bougival.

Bougival. Les Frênes.
Thursday, September 23, 1875.

My dear friend,

Verne's book is implausible—but that doesn't matter: it's amusing.[2]
The implausibility lies in the Khan of Bokhara's invasion of present-day
Siberia—that's the same thing as if I were to portray France invaded by
Holland. It would really be better to stress the personal dangers that the
Tsar's brother risked. I'm sorry that Verne made his heroine a *Livonian-
Russian*: the fact is that the Livonians are no more Russians than the
Germans are. But that's a minor detail that will pass unnoticed.

I very much hope that Mme Hetzel's accident has no serious
consequences; do you have polished stairs, too? France is terrible in that
way. I'll try to arrange a luncheon with "commentaries" for next week.

Until then I clasp your hand firmly and remain

Your devoted J. Tourguéneff.

Letter 279 (3725). To Emile Zola.[1]
September 14/26, 1875. Bougival.

Bougival. Les Frênes.
September 26, 1875.

My dear friend,

Your letter of the 8th didn't reach me until the 20th! The mail has been
playing pranks on me like that for some time. I'm writing you in the hope
that my letter will find you still at St. Aubin. I have no doubt but that the
sea air is good for your wife, and I'm happy to see that you're working and
finishing up some books. There are still people, after all, who work
indefatigably!

Poor Flaubert is in an absolutely pathetic psychic state: just as you say, all of his friends must draw close around him this winter *if he comes to Paris,* but that's not at all certain yet. It's an abominable cruelty of fate to up and strike the man of the world the least capable of living by his labor.

Stasyulevich, whom I've seen a number of times during his short stay in Paris, also regretted not having been able to make your acquaintance; he has come to terms with Charpentier for the new volume.[2] By the way, do you have any objections to your full name being placed under the feuilletons in *The Messenger of Europe?* He requested that I ask you. The last one (on the Goncourt brothers) is excellent. Their novel will have to be translated, and Stasyulevich has already put his hooks in *Renée Mauperin.*[3]

What?! Poor Goncourt[4] is having financial difficulties too? That's stupid and unjust.

I'm staying here another month or six weeks, but I come to Paris often, and I hope to be able to clasp your hand.

Iv. Tourguéneff

Letter 280 (3758). To M. Ye. Saltykov.
October 28/November 9, 1875. Bougival.

Bougival. (Seine-et-Oise.) Les Frênes.
October 28/November 9, 1875.
Tuesday.

Your letter made me very happy, dear Mikhail Yevgrafovich, for I was beginning to be worried. I consider that letter the nicest gift for my birthday today. (I've turned 57—a respectable age, as you can see.) I'm glad that you found a place in Nice that suits you—I'm just afraid that the dear and funny Mrs. Danilova[1] might up and ask you for money![2] But that's only a minor problem for you if you have the strength and firmness of will. But you're more stern than you are firm! Especially in the matter of a refusal.

I'll move on to your latest story in *The Notes of the Fatherland.* I received the October issue yesterday—and of course I immediately read "A Family Tribunal," which I was extraordinarily pleased with. The characters are drawn strongly and accurately: I'm not speaking of the figure of the mother, who is typical—and has appeared in your works before—she was obviously taken from real life. But the drunken and lost "simpleton" is especially good. The character is so well done that one can't help wondering why Saltykov, instead of doing sketches, doesn't write a large novel with a grouping of characters and events, with a guiding idea and broad execution?[3] But one could respond that to a certain extent it's others who write novels and povests—but what Saltykov does is done by him and no one else. Be that as it may, I liked "A Family Tribunal" very much, and I impatiently await its continuation—the description of "Little Judas" triumphs. You complain that you have to write and work a great deal; but I, sinner that I am, instead of feeling sorry for you, envy you (of course, on the condition that the work doesn't injure your health). I have so completely forgotten both how to work and write, and it's doubtful that I'll be able to come to terms with my sloth and my indifference. And you also shouldn't complain that Mother Russia accompanies you everywhere: she'll still have to undergo your operations for a long time yet—and therefore even though she screams, still she comes at you in the form of various "Prince" Rekins and "Marquise" Baratynskys.[4] That milieu won't produce anything anyway: it's so$<--->$. That means that there's no point in relying on others.

I haven't seen your enemy Sollogub[5] since the time of that famous scene: but he's still here, and they say that he's lost his comedy again—and, imagine!—is again looking for it. What eccentrics there are!

Annenkov has finally returned to Baden-Baden and has settled in at Sophienstrasse, No. 4. I'm certain that your letters to him got lost; otherwise he definitely would have answered you: he's a punctilious person and he likes you.

By the way, I'll be writing to him tomorrow.

And what do you have to say about the Moscow catastrophe with Strusberg and so on?[6] Typical! My publisher Salayev lost 55,000 silver rubles in that scrape.

I'll be here another week—and then I'm moving to Paris, 50, rue de Douai. Please use that address for your letters.

I send my regards to your loved ones and clasp your hand cordially.

Your devoted Iv. Turgenev

Letter 281 (3817). To M. Ye. Saltykov.
January 3/15, 1876. Paris.

Paris. 50, rue de Douai.
Saturday, January 3/15, 1876.

I received your letter yesterday, dear Mikhail Yevgrafovich—and, as you see, I'm not tardy in answering. Your letter—it's not at all "stupid" or "crude," as you put it, but on the contrary, very good and very intelligent—made me very happy: it speaks of a certain vitality and better health—which forms a sharp contrast to your earlier gloomy missive. (By the way—now I'm not at all well: I've been in bed for five days, forced there by gout.) In addition, your sketch for a humorous story about Nicholas' correspondence with Paul de Kock delighted me: you absolutely *must* write it—for it will be a pearl of the first magnitude.[1] I also read "The Way You Would with Relatives" and enjoyed it very much: the old woman who weeps at the rising of the sun is what the French call "une travaille"[a find], and in general the entire character is superb. Only a great talent is capable of arousing the reader's sympathy for her without softening a single one of her traits.

Well, and now I'll say a couple of words about *Fathers and Sons,* since you spoke of it. Can you really imagine that everything that you reproach me for hasn't already occurred to me? That's why I wouldn't like to disappear from the face of the earth without finishing my long novel, which, it seems to me, ought to clear up many misunderstandings and place me where I ought to be.[2] I'm not surprised, by the way, that Bazarov has remained a mystery for many people; I myself can't really imagine how I wrote him. It was—don't laugh, please—fate, something stronger than the author himself, something independent of him. I know only one thing: I had no preconceived idea or tendency; I wrote naively, as though myself surprised at how it was turning out. You mention the heir's tutor;[3] but it was precisely after *Fathers and Sons* that I became more removed than ever from that circle, to which I never actually belonged and to write or work for which I would have considered stupid or shameful. Tell me in all honesty: could anyone really be offended by being compared to Bazarov? Don't you yourself notice that he's the most sympathetic of all my characters? "A certain subtle odor" has been added by my readers; but I'm ready to confess (and I've already done so in print in my "memoirs") that I didn't have the right to give our reactionary scoundrels the chance to latch onto a tag—a name; the writer in me ought to have made that sacrifice to the citizen—and therefore I recognize as justified both the young people's alienation from me and every sort of censure... The question that arose was more important than artistic truth—and I should have known that ahead of time.

All that I can do is say once again: wait for my novel—and in the meanwhile don't be angry that I write light and insignificant things in order not to get out of the habit of holding a pen ... Who knows, perhaps I'm still fated to scorch the hearts of men.

All the same I won't be an entertaining writer such as I.A. Goncharov. I'll sooner become a boring writer.[4]

Well, enough, though!

No one has been freezing here and we've probably had less snow than you have in the south; but stay in Nice until the spring, get better—and then come up here. I'll be very happy to see you.

I send my regards to your family and clasp your hand cordially.

Your devoted Iv. Turgenev

Letter 282 (3824). To Hippolyte Taine.[1]
January 8/20, 1876. Paris.

50, rue de Douai.
Thursday, January 20

My dear Taine (you'll allow me to forego the Monsieur, won't you?), I have profited by the forced leisure just afforded me by an attack of gout in order to read your books, and I beg you to accept my most sincere congratulations. It's the work of a master, from which even those who attacked it will be extracting handfuls of material. You have produced something which will endure and which will be useful—two things that don't always go together.[2]

If I can go out on Tuesday, I'll come to clasp your hand and have a serious chat.

In the meantime I beg you to believe in my most sincere regards.

Iv. Tourguéneff

Letter 283 (3837). To P.V. Annenkov.
January 19/31, 1876. Paris.

Paris. 50, rue de Douai.
Monday, January 31, 1876.

Dear Pavel Vasilievich,

I just finished reading the part of *My Past and Thoughts* in which Herzen relates the story of his wife and Herwegh, her death, and so on.[1] You know that this is a manuscript and that the question is whether it should be published or not—out of respect for the remaining family and foreseeing the unavoidable scandal that Herwegh's widow[2] will not fail to raise. (Tata[3] entrusted me with the manuscript.) For my part, I'm definitely against publication, although as a reader I can't help but regret that, since it's all written with fire, tears, and blood—and even now I find myself in that state of nervous trembling that Herzen's confessions always incite in me. Are you familiar with the manuscript? Do you want me to ask Tata's permission to send it to you? Your opinion in this matter would be weighty—decisive, one might say. Write me a word or two.[4]

My gout is almost completely gone—but I've caught a bit of a cold—and I'm sitting in seclusion with a rather strong case of bronchitis; and I've quite lost my voice. But these are all minor problems.

The Senate elections turned out so-so: not very good and not very bad. The Republic will still have a majority, though a small one.[5]

Louise[6] is better, but she still has her arm in a sling. Everyone else is well and sends you regards.

And I send my regards to all your family and clasp your hand firmly.

Your devoted Iv. Turgenev

Letter 284 (3968). To Gustave Flaubert.[1]
June 6/18, 1876. Spasskoye.

Spasskoye.
(Oryol Province, City of Mtsensk.)
Sunday, June 18, 1876.

I've been at my Patmos since this morning and I'm as sad as can be. (Have you ever noticed that it's generally at such moments that one writes to one's friends?) It's *32 degrees Réamur*[2] in the shade—and along with that—thanks to a cold snap of *9 degrees below zero*[3] on May 21st—all the greenery in the garden is speckled with little dead leaves that make one think vaguely of the corpses of dead children—and my old linden trees give a meager and paltry shade that is painful to see. Add to that the fact that my brother, who was supposed to wait for me in order to arrange some financial matters that are very important for me, left for Carlsbad five days ago; that I believe that I'm going to have an attack of gout (that's what happened to me at the same time and place two years ago); that I'm almost certain that my estate manager is robbing me—and that I won't be able to get rid of him—and you see what the situation is. Mme Sand's death[4] has also caused me much, much grief. I know that you went to Nohant for the funeral—and I, who was going to send a telegram of condolence in the name of the Russian public, was restrained by a sort of ridiculous modesty, by the fear of *Figaro,*[5] of the publicity—of absurd things! The Russian public was one of those on which Mme Sand had the greatest influence— and it ought to have said so, damn it—and I had the right to do so, after all. But you see how things turned out!

Poor, dear Mme Sand! She loved both of us—especially you—and that was natural. What a heart of gold she had! What an absence of any petty, false feelings—what a marvellous person and what a kind woman she was! Now all of that is over there, in that horrible, insatiable, mute, beastly hole that doesn't even know what it is devouring.

But there's nothing that can be done and let's try to keep our chins up.

I'm writing you at Croisset—I assume that you're there—have you gotten back to work? If I don't do anything here—that will mean that it's all over. There is a silence here the likes of which nothing can convey; there are no neighbors for twenty kilometers in any direction—everything is listless from immobility! The house is wretched—but not too hot—and the furniture is good. An excellent desk and a double chair made of cane. For example, there's a dangerous sofa here—as soon as you're on it, you're asleep. I'm going to try to avoid it. I'll begin by finishing up "St. Julien."[6]

136

In the corner of my room there is an old Byzantine icon, all black, framed in silver, and all one can see is a large, sad, rigid face—it bothers me a little—but I can't have it removed—my servant would consider me a pagan—and here that's nothing to joke about.

Write me a few words that are a little more cheerful than the ones herein. I embrace you and remain

Your old friend Iv. Tourguéneff.

P.S. Do you know that the Circassian Hassan who executes ministers in pairs, like partridges, inspires a certain respect in me?[7]

P.P.S. My most cordial regards to your niece and her husband.[8]

Letter 285 (3878). To V.L. Kign.[1]
June 16/28, 1876. Spasskoye.

Village of Spasskoye-Lutovinovo.
(Oryol Province, City of Mtsensk.)
Wednesday, June 16, 1876.

I received your letter here, Vladimir Ludvigovich: it was forwarded to me by the editorial office of *The Messenger of Europe*. I regret that I didn't read your piece in *The Week*. I could have judged about your talents de visu [at sight]. But people such as Skabichevsky[2] and G. Uspensky[3] aren't about to talk nonsense: you can believe them. But you've set me a difficult task: how can I tell you in a short letter how I work, and how one ought to work in general, and what objective writing is, which you even go so far as to call epic! The figurative language in your Balzac quotation is not as murky as you suppose: he simply meant that it is sometimes amusing to think up a plot because a certain play of the imagination goes on there—but bringing it to fruition—getting it all down on paper—is difficult and bothersome. As for the question of whether there is objectivity in your talent, here's what I have to say: if the study of the human physiognomy, of other people's lives interests you *more* than the exposition of your own feelings and ideas; if, for example, you find it more pleasant to convey accurately and faithfully the external appearance not only of a person, but of a simple thing, than to express eloquently and passionately what you experience at the sight of

137

that person or thing—then that means that you are an objective writer and can take up a povest or a novel. As for work, without it, without painstaking work any writer or artist definitely remains a dilettante; there is no point in waiting for so-called blissful moments, inspiration; if it comes, so much the better; but you keep on working anyway. And you must not only work on your own piece, so that it expresses exactly what you wanted to express and exactly in the way and form that you wanted; in addition you must read and study ceaselessly. Try to penetrate everything around you, try to grasp life not only in all of its manifestations—but to understand it, to understand the laws that guide it and which don't always come to the surface; you must go beyond the game of chance happenings to achieve types—and with all of that remain always faithful to the truth, not be satisfied with superficial study, shun effects and deceitfulness. The objective writer takes a great burden upon himself: his muscles must be firm. That's the way that I used to work—even then not always; now I've gotten lazy—and old.

Look at what a storm I've talked up—and in the final analysis there's only one conclusion: if you have an objective talent, you have it. If you don't—you can't procure it. But in order to find out whether you have it, you need to put yourself to the test; then you'll be able to tell.

I wish you, my "literary grandson," all possible success and remain

always at your service,

Iv. Turgenev.

Letter 286 (4081). To Ye. A. Cherkasskaya.
November 9/21, 1876. Paris.

50, rue de Douai.
Paris.
Tuesday, November 9/21, 1876.

Dear Princess, I beg you to forgive me for not having immediately answered your letter containing the two translations of "Croquet";[1] I was terribly busy with finishing, copying, and sending off my novel,[2] which only today went to Russia. I'm very grateful to you for remembering me at such a troubled time.[3] Mrs. Baratynskaya's[4] translation is very accurate and good; Count Orlov-Davydov's is quite the contrary. I don't know whether you're aware that a translation (prose, from the French) was sent to the *Daily News* to be published; but "on second thought" the editors rejected it—"because it may hurt the feelings of the Queen." No other journal would even have thought of publishing that piece.

As for your hint that I ought to continue in the same vein—I'll tell you that I composed "Croquet" almost unconsciously, while on the train from Moscow to Petersburg; I don't regret it in the least—but writing poetry isn't my business (which the rather wooden verses in "Croquet" prove); do you mean to tell me that you don't have some young poet in Moscow?

You know that I'm not a Slavophile and never will be; therefore I cannot sympathize deeply with the movement sweeping Russia, because it is an exclusively religious one; but I recognize its strength and elemental magnitude—and I myself desire war as the only way out of this agitated darkness; moreover, being an eyewitness to all of Europe's hatred for us, one can't help but go deep into oneself and recognize that Russia has the right to act as she pleases. I bow down before I.S. Aksakov's self-sacrifice[6]—but I see no reason to become embroiled myself. The massacres of Bulgarians have offended my humanitarian feelings: it's all that I think about—and if this can't be helped in any other way than through war— well, then it's war! If the murdered Bulgarian women and children weren't of the Christian faith and of our blood—my indignation against the Turks wouldn't be any the less. To leave things *as they are,* not to secure the future for those unfortunate people would be *shameful*—and, I repeat, that's hardly possible without war. But, according to the latest news, that war of salvation won't take place—and we'll be left holding the bag again.

I read in the newspaper of Prince Cherkassky's appointment.[7] Is it true? If so, I wish him every sort of success—and above all, good health.

I hope that your health hasn't suffered too much from all the worries that you must have been subjected to recently. I can't complain myself: my gout is lying low—for the time being. I hope to see you at the end of January—I'll be coming to Petersburg and will probably get to Moscow, too. I send my regards to all our mutual acquaintances and clasp your hand firmly.

Your sincerely devoted Iv. Turgenev

Letter 287 (4108). To M.M. Stasyulevich.
November 28/December 10, 1876. Paris.

50, rue de Douai.
Paris.
Sunday, Dec. 10, 1876.

Dear Mikhail Matveyevich, it's very kind of you to send me daily reports on the progress of the printing and so on.[1] I'm awaiting today's proofs and will send them right back. You don't mention whether you received the corrected proofs, but I don't doubt that they arrived on time. The French translation of *Virgin Soil* won't come out earlier than February or March and not in the *Revue des 2 Mondes,* but probably in the *Temps* instead; therefore you have no reason to fear a repetition of the prank that *The Voice* pulled.[2] The German translation is in your hands. Please tell me whether you'll accept Mrs. Blaramberg's[3] short story[4] that I sent you. I imagine that you could publish it in the *March* issue along with my translation of Flaubert's legend.[5] Let me know.

I'm very glad that your wife liked my Fomushka and Fimushka.[6] Give my regards to her as well as to the rest of our friends.

I clasp your hand and remain

Your devoted Iv. Turgenev.

Letter 288 (4118). To P.V. Annenkov.
December 4/16, 1876. Paris.

Paris. 50, rue de Douai.
Saturday, Dec. 16, 1876.

Dear Pavel Vasilievich,

I'm just on my way to my daughter's (she lives near Châteaudun) and I'll spend three days there—and therefore I can only dash off a couple of words in answer to your letter. To be precise—please send me Wagner's works—no matter what they cost—because I have a 100-franc bet with a

Wagnerophile here who claims that he never wrote any such pamphlet, and that it's all slander created by the French and so on.[1]

So far everything it going swimmingly with my novel;[2] we'll see what the public says.

Do you know, by the way, why we're ready for peace?[2] It turns out that try as hard as we may, we can't produce more than *130,000* troops—and the Turks have three times as many.[3]

Marvellous results for reforms so long under way!

I'm glad about your good health—I'm not displeased with my own health either. I send my regards to your loved ones and remain

Your devoted Iv. Turgenev.

Letter 289 (4131). To Ludwig Pietsch.[1]
December 16/28, 1876. Paris.

50, rue de Douai.
Paris.
Thursday, Dec. 28, 1876.

Happy New Year, dear Pietsch! Many thanks for your letter. I fear that this will be a bad year for Russia. I'm definitely going to Petersburg at the *beginning of February*—and if you want to or can, we'll leave Berlin together.

I sent you the book that you wanted, "sous bande" [parcel post]. It wasn't easy to find. But your enclosed *package* (I mean the photograph) was *not* there. But I'm still counting on it.[2]

Everyone here is alive and well; Kathi[3] really did send your nice and friendly article about Paul[4] to Mme Viardot.[5] You remain a reliable old friend!

"A propos de photographies" [speaking of photographs], tell Julian Schmidt, if you see him, "que je ne me tiens pas quitte" [that I don't consider myself not liable] for Zola's and Flaubert's photographs, which I promised him. He'll receive them—no matter what.[6]

I wrote to Storm[7] and thanked him graciously for his *Aquis submersus,* which he sent me in a most elegant edition. The story is delicate and tender; but how in Heaven's name, for instance, is it possible to make a boy sing about heaven and angels *just* before he drowns! Any good children's song would have made ten times the impression. Germans are *always* guilty of two errors when they narrate: clumsy motivation and a thoroughly damnable idealization of reality. Grasp truth simply and *poetically*—and the Ideal will come about on its own. No, the Germans can conquer the whole world; but they've forgotten how to narrate . . . actually, they never really knew how to. If a German author tells me something touching—he can't resist pointing at his own weeping eye with one finger— and with the other giving me, the reader, a modest sign that I ought not leave unremarked the object that touched him.

In Petersburg the cold has reached *40 degrees*—we're having a thaw here—how about in Berlin?

Regards to all our friends and to your family; I clasp your hand and remain

Your devoted Iw. Turgénjew.

Letter 290 (4164). To S.K. Bryullova.[1]
January 4/16, 1877. Paris.

50, Rue de Douai.
Paris.
Tuesday, Jan. 4/16, 1877.

Dear Sofia Konstantinova, I kept postponing a reply to your kind, intelligent letter, because I didn't want to limit myself to a few words of gratitude and so on, and there was no time. But it would be unforgivable to delay any longer—and so here—tout chaud, tout bouillant [all hot and boiling]—is what I have to say.

First of all, your letter brought me great happiness; following upon your father's letter,[2] it was a pledge of the fact that I wasn't entirely mistaken—and that what I've written has a right to exist.[3] After all the doubts expressed by others—and more importantly, after my own doubts and hesitation—this is really a great source of joy. What I'm concerned with here isn't my literary vanity, which was never too strong in me, but rather with another, more serious feeling. Consequently, you can appreciate how pleased your opinion—precisely yours—made me. Now the public will express its opinion: I won't be indifferent to it; but my harvest is already in.

In my letter to Konstantin Dmitrievich I explained the reason that made me depict the popular element in *Virgin Soil* in *that way;*[4] by the way, under the influence of your words, I added two or three additional strokes.

But now I have to express a certain disagreement with you. (I hope that you won't attribute this to an authorial mania that lingers lovingly over the worst and weakest offspring.) You speak of various of my insignificant trifles, mentioning, among others, "Knock ... Knock!" Just imagine—I consider that piece not exactly successful—its execution perhaps is insufficient and weak—but one of the most serious ones that I've ever written. It's a study of a suicide, specifically a Russian one, contemporary, conceited, dull, and superstitious—and an absurd, showy suicide—and it made for a subject that is just as interesting and just as important as any public or social question can be. I repeat that I most likely failed to analyze everything and put it forward in a sufficiently vivid light; but I assert once again that such subjects are not in the least inferior to any others! Don't forget that a Russian suicide is unlike a European or an Asiatic one; and pointing out that difference in an accurate, artistic way is worthwhile because it adds a document to the elaboration of the human physiognomy—and, properly speaking, all poetry, beginning with the epic and ending with the vaudeville, has that as its subject and no other.

"Wow!" you'll say, "what an oratio pro domo sua"[oration about my home, i.e., myself]! And therefore, je n'insiste plus [I won't press the point any longer].

I'll probably come to Petersburg in a month or five weeks—and then we'll see each other often, of course. In the meantime, please give my cordial regards to your husband[5] and your parents—and accept the expression of the sincere attachment with which I remain

Your devoted Iv. Turgenev.

Letter 291 (4184). To A.P. Bogolyubov.[1]
January 21/February 2, 1877. Paris.

50, Rue de Douai.
Friday, Feb. 2.

Dear Alexey Petrovich, allow me to appeal to your invariable indulgence, which I do all the more willingly inasmuch as the bearer of this note, Sergey Ivanovich Taneyev,[2] is most worthy of it. He is a young compatriot of ours, an excellent pianist, and a fine fellow; he intends to spend the whole winter in Paris—but he somehow managed to take an apartment behind the Odéon—and all his friends and acquaintances live in our neighborhood. He's been walking around and looking for two days now—and he can't find anything. Please be so kind as to give him some practical and businesslike advice—and perhaps you might know of an apartment of the sort that he's seeking? I'll be very grateful to you—and Taneyev will be ready to reward you by delighting your ears with all sorts of harmonies and melodies. I wouldn't have troubled you if I didn't know your bottomless kindness. You yourself are to blame.

I clasp your hand cordially and remain

Your devoted Iv. Turgenev.

Letter 292 (4240). To N.S. Turgenev.
March 7/19, 1877. Paris.

50, Rue de Douai.
Paris.
Monday, March 7/19, 1877.

Dear brother,

It seems to me that I've been writing to you rather often lately, but in your last letter, dated March 1/13, you complain about my silence and ask about my health. It isn't bad, although recently I suffered a rather seriously swollen cheek and neuralgic headaches; but none of that is really important—and my gout has only nipped at me a little bit.

As for the review of my novel that you cut out and sent me, I didn't learn anything new from it. There's no doubt, as you say, that *Virgin Soil* is a failure; and I'm beginning to think that its fate is well deserved. It's impossible to imagine that *all* the journals entered into some sort of conspiracy against me; rather, I ought to admit that I made a mistake, took on a labor that was beyond my strength, and fell under its weight. One really can't write about Russia without living there. It would have been better if I'd fallen mute several years ago; but in any event, this latest lesson won't have been in vain: my literary career is finished forever—and my name will never again appear under an independent work. This isn't such an easy thing to do; life from now on looks somewhat empty; but, as they say, you need to be able to look the devil—or perhaps the truth, in the eyes. Diderot said somewhere that "avant sa mort, l'homme suit plusieurs fois son propre convoi" [before his death, man follows his own funeral procession many times]; well, and so have I had to walk behind my own literary coffin. I'll find some other activity for myself; and then real old age will set in . . . And the petty daily worries about preserving my life and so on will swallow up all other interests.

I'm still coming to Russia—before Carlsbad, i.e., at the very beginning of May—or even the end of April. I very much hope to find you still in Moscow . . . and until then I embrace you heartily and remain

Your loving brother Iv. Turgenev.

Letter 293 (4259). To F.M. Dostoevsky.
March 28/ April 9, 1877. Paris.

Paris. 50, Rue de Douai.
Monday, Mar. 28/Apr. 9, 1877.

My dear Fyodor Mikhailovich!

Mr. Emile Durand,[1] a good friend of mine and a well-known writer and authority on the Russian language, has been commissioned by the editors of the *Revue des Deux Mondes* to compile monographs (biographical and literary-critical) on the leading representatives of Russian letters—and has gone to Russia for that purpose. You, of course, are in the forefront in this regard—and he has asked me to provide him with a letter of introduction to you, which I undertake with all the more willingness, inasmuch as the acquaintance with Mr. Durand, a highly conscientious, educated, and intelligent person, cannot but give you pleasure.

I decided to write you this letter in spite of the misunderstandings that have arisen between us and as a consequence of which our personal relations have been severed.[2] I am certain that you do not doubt that these misunderstandings could not have any influence on my opinion of your first-class talent and the lofty position which you rightfully occupy in our literature.

In hopes of a warm reception for Mr. Durand and of your sympathy for the goal of his journey, I beg you to accept the assurance of the perfect respect with which I have the honor of remaining your most humble servant.

Iv. Turgenev

Letter 294 (4267). To Ya. P. Polonsky.
April 7/19, 1877. Paris.

50 Rue de Douai.
Paris.
Thursday, Apr. 7/19, 1877.

Dear Yakov Petrovich,

Your poem (in which there are remarkable lines such as, for instance:

"The damp haze of the whining night
Looks in through the window and floods the eyes"[1])

produced a profound melancholy in me; so that you might understand why, I'm copying out a few lines from my diary for you:

"*March 5/17. Midnight.* I'm sitting at my desk again; downstairs my poor friend is singing something in her quite cracked voice;[2] and in my soul it's darker than a dark night ... It is as if the grave were hurrying to devour me: the days fly past like some mere moment, empty, aimless, colorless. You look: and it's time to flop into bed again. I have neither the right nor the urge to live; there is nothing more to do, nothing to expect, or even to desire..."

I won't copy out any more: it's already melancholy enough. You forget that I'm 58, and she's 55; not only can she not sing—but for the opening of the theater that you describe so eloquently, she, the singer who once upon a time created the role of Fidès in *Prophète,* wasn't even sent tickets: what would be the point? After all, there's been nothing to expect from her for a long time now... And you speak of the "rays of fame" and "the charms of song..."[3] My friend, we're both two fragments of a vessel long since shattered. I, at least, feel like a retired chamber pot...

You can now understand how your verses affected me. (I beg you, however, to destroy this letter.)

There's only one good thing in all of this, though you don't write anything of it: your awful illness has probably passed—and you're left with just your old complaints, which are truer than friends and don't abandon a person.

The proximity of war doesn't help me to feel especially cheerful either. But we'll soon talk about all this in person. We'll see each other in two weeks—since I'm leaving here soon—and until then I embrace you heartily and remain

Your devoted Iv. Turgenev.

Letter 295 (4268). To William Ralston.[1]
April 7/19, 1877. Paris.

50, Rue de Douai.
Paris.
Thursday, April 19, 1877.

My dear friend,

There is decidedly no French separate book about *nihilism* in Russia—but in the "Revue des Deux Mondes" there has appeared in 1876 or 75 an article intitulated "Le Nihilisme en Russie" by Alf. Rambaud or Leroy-Beaulieu (I am not quite sure of the name of the author)—which I have read and found good and exact enough.[2] I have not been able to put my hand on it, I have given to my bookseller the commission to find it out—but I have not yet received an answer. I imagine, it will be easy for you to find it in the "bibliothèque" of the British Museum.

The trial of the revolutionists is sad enough—certainly;[3] but you are in a mistake if you imagine that the young girls resemble Mashurina rather than Marianna.[4] Some of them are very handsome and interesting—and (as there still exists in our jurisprudence the barbarous custom of a *bodily* examination of prisoners accused of crimes) they have been found *all* in a state of virginity. There is a matter for serious réflexion. I send you in this letter a very touching piece of verses by Mlle Figner,[5] a very pretty blondine of 22 years—but in the last stage of phthisis (that explains the last couplet but one)—she did not defend herself nor take an advocate—and was condemned to five years hard labour in Siberia—in the mines. Death will evidently soon release her.[6] I send you likewise a letter (by Zsvilenef) which has been read during the trial—I received it from an unknown person with the remark that it could have been written by *Solomine*.[7] Russian statesmen ought to think of all that—and come to the conclusion that the only way of stopping the progress of revolutionary propaganda in Russia—is to grant a constitutional reform. But all these considerations will now be swallowed by the turbid waves of wars. My conviction is that we stand on the threshold of very dark times . . . There is nobody who can predict what shall come out of all this.

I leave Paris on the fifth of May—and come back—if nothing happens—in the middle of July.

Wishing you good health and good spirits, I remain

Yours very truly, Iv. Tourguéneff.

Letter 296 (4299). To Pauline Bruère.[1]
May 4/16, 1877. Paris.

50, Rue de Douai.
Paris.
Wednesday, May 16, 1877.

Dear Paulinette,

You probably weren't expecting to receive a letter from me in Paris dated May *16*—you probably thought that I'd left; nor was I expecting any such thing; I reckoned on leaving here Saturday, at the latest; but I reckoned without gout. It attacked me eight days ago in *both* feet at once; it kept me in bed for a week—and although I can walk about my room after a fashion—I haven't yet been able to go down the stairs; so you can see that I can't say for certain when I'll be on my way to Russia. However, since, all in all, I feel fine, I quite hope that that will take place in a week—next Wednesday, but I needn't tell you how upset I am over this inconvenience.

I saw your mother-in-law quite a while ago and she spoke to me, of course, of the money that she lent you and which I promised to return to her. I'm in the habit of keeping all my promises; but I confess that it is harsh that it is I and always I who must do everything. Because—really—our shares are not equal. Besides the dowry of 150,000 francs that I gave you and which has disappeared—I give and keep on giving—including money to cover your husband's pledges and from hand to hand; and what have Gaston's parents—his mother—what have they done? To be quite precise—absolutely *nothing*. The factory that was evaluated at 50,000 francs has been found to have no value; and then the famous debt of 35,000 that was kept hidden from me and which again disappeared into his parents' pockets ... And after all of that they find that they can't *loan* you 3,000 francs—and they remind me almost as though it were a debt—that I'm obliged to reimburse them for that too! Really, that is going too far. It reminds me of the Spanish proverb about sharing like brothers: "mine for me—and yours for both of us." If your parents-in-law had contributed even one-fourth of what I have!

I'm not telling you this to upset you; but it was bothering me, and I didn't want to keep it from you. Now it's all over.

I won't leave without seeing Mme Delessert and speaking to her again about you and Gaston. Jules Simon is out; it's likely that Mme Delessert's friends will come to power and perhaps it will be easier for her to do something.[2]

I'll write you as soon as I talk to her; until then I embrace you all—and wish you good health and "bonnes affaires!"

Iv. Tourguéneff

Letter 297 (4415). To A.P. Borodin.
October 27/November 8, 1877. Paris.

Paris. 50, Rue de Douai.
Thursday, Oct. 27/Nov. 8, 1877.

My dear Alexander Prokofievich,

The day before yesterday Mrs. Lukanina[1] came to see me with a letter from you—and yesterday she read me from her copybook "The Old Nanny's Story," which she's sent to you. I was struck by that work—there is so much life, intelligence, and poetry in it—and I would very much like to see it published in *The Messenger of Europe*—if you don't see any obstacles to that on your part. I wrote Mr. Stasyulevich, the editor of *The Messenger of Europe,* yesterday—and alerted him that you would be delivering Mrs. Lukanina's manuscript. I have no doubt that when he reads it, even without my recommendation, which was expressed in the strongest terms, he'll be especially anxious to print such a remarkable piece in his journal. I hope that you haven't yet had time to make any other arrangements—and that you'll agree with me that *The Messenger of Europe* is the sort of organ in which it's best for a beginning writer to appear. I would be very obliged if you would let me know that outcome of your meeting with Mr. Stasyulevich.[2]

Personally I'm very grateful to you for my acquaintance with A.N. Lukanina: as far as I can judge, she is a very intelligent, sympathetic, and good woman.

From a material point of view as well, having this story published in *The Messenger of Europe* will be much more advantageous for her than lessons and similar work that is unreliable and difficult to come by here.

I very well recall our meeting at Mr. Stasov's;[3] I can tell you, by the way, that this fall Mrs. Viardot, who is quite interested in Russian music, and her daughter played through the four-hand piano transcription of your Second Symphony that I brought back from Russia—and she had the highest praise for your work, which she plans to introduce to local musicians.

I expect to come to Petersburg at the end of this year—and I hope to have the pleasure of renewing our acquaintance; and until that time I beg you to accept the assurance of the profound respect and devotion

of your humble servant Iv. Turgenev.

Letter 298 (4543). To Ya. N. Polonsky.
April 17/29, 1878. Paris.

50, Rue de Douai.
Paris.
Monday, Apr. 17/29, 1878.

Dear Yakov Petrovich,

I received your letter today—and am answering it today: see how punctual I am? And for even greater punctuality, I'll answer point by point.

1) I'm writing you from my bed. A very bad attack of gout in both knees felled me 12 days ago—and I don't know how much longer I'll still have to be in bed. I'm sorry that only in this regard am I growing to resemble Heine.[1]

2) Your complaints about my literary silence are very kind and well-intentioned—but they don't change the essence of the matter. In order to write—especially now—one must live in Russia; I can't live there on a regular basis; ergo: I shouldn't write. Nor does it mean anything that one hears voices allegedly raised in regret over this: if I were to try to draft so much as a line those same voices would cry out: "See, the old phrase-monger, he couldn't hold out!" All in all, I ought to stay as far away from literature as possible now—they say, for instance, that Pushkin's sons are planning to come to Paris to beat me up for publishing their father's letters.

If that's so, they ought at least to start with their own sister, who gave me permission to do that.[2]

3) Though I'm not at all ruined, my finances were in such bad shape that I really was forced to sell my picture gallery. I did that and suffered a defeat like that at Sedan;[3] I expected to lose 6,000 francs on them, and lost 12,000. The time was poorly chosen—in addition to which my friends—especially the Russians—were singularly and foppishly unsupportive.

To hell with them and the pictures! (I didn't sell my Rousseau, however.)[4] But as regards you, dear Yakov Petrovich, I will consider it my special good fortune to be your creditor to the end of my days—and therefore there's no reason for you to worry; besides, I'm still a long way from poverty.

4) I think of the poor Baroness Vrevskaya daily, with a special feeling of grief and sadness—and your poem in *New Time* brought tears to my eyes.[5] She was a marvellous person—and so profoundly unfortunate!

5) You're wrong in thinking that I haven't been reading your novel. As soon as each yellow supplement to *The Week* appears, I devour *Accidentally* first thing—and am very pleased with it; in spite of Gaydeburov's criticism.[6]

6) You and I agreed not to talk about Chernyayev.[7]

7) I'll receive Chuiko with all due warmth.[8] Vengerov is a coxcomb, but not without sensitivity.

8) You couldn't have liked the bust of me (by Zabello[9])—because, just between the two of us, it's <--->.

9) As soon as I get back on my feet I'll leave for Carlsbad—and beyond that I don't know anything.

I send regards to your family and embrace you.

Iv. Turgenev

Letter 299 (4561). To L.N. Tolstoy.
May 8/20, 1878. Paris.

> 50, Rue de Doaui.
> Paris.
> Monday, May 8/20, 1878.

Dear Lev Nikolayevich,

I didn't receive the letter that you sent me poste restante until today.[1] It made me very happy and touched me. I'm more than willing to renew our former friendship and I clasp firmly the hand that you extend. You are quite right in assuming that I have no hostile feelings towards you: if they did exist, they've long since disappeared[2]—and all that remains is the memory of you as a person to whom I was sincerely attached—and as a writer whose first steps I managed to welcome before anyone else, and each new work of whose always attracted my liveliest interest. I'm heartily glad for the cessation of the misunderstandings that arose between us.

I hope to come to Oryol Province this summer—and then we'll see each other, of course. And until then I wish you all the best—and once more clasp your hand cordially.

> Ivan Turgenev

Letter 300 (4607). To A.A. Fet
August 21/September 2, 1878. Spasskoye.

> Village of Spasskoye-Lutovinovo.
> Monday, Aug. 21, 1878

Dear Afansy Afanasievich,

I was sincerely happy to receive your letter. The only good thing about old age is that it gives us the chance to wash away and destroy all our past squabbles—and, bringing us closer to ultimate simplification, it simplifies all of life's relationships. I gladly clasp your outstretched hand—and I'm certain that when we see each other in person we'll find ourselves just as good friends as we were in ancient times.[1] But I don't know when that meeting will come about: I'm leaving directly for Paris in about a week. Perhaps this winter in Petersburg or Moscow; or perhaps you'll drop in on us in our little village of Paris?

But be that as it may, I repeat my greeting and thanks.

Give my cordial regards to Maria Petrovna. If I'm not mistaken, her face flashed by me in a train car at the station beyond Oryol. I was returning from Maloarkhangelsky District—and she was probably on her way to your new estate.[2]

Once again—I wish you all the best, beginning with good health, and remain

Your devoted Iv. Turgenev.

Letter 301 (4663). To L.N. Tolstoy.
November 15/27, 1878. Paris.

50, Rue de Douai.
Paris.
Wednesday, Nov. 15/27, 1878.

Dear Lev Nikolayevich, I too failed to answer your letter of October 27 right away. I've had rather sad things to attend to lately: my old friend Khanykov died in Rambouillet, near Paris; I had to have his body moved and buried and see to the matter of his will. In addition, I caught a slight cold and had a terrible headache for two days. But all of that is past now— and I can have a chat with you.

I'm glad that you're physically well—and I hope that the "mental" illness of which you write has passed, too. I used to be familiar with it, as well: often it would appear in the form of inner unrest before beginning a work; I imagine that that sort of unrest is what happened to you, too.[1] Although you beg me not to speak of your writings—still, I can't help but point out that I've never had occasion to laugh at you "even a little bit";[2] I've liked some of your works, disliked others, and others, such as *The Cossacks,* for instance, gave me great pleasure and evoked wonder in me. But why on earth would I laugh? I had imagined that you had long since gotten rid of such "retrograde" feelings. Why is it that only writers experience them—and not painters, musicians, or other artists? It's probably because more of *that* part of the soul that it's not quite appropriate to expose nonetheless enters into a work of literature. Yes, but at our age, when we're no longer young writers, it's time to get used to that.

That I'm not writing anything here is, unfortunately, true. In saying "unfortunately," I don't mean "in general," but in regard to myself. Because I'm overcome by ennui. Living abroad, I've ceased being able to write (at least I attribute my inaction to life abroad), and as you well know, one can't force oneself in this matter. We'll wait and see what happens.

The English translation of *The Cossacks* is accurate—but dry and "matter of fact," just like Mr. Schuyler himself, who was here a few days ago on his way to Birmingham, where he has been appointed Consul.[3] I haven't seen the French translation; I'm afraid that it really did turn out to be unsuccessful, since I know the ways and habits of our Russian lady translators.[4] On the one hand, I'm afraid and on the other—I'm almost glad: that means that it will still be possible to translate your povest and publish it here.[5]

You've been hunting rabbits—and I've done some hunting this fall, too. I went to England to visit a friend whose estate is located between Cambridge and Oxford—and I bagged a decent number of pheasants and partridges and so on.[6] But that sort of hunting—without a dog—is really rather monotonous. You need to shoot superbly in that case; and I was always a mediocre shot . . . besides, I'm out of the habit. By the way, I visited both universities: Cambridge and Oxford. Those English educational institutions are a very strange and clever thing! And how they hate us![7]

Chaikovsky's *Eugene Onegin* has arrived here in a piano score. Mrs. Viardot has begun playing through it in the evenings. It's undoubtedly remarkable music; especially beautiful are the lyrical, melodic spots. But what a libretto![8] Just imagine: Pushkin's verses about the characters are placed in their own mouths. For instance, he says of Lensky:

"*He sang* the prime of faded life
At just short of age eighteen"

and in the libretto we find:

"*I sing* the prime of faded life" and so on.[9]

And it goes on like that almost continually.

Chaikovsky's reputation has grown here a great deal since the Russian concerts at the Trockadero;[10] and in Germany he's long enjoyed attention, if not exactly respect. At Cambridge an Englishman, a professor of music, told me quite seriously that Chaikovsky was the most remarkable musical figure of the present time. My mouth fell open.

Well, enough, however. Thank the Countess for her greetings. I send regards to all your family—and embrace you.

Your devoted Iv. Turgenev

Letter 302 (4727). To A.V. Toporov.
January 11/23, 1879. Paris.

50, Rue de Douai.
Paris.
Thursday, Jan. 11/23, 1879.

Dear Alexander Vasilievich,

I have sad news to relate to you: last Sunday my brother died at his Tula village. Although he left his entire estate to his wife's relatives[1]—still, it's likely that I'll soon have to go to Russia, since, as he told me, he willed me 100,000 rubles of his sizeable capital, and I'm not at all certain that when the seals are removed and so on, the heirs won't try to arrange things so that the money evaporates. And therefore—expect me shortly. I would have left immediately—but I had an attack of gout a week ago—and I still can't leave the house—though I'm out of bed. In any event, you'll be notified in advance. I've begun receiving *The Russian Truth* and *The Stock Exchange News*.

Last night a telegram came from Savina[2] (the actress), in which she asked my permission for her to make necessary cuts in my comedy *A Month in the Country*, which she has selected for her benefit performance on January 17/29. I don't understand why on earth she took it into her head to pick that play, which is impossible in a theatrical sense! One Moscow actress, Vasilieva,[3] tried it several years ago,[4] in spite of my repeated warnings, and she earned a gala fiasco. The same thing awaits Madame Savina. Of course I answered her—also by telegram—that I give my permission for any and all cuts; but since I don't know her address—I addressed the telegram to the Alexandrisky Theater. When you get this letter, please go to see her (it will be easy for you to find out where she lives)—and, using my name, repeat my permission, if for any reason the telegram didn't reach her. You may also repeat my regret and disapproval, which, by the way, I expressed in the telegram.

Have you received any answer from Beggrov?[5]

Give my regards to everyone, beginning with the Samarskys,[6] and accept the assurance of my sincere friendship.

Iv. Turgenev

Letter 303 (4753). To Pauline Bruère.[1]
February 1/13, 1879. Paris.

> 50, Rue de Douai.
> Paris.
> Thursday morning.

My dear Paulinette,

I just received your letter and I'm replying with just a few words— because I'm leaving tomorrow for Russia, where I'm going to try to gather a few crumbs from my brother's large fortune (you know, I think, that he just died)—a fortune which he left to his wife's relatives. Those relatives are displaying the intention of hoarding even that little bit that my brother willed me—and I have to be there to defend myself.[2]

As for your questions—I have only one piece of advice to give you. While deploring the ill luck that seems to pursue you, *hang on to your factory*. I am absolutely powerless to do anything for you. Quite recently I tried to solicit a position (ten times promised) for my poor friend Flaubert, who finds himself completely ruined—and I was met with a brutally boorish rejection.[3] I'll never involve myself like that again. I repeat—I am absolutely powerless—and I'll be grateful if you'll never return to this topic.

I'll write to you from Moscow—I'll let you know if everything there goes to the devil, too. In the meantime I embrace you all and wish you all the best.

Iv. Tourguéneff

P.S. I paid Mme Innis 124 francs for you.

Letter 304 (4768). To A.V. Toporov.
February 20/March 4, 1879. Moscow.

Moscow. Crown Office.
Tuesday, Feb. 20, 1879.

Dear Alexander Vasilievich,

I hasten to inform you that my affairs are becoming clearer: my brother's new will is so brilliantly drawn up (by Mr. Malyarevsky himself[1]) that you couldn't even pass a needle through it, as they say: instead of 100,000 rubles I get a little over 60 thousand. But I'm happy even for that: given his influence over my brother, Malyarevsky could have left me with nothing. The will is to be confirmed on the 25th in the local Circuit Court; my rights to the inheritance will be confirmed as well. Tell the good Samarsky about all of this, since he's involved in this whole business.

I really am having luck—just as you predicted: on Thursday the young professors here threw me a dinner with sympathetic "speeches"—and the day before yesterday at a meeting of the Admirers of Russian Letters the students gave me such an unprecedented reception that I was nearly stupefied—applause for five minutes, a speech addressed to me from the gallery, and so on and so forth. Society has promoted me to the ranks of the respected. The young generation's return to me made me very happy, but it agitated me quite a bit as well. I don't know whether it's because of that, but my right knee has been hurting since yesterday—and I can hardly walk...Perhaps this won't be a real attack.

I'll be in Petersburg again at the end of the month; until then I wish you all the best and I clasp your hand firmly.

Your devoted Iv. Turgenev

Letter 305 (4824). To P.V. Annenkov.
April 12/24, 1879. Paris.

> 50, Rue de Douai.
> Paris.
> Thursday, April 12/24, 1879.

My dear friend Pavel Vasilievich, I don't doubt even for a moment that you'll believe me when I declare the following: during all the unexpected occurrences that happened to me in Russia,[1] I thought of you constantly—even though I didn't keep my promise to write you from Moscow; and ever since coming back here I've been asking myself constantly—and not without reproach: "Why is it that I haven't been writing to Annenkov?"—and when your letter came today, I already had pen in hand, poised over the very same sheet of paper that it's running across now. Well, and now—what can I tell you? So much has accumulated that there would be enough for a whole brochure. If you were sitting before me at this moment I could manage it all in a couple of hours—and more importantly—would show you the mass of interesting documents that I brought out from Russia (some of them, as for instance the address by the Kharkov students, another address by the Kharkov professors, Zemstvo members, and so on, had already been sent to me here).[2] And I *will* do that, since I'm quite certain that before two months have passed, we'll see each other . . . Perhaps on your way to Baden you'll make a detour to Paris—or more accurately, Bougival? I'd like to be able to express the feeling that I brought back from Russia in a single word. Perhaps that word is *compassion*—profound compassion for our marvellous young people— male and female—who are simply suffocating from a lack of air, like a bird under a pneumatic bell jar. Any satisfaction of literary vanity disappears and is dissipated in that ardent feeling—as is even that joy which the universal expression of sympathy cannot but arouse in a soul grown old . . . All that enthusiasm, the hopes and expectations . . . what sort of an outlet can there be for them? Especially after the outrage that occurred a few days ago?[3] Now everything will be driven underground again . . . But how can you reconcile yourself now to what was barely tolerable twenty or thirty years ago? . . .

And how they begged me in Russia to return there, to remain there— not in order to become a "leader," of course (that's not in my nature—nor would the present conditions allow it), but a central point, a banner . . . In spite of my advanced years (you may have noticed that in the papers they kept referring to me as "venerable")—I might decide to pluck up all the roots that I've put down here—but why, to what purpose? I was born too late—or too early; I could only be a hindrance now—either to myself, or to others. I'm not making myself very clear; but you and I are berries from the same field—you'll understand me after only half a word—and will even complete in your own thoughts what I myself haven't even thought through to the end.

Moving on to the other question, I can tell you that the result of my *business* trip was the following: instead of the 100,000 rubles promised by my deceased brother, I got a little more than half of that... But I'm satisfied even with that much. There occurred some curious confrontations which I would make use of if I were Shchedrin.[4]

As for my health—I also have reason to be satisfied. My gout nips at me from time to time—and my heart plays pranks; but in the final analysis, my system seems to have settled down (true, in an elderly way). You don't mention either your health or how you all are. I assume, along with diplomats, that "absence de nouvelles—bonne nouvelle" [no news is good news].

I'll write you again soon; but for now I send my regards to your whole family—and embrace you cordially.

Your devoted Iv. Turgenev

Letter 306 (4877). To P.V. Annenkov.
June 12/24, 1879. Bougival.

> Bougival.
> Les Frênes.
> Chalet.
> Tuesday, June 12/24, 1879.

I returned here the day before yesterday, dear Pavel Vasilievich—and I don't think that I'll be going anywhere now until October. The ceremony at Oxford was accomplished successfully:[1] there were nine of us new doctors in red tunics and quadrangular caps (including the Crown Prince of Sweden, a very tall young fellow with a silly French face)—there were scads of people—especially ladies—in the round hall with a cupola where these "commemorations" take place: the same sort of Doctor introduced each of us in turn to the Vice-Chancellor—first exalting each of us in Latin; the students and the audience applauded—the Vice-Chancellor greeted us in Latin, too, shook our hands—and we went to take our seats. I frankly confess that when it came to my turn, my heart was beating very strongly. It was a most unusual business for the likes of us!

I was told that one day the students (undergraduates) allow themselves all sorts of pranks—it's something like university saturnalia; and since anti-Russian sentiment is still very strong in England[2]—catcalls might have been expected; but nothing of the sort occurred—as a matter of fact, the *Times* noted that I was applauded more than the others . . .[3] In addition to which the weather was marvellous that day, and you probably are aware of what an enchanting city Oxford is—it's one of a kind. I made many new acquaintances and in general I can't say enough about what a friendly reception the English gave me. The professors there made me a gift of my red robe and cap—and, in accordance with the wishes of our local ladies, I'm going to have my picture taken in that slightly motley garb—and I'll send you a copy signed "J. Tourguéneff, D.C.L." Now all that has to happen is for the Russian journals to rake me over the coals apropos of this—and then everything will sink into Lethe, leaving a pleasant memory, however.

Well—and what can we say about the demise of the Prince Impérial?[4] It really does often seem that the fate which rules us seeks to entertain through spectacular dramatic effects! If an author such as myself had thought up *such* a conclusion—everyone would exclaim "What an unnatural antithesis!" A birth to the accompaniment of cannon fire, in a palace, in a golden cradle—at the center of the world—and death in a South African backwater at the hands of a savage half-gorilla! All sorts of things happen . . . but you could add along with Gogol: "rarely, but they happen."[5]

This is an irreparable blow for the Bonapartists; whether the Republic will manage to make use of this "great helmet" is another question.

Let me hear from you. Everyone here send regards; I too send my regards to all your family and embrace you.

Iv. Turgenev, D.C.L.

Letter 307 (4911). To Gustave Flaubert.[1]
July 26/August 7, 1879. Bougival.

> Bougival.
> Les Frênes
> Chalet.
> (Seine-et-Oise).
> Thursday, August 7, 1879.

My dear friend,

It has been decidedly too long since I had any news from you. Write me a few words about what you're doing, how you are, etc., etc. As for me, I'm fine physically; you can get an exact idea of my spiritual state by lifting up the lid on a cesspool and looking inside; but it must not be an English "water closet": they're generally clean.

All my little world here sends you regards; I do too—from the depths of my *spleen*—because I love you, you know.

> Your Iv. Tourguéneff.

Letter 308 (5022). To P.L. Lavrov.
November 15/27, 1879. Bougival.

> Bougival. Les Frênes.
> Thursday, Nov. 27. 1879.

Dear Lavrov,

I'm still here, but I'll soon be moving to Paris—I'll let you know right away when I do. I'm writing you now, however, in connection with a somewhat unpleasant matter. That Russian, whose last name I don't even know,[1] and for whom I arranged work, at your recommendation, at the Chamero Printing Plant (Rue des Saints Pères, 19), took it into his head to go to a meeting of Humbert's constituency, where his outcries attracted the attention of the police, who immediately recognized that he was a

Russian—traced him to the printing plant—and gathered information about him, learning among other things that I had recommended him. (The police know me "comme le loup blanc" [like the white wolf, i.e., very well]—and keep me under constant observation—since in their eyes I'm the very womb of nihilists.) Since he isn't French, that Russian had no right to be at the constituency meeting and as a consequence of that, he will be subjected to inevitable deportation at the slightest relapse, the more so as they're dissatisfied with him at the printers' too, since he's begun to be absent quite often. Couldn't you meet with him and point out to him the rashness of his actions? He'll harm both himself and his other confrères in exile who are only tolerated here because they don't embroil themselves in local politics. Do this in secret, since this was told to me in secret, too.

I clasp your hand cordially.

Iv. Turgenev

Letter 309 (5142). To P.V. Annenkov.
April 24/May 6, 1880. Moscow.

> Moscow.
> Prechistensky Boulevard,
>   Crown Office Building.
> Thursday, Apr. 24/May 6, 1880.

Dear Pavel Vasilievich, I imagine that this letter will catch you just as you are about to depart for Baden-Baden—and therefore I'll limit myself to a few words: come, come quickly—because the Pushkin Commemoration (which will last three days: May 25, *26,* 27)[1] is inconceivable without you and everyone is waiting for you with the greatest impatience. At the dinner on the 26th you will definitely have to give a short speech apropos of any Pushkin work that you want; and you're already listed along with Goncharov, Dostoevsky, Ostrovsky, Pisemsky, Potekhin,[2] Polonsky, Maykov, I.S. Aksakov, Tikhonravov,[3] your friend Bartenyev and your humble servant and others. Any undesirable elements will be eliminated. I myself arrived here last Friday (N.B. The very next day a telegram about Tolstoy's ouster[4] arrived—I have yet to see such an explosion of general rejoicing)—I'll remain here until Monday—then go to Spasskoye—and be back here again at my friend Maslov's on the 24th. On the way I'll visit Lev Tolstoy and try to persuade him to come, in which endeavor it's unlikely that I'll be successful.[5]

And so, we'll see each other soon! I send my regards to all your family and embrace you.

Iv. Turgenev

Letter 310 (5143). To V.P. Gayevsky.[1]
April 24/May 6, 1880. Moscow.

Moscow.
Prechistensky Boulevard, Crown
Office Building.
Thursday, Apr. 24, 1880.

Dear Victor Pavlovich,

I haven't been able to write you anything about the Pushkin Commemoration until now because the program wasn't definitely arranged until yesterday. Here it is: on the 25th (the eve of the unveiling)[2] in the morning—an open meeting of the Society of Admirers of Russian Letters, chaired by Yuriev,[3] with speeches. The morning of the 26th—the unveiling of the monument—then a grand dinner, chaired by Grot,[4] for men of letters, delegates from the University, and so on—with separate short speeches (and toasts). Speeches will be given only by those people whose names will be on a list compiled by the committee, by which means any *undesirable elements*[5] will be eliminated. Here are the people in Petersburg whom the Committee invites to give these short speeches: Goncharov, Dostoevsky, Saltykov, Potekhin, Polonsky, Grigorovich, Pypin, Maykov. It goes without saying that as the president of our Society, you will receive an invitation, too, just as will universities, learned societies, the editorial committees of journals and so on. It may be that some of the people mentioned by me won't want to attend and give talks: please try to persuade them (for instance, Goncharov, without whom a Pushkin

Commemoration would be incomplete). In this connection we must lay aside all vanity, apprehensions, and extraneous considerations. I even assume that since we can be certain that no discordant voices à la Katkov will be there to hinder us, we ought to banish any thought of a separate Petersburg dinner, which would be like mustard after supper. Talk to Stasyulevich about this. Governor-General Dolgorukov[6] will be among the guests and has promised not only every assistance, but the widest latitude in our speeches as well. The following people from Moscow will speak: Ostrovsky, Pisemsky, I. Aksakov, Bartenyev, Tikhonravov, and others. I'll try to persuade Lev Tolstoy, whom I'll be seeing very soon. (I'm going to the country on Tuesday—but I'll be back here by the 23rd.) On the 27th a grand musical and theatre evening will be held (the actor Samarin[7] and N. Rubinstein have undertaken to arrange it)—and if there is a great demand, it will be repeated on the following day. It would be very much to be desired that all our literature gather together for the Pushkin Commemoration.

I conclude with a request that concerns you personally and which I forgot to convey to you during my stay in Petersburg. I have a good friend in Paris, Mr. Commanville,[8] who owns a large lumber factory. He concluded a contract with Mr. Sollogub (the son)[9] for the purchase of large forests in the Caucasus and the delivery of logs to Le Havre. Up until now everything has been going well: but since Mr. Sollogub doesn't enjoy too reliable a reputation—Mr. Commanville, in case of any vacillation, misunderstanding, or failure to deliver, would like to have a lawyer in Russia, un homme de loi [a man of law], to whom he could entrust the affair. Upon Stasyulevich's advice I suggested you to him, since, as it is, you are a lawyer for the French Embassy. So, if Mr. Commanville should appeal to you for advice and directions, you may be assured that he is a quite solid person on whom you may rely and for whom I can vouch. I hope that you won't find anything in this that contradicts your interests or the merit of your position.

Please accept, dear Viktor Pavlovich, the assurance of the complete respect and devotion

Of your Iv. Turgenev.

Letter 311 (5163). To Emile Zola.[1]
May 11/23, 1880. Spasskoye.

Spasskoye (City of Mtsensk.)
Sunday, May 11/23, 1880.

My dear Zola,

I thank you for having thought of me. It was like a handshake from a friend. I received the blow in a most brutal fashion, here, three days ago, while reading a feuilleton in *The Voice*.[2] I do not need to tell you of my sorrow: Flaubert was one of the people whom I loved most in the world. It isn't only a great talent that has left us, but a superior being, and a center for us all.

I'll arrive in Paris in three weeks at the latest. I'll see you there, and we'll talk about the publication of his novel that he was unable to finish and which *must* appear.[3] Until then, I clasp your hand very cordially and remain

Your devoted Iv. Tourguéneff.

Letter 312 (5175). To M.G. Savina.
May 10/31, 1880. Spasskoye.

Village of Spasskoye-Lutovinovo.
(Oryol Province, City of Mtsensk.)
Monday, May 19, 1880.

Dear Maria Gavrilovna!

It is incredible. The weather has been divine for three days now, and from morning till evening I stroll around the park or sit on the terrace, trying to think—and I do think—about various subjects—but down there, somewhere at the bottom of my soul, a single note keeps sounding. I imagine that I'm meditating on the Pushkin Commemoration—and suddenly I notice that my lips are whispering: "What a night we would have spent...And what would have happened afterwards? The Lord only knows!"[1] And to this is immediately added the realization that that can never be and that I will end up departing for that "unknown land" without taking with me the recollection of something that I hadn't ever experienced. For some reason it often seems to me that we will never see each other again: I never did believe and still don't believe that your trip abroad will take place, I won't arrive in Petersburg for the winter—and you are just wasting your time in reproaching yourself by calling me "your sin." Alas, I will never be that. And even if we do see each other in two or three years—I'll be an old man by then, you surely will have settled down for good—and nothing will remain of what was. For you that's not such a loss...your whole life is ahead of you—mine is behind me—and that hour that we spent in the train car, when I almost felt like a twenty-year-old youth, was the last flare-up of the lamp. It's even difficult for me to explain to myself what feeling you inspired in me. I don't know whether I'm in love with you; that used to happen to me in quite a different way. This unquenchable desire for merging, for possession—and for giving up of oneself, where even sensuality is consumed by a delicate fire...I'm surely talking nonsense—but I would have been unspeakably happy if...if...But now, when I know that that is not to be, I'm not exactly unhappy, I don't even feel any special melancholy, but I'm profoundly sorry that that lovely night is really lost forever, without having touched me with its wing...I'm sorry for myself—and I make bold to add—and for you, as well, because I'm certain that you too would not have forgotten the happiness that you would have given me.

I wouldn't be writing all of this to you if I didn't sense that this is a farewell letter. Not that our correspondence has ceased—oh, no!—I hope that we'll hear from one another often—but a door that was half open, that door behind which I seemed to glimpse something mysteriously wonderful, has slammed shut forever...Now it's quite definite that le verrou est tiré [the bolt has been drawn]. No matter what happens—I will no longer be this way—nor will you.

Well, and now that's enough. What *was*...(or wasn't)—is now gone—and forgotten. Which doesn't prevent me from wishing you all the best in the world and kissing your dear hands in my thoughts. You needn't answer this letter...but do answer the first one.[2]

Your Iv. Turgenev

P.S. Please don't be alarmed for the future. You will never receive another letter *such as this one.*

Letter 313 (5202). To M.M. Stastyulevich.
June 13/25, 1880. Spasskoye.

> Village of Spasskoye-Lutovinovo.
> (Oryol Province, City of Mtsensk.)
> Friday, June 13, 1880.

Dear Mikhail Matveyevich, just try not to be superstitious after you hear this! About 8 years ago, arriving in Vienna for an exhibit, on the 13th of June, a Friday, I hurt my knee as I was getting out of a carriage—I had a sudden attack of gout—and I was in bed for 3 weeks; 4 years ago also on the 13th of June and also on a Friday I slipped and fell on the stairs—and I again had an attack of gout that kept me immobile for about a week; and now today, again the 13th of June and again on a Friday—I've had another attack of gout—without any reason whatsoever—that has put me in bed!! I don't know when I'll be able to leave here—and our dinner has receded into the misty future . . . There's only one thing I can do: inform you about my arrival by telegram . . . and until then: patience!

I don't know who of your staff will be writing about the Pushkin Commemoration, but it wouldn't hurt to point out the following to him: both in Iv. Aksakov's speech and in all the newspapers it says that I personally was completely won over by Dostoevsky's speech and that I thoroughly approve of it.[1] But that is not so—and I haven't yet said: "Thou hast conquered, Gallilean!" That very brilliant, smart, and—for all its passion—clever speech rests entirely on a conceit, but a conceit that is extremely flattering for Russian vanity. Pushkin's Aleko[2] is a purely Byronic figure—and not at all an example of a contemporary Russian wanderer; the characterization of Tatyana[3] is very subtle—but can it really be that only *Russian* wives remain faithful to their elderly husbands? And the main thing is: "We shall say the final word to Europe, we will make a gift of herself to her—because the genius of Pushkin recreated Shakespeare, Goethe, and others"?[4] But after all, he *recreated,* not *created*—and it's certain that we'll no more create a new Europe than he created Shakespeare and others. And what's the point of this *all-man* whom the audience applauded so violently? But it isn't even at all desirable to be him: it is better to be an original Russian than this faceless all-man. It's the same old pride again under the guise of humility. It may be that for Europeans the sort of assimilation that can be elevated to a work of universal genius is more difficult because they are more original than we are. But it's understandable that the audience was thrilled by these compliments; and the speech really was remarkable in its beauty and rhythm. I think that something of this sort ought to be said. The Messrs. Slavophiles have not yet swallowed us up.

In conclusion, farewell. I haven't yet untangled my affairs—but there is some hope. Perhaps we shall soon see each other . . . But for now, like Socrates, I only know that I know nothing.

I clasp your hand cordially.

Your Iv. Turgenev

Letter 314 (5242). To A.V. Toporov.
August 9/21, 1880. Bougival.

> (Seine-et-Oise.)
> Bougival.
> Les Frênes.
> Chalet.
> Saturday, Aug. 9/21, 1880.

Dear Alexander Vasilievich,

When you receive this letter, please be so kind as to buy a copy of V. Krestovsky's[1] *Petersburg Slums* and send it to me at my address here in Paris right away. Also let me know whether you finally received the ill-fated pills and sent them to N.S. Tikhonrarov in Moscow.[2] Did you subscribe to *The Deed?* I don't know how much of my money you have left—but in any case I'm writing my estate manager to send you 50 rubles.

M.G. Savina is probably in Petersburg already. It may be that you'll see her—but I ask you *not* to give her my regards. Her not wanting to see me is quite understandable; but elementary politeness should have prodded her to write me a word or two. I wish her every success; but she has ceased to exist for me.[3]

I clasp your hand cordially.

Your devoted Iv. Turgenev

Letter 315 (5315). To P.V. Annenkov.
November 22/December 4, 1880. Paris.

> 50, Rue de Douai.
> Paris.
> Saturday, Dec. 4, 1880.

Dear Pavel Vasilievich,

The package containing "Old Portraits" just arrived; I needn't tell you how happy your reaction made me. I can honestly assure you that before it came I didn't at all know what sort of thing I had written—and if you advised me against publishing this study, I wouldn't have been surprised! That is the explanation for my letter to Stasyulevich as well; I really wasn't "sentimentalizing." Now, of course, that letter will be destroyed—all that will be kept are a few lines about the form of first-person narration as one that is more convenient and which gives me greater freedom.[1]

And now about the coachman. In reality that story happened and concluded just like that (I didn't even change the name [Ivan]). That's not yet any proof, however: reality teems with chance happenstances that art should exclude; but that fact occurs to me that *almost never does a Russian* murderer commit suicide—especially among the peasantry, while in Europe that happens all the time. I'm afraid of giving the suicide a European coloration. But since I believe in your critical sense almost blindly—I intend to give myself two or three days for pondering this before I send the piece off to Stasyulevich—and then I'll make up my mind—one way or the other.[2]

I have several similar studies ready in my head: they may now see the light of day, too. At the beginning of my career the success of "Khor and Kalinych" gave birth to *The Notes of a Hunter;* it would be curious if "Old Portraits" turned out to be fruitful, too—at the very end of that same career.[3]

Once again I thank you sincerely for your swift reaction; I send my cordial regards to your wife, kiss the children, and embrace you.

> Your Iv. Turgenev

Letter 316 (5574). To K.N. Boborykin.[1]
November 21/ December 3, 1881. Paris.

To His Excellency the Governor of Oryol

Paris. 50, Rue de Douai.
Nov. 21/ Dec. 3, 1881

Esteemed Konstantin Nikolayevich,

Allow me to take advantage of our long-standing acquaintance and appeal to you with the following request.

The Jews residing in Oryol Province are being expelled. I will not go into a discussion of the reasons that have prompted the government to take such a measure, but surely you will agree that it sometimes acquires the appearance of flagrant injustice and undeserved oppression.

Such expressions certainly apply to the situation of the two sisters of a good friend of mine, the artist Zilberman,[2] who works here in Paris in the studio of the well-known Antokolsky. These sisters—Maria Isaakovna Itsikson and Olga Isaakovna Tsekhnovicher—are both widows; they have lived in Volkhovo since early childhood, and since they do not possess any means, they earn their livelihood as seamstresses. (They have passports and craft documents.) They both have children: one has five, the other four, and they all go to school. They have now been given written instructions to leave Oryol Province within a month. But to force these two women and their small children to leave their nest of many years would not only mean ruining them financially, but condemning them to death by starvation. Of course governors must be the first executors of laws—but they have been given the authority to mitigate the application of those laws when they see fit to do so. I dare to think that in regard to these two poor widows, esteemed Konstantin Nikolayevich, you will find it possible to make use of just that authority—and will give them the means to remain, if only temporarily, on the brink of the abyss into which they must inevitably fall without your intercession.[3]

This is what my request to you is. In the hopes that you will not find it an immodest one, I beg you to accept the assurance of the feelings of profound respect with which I remain

Your sincerely devoted Ivan Turgenev.

171

Letter 317 (5630). To P.V. Annenkov.
January 8/20, 1882. Paris.

Paris. 50, Rue de Douai.
Jan. 20, 1882.

Dear Pavel Vasilievich,

First of all, a few words about the translation of *Onegin*.[1] Did you read my letter?[2] It was very sharply worded—but why should Mikhailov be exasperated? And there was no *apostrophe* in it. I wrote "Dear Mr. Mikhailov" because I couldn't remember either his first name or patronymic, and I could hardly write "Dear Mikhailov." It's quite true that Pushkin needs to be translated in verse; no one pays any attention to prose translation—because there exists an *extraordinarily accurate* French prose translation of *Eugene Onegin*—namely, the translation that *Viardot and I* made and published in *Revue Nationale* about 20 years ago;[3] and it has remained so unnoticed that it didn't prevent the appearance of that outrageous translation from which you cite the "Tanbur poet"[4]—but on the other hand, a verse translation ought to be done by a poet. You say that I ought to have been more indulgent toward the labor of an elderly man who desired to fill his leisure time with something; but it is precisely out of respect for that elderly man that I should have tried to dissuade him from such a hopeless business; the more so as, as was already proved by the Heine translation, that elderly fellow can manage Russian verses and is not altogether lacking in talent for translation;[5] why doesn't he tackle a French or a German poet? The result would be something pleasant and useful. But for a person unfamiliar with the grammar of the language into which he is translating to translate *Pushkin*—excuse me, but that's a crime: c'est plus qu'un crime, c'est une faute [it's more than a crime, it's a mistake]. To this day I am grateful to Herzen for having taken the manuscript of a narrative poem that I'd read him and thrown it into the fire; I would like to convince Mr. Mikhailov that it was sympathy alone for him that impelled me to give him similar advice. But, anyway, he can do as he sees fit.[6] No, my dear friend, one cannot allow everyone, however many want, as you say, to play and frolic around Pushkin; they put railings around marble fences, after all.

And now—enough of that!

As you are aware, there occurred a financial and political crash here yesterday—and Gambetta, as little as two months ago the most popular man in France and in the House, has gone flying head over heels into the mud.[7] An instructive case! "Everything on earth is so changeable."[8] What will be the outcome of all this? "Wise Oedipus, decide!"[9] I'm not about to.

Everyone here is well; Marianne's[10] condition is excellent. I'm well too. I send my regards to all your loved ones and clasp your hand cordially.

Your devoted Iv. Turgenev.

Letter 318 (5633). To V.V. Stasov.
January 9/21, 1882. Paris.

Paris. 50, Rue de Douai.
January 9/21, 1882.

Your letter very much surprised me, dear Mr. Stasov. But since I am ready to believe that is was occasioned not so much by the enthusiasm that Sarah Bernhardt evoked in you as by sympathetic concern for me, I will answer you—briefly.

You reproach me, claiming that I offer my hand to Mr. Suvorin and that this stains my reputation. I know Mr. Suvorin as a person just as well as you do—and I have never offered him my hand and never will—just as I never offered it to Mr. Katkov;[1] and the only thing that can stain a person's reputation is an ugly act on his part, not the first scandalmonger who comes along. I expressed my views on Mr. Suvorin's article about Sarah Bernhardt in a private letter to Grigorovich[2]—and I could hardly have expected, of course, that it would become common knowledge; I regret that. But I'm not in the habit of renouncing my opinions even when, though stated in a cordial, private conversation, they become public. Yes; I find Mr. Suvorin's evaluation of Sarah Bernhardt true and just. She is an intelligent, adroit woman who knows all the subtleties of her métier, is blessed with an exquisite voice, with good schooling—but she utterly lacks any *nature* or any artistic temperament (for which she tries to substitute Parisian lewdness), she has been corrupted by chic (pourrie de chic), publicity, and posing, she does not have a spark of what is called talent in its highest sense. Her carriage is that of a chicken—she has no silent acting whatsoever—and her gestures are angularly-piquante—it all reeks of the boulevard, *Figaro,* and patchouli. As you can see, in my opinion Mr. Suvorin was rather indulgent. You quote E. Zola as an authority, although you rebel against authorities in general; allow me to cite G. Augier, who told me the following, word-for-word: "Cette femme n'a aucun talent; on

173

dit d'elle que c'est un paquet de nerfs—c'est un paquet de ficelles" [That woman has no talent; they say of her that she is a bundle of nerves—she's a bundle of cheap tricks]. "But then why the world-wide reputation?" you'll ask. And what do I care? I speak upon consideration of my *own* feelings, and I'm very glad when I find confirmation of that in another's feelings.

As for the other subject of your letter, I cannot even possibly imagine how I would exert pressure on Mr. Stasyulevich and on the contents of both of his publications. And don't you yourself contribute to both of them?[3]

Accept the assurance of my respect.

Iv. Turgenev

Letter 319 (5665). To Zh. A. Polonskaya.
February 22/March 6, 1882. Paris.

50, Rue de Douai.
Paris.
Monday, March 6, 1882.

Dear Zhozefina Antonovna,

I received your letter a week ago and haven't gotten around to answering it until now; but you will surely forgive me when you find out that in the course of the week my old friend Viardot suffered a pulmonary stroke from which he nearly died—Marianne gave birth to a daughter (Suzanne) after forty hours of torment—and, lastly, my daughter was forced to run away from her husband with two children, I had to hide her here, etc. Viardot has begun to show such improvement, thank God, that there is hope for his recovery, Marianne and her baby are doing well—and I found a refuge for my daughter where her husband won't be able to find her.[1] There's a lot of fussing about ahead—but at least I can catch my breath—that is to say, I haven't slept for six nights running. That hasn't affected my health, however. I'll limit myself to these few lines for now—I'll write you in more detail tomorrow or the day after—and in the meantime I embrace you all very heartily and remain

Your Iv. Turgenev.

Letter 320 (5676). To Pauline Bruère.[1]
March 4/16, 1882. Paris.

50, Rue de Douai.
Paris.
March 16, 1882. 11:00 P.M.

My dear Paulinette,

The good Mlle Arnholdt has just arrived and brought me up to date on everything.[2] I'm very happy to learn that you are well installed. But allow me to make the following recommendations:

a) Stay calm—don't show yourself too much, speak little, and don't make any acquaintances. Understand that your husband will have a very thorough search conducted—and if he were ever to discover your retreat, whether through a commercial traveller or in some other way, nothing will be able to save you from his claws, as you say. It's folly to think of writing to him or to Mr. Pol—I am pretending ignorance of your whereabouts—he has already sent me a summons through a process server, and if he had reason to suspect my knowledge, he would initiate a court case immediately.

b) Live on the strictest possible budget. It's absolutely impossible for me to give you more than *400 francs* a month. You will have to manage on that and you shouldn't count on a *single sou more.* Keep your account book very accurate.

c) Don't forget that you no longer have anything—you can't make any claims *at all,* because you have put yourself in an unequal position—and you ought not to think of anything except being forgotten. You made the mistake of selling Mr. Pol Chamerot's[3] promissory note—he has already given notice through a process server that he has taken your place—and Chamerot has told me that he has no choice but to pay him your 1500 francs a year. The same thing applies to Jeanne's bonds; it's your husband who is the administrator of your usufruct and he can dispose of it as he pleases. Georges' bond is in my hands, but it's impossible for me to receive the revenue from it, because the company will only pay it to your husband or to the person to whom he cedes his rights. And so that revenue must accumulate in my hands *without being paid to me*—until your son's majority or the death of your husband, which is as far away as it could possibly be, since he has never felt better and no longer speaks of suicide, now that the thing has been done.

175

d) He has the perfect right to sell all of your effects, jewelry, etc., etc., down to the last garment. In the eyes of the law you are dead—and I repeat—you cannot demand or insist on anything. Come to terms with this idea that you have absolutely nothing, that all of your rights and possessions are quite lost forever. You see with what prudence you must watch every sou.

Try to keep yourself occupied, work on clothes for the children and for yourself, educate your children. Take care that no one at the hotel doubt that you have a live husband; invent some story, moreover, one of which you will tell as little as possible. Let them think that your husband has been exiled, that he has emigrated to America, let them think, moreover, that there is a bit of mystery in your affairs. Don't ever answer inquiries; try to see to it that no one makes any of you. For Heaven's sake, don't chatter and don't ever tell anyone anything. The slightest suspicion, a chance word—spreads like a spot of oil. A telegram is sent off very quickly and you'll see your husband crashing down on you like a bomb. You have always been afraid of trifles—now you have real fears and don't ever forget that you have a sort of sword suspended over your head. After what Mlle Arnholt told me I'm afraid that Soleure is not a sufficiently isolated place. There are some words in your letter that make me shudder: "We are installed in a charming manner. *The society is suitable,* we'll take *endless* walks, things will go *swimmingly.*" But Good Lord! You must not see people, you must not keep showing yourself outside, etc. One really might think that you had no doubts about your position.

"Conceal yourself and be silent"—that is your rule of conduct.

I'll try to send you some music through Annenkov. You could let me know two or three pieces that you would like.

In closing I embrace you and your children and may God grant that all go well.

Mlle Arnholt told me that she left you about 750 francs. That is for six weeks beginning March 15.

I'll try to send you another small sum for clothes for you and the children.

I.T.

Letter 321 (5720). To Zh. A. Polonskaya.
April 8/20, 1882. Paris.

Paris. 50, Rue de Douai.
8/20 April, 1882.

Dear Zhozefina Antonovna,

I've been hesitating all this time; but now I have to relate a not very pleasant bit of news. I have come down with an illness called "angine de poitrine [angina pectoris]."[1] It's actually a gouty neuralgia of the heart. It doesn't present any danger—but it forces one to lie or sit quietly; not just going up the stairs, but even simply walking or even just standing on one's feet causes very strong pains in the shoulders, shoulder blades, and the entire chest—and then difficulties in breathing arise. I decided to consult Charcot.[2] He prescribed medicine, ordered me not to move from the spot— and declared in advance that this illness, like all neuralgias, is rather stubborn and capricious—and that it's absolutely impossible to predict when I'll be able to leave here—but in any event it will be no earlier than in six weeks. You can imagine how that has affected me and distressed me. It's such a stupid situation: an absolutely healthy person who can't move from the spot, can't stand on his feet, and Lord only knows how long this will continue.

And therefore I suggest that as soon as you and your family find it possible, go to Spasskoye and settle in there—and await my arrival: I'll write N.A. Shchepkin[3] immediately and have him take all the necessary steps and make the essential dispositions as though for my own arrival. It will be pleasant for me to think that you're waiting for me there—and I think that that idea will facilitate my recovery. Write me of your decision immediately.

I received a long letter from Yakov Petrovich[4] about his drama—and I could say a great deal and explain the reasons for my views—but I'll put that off for another time. In a few days an artist is supposed to bring me the trial illustrations for *The Grasshopper*.[5]

I'm glad at least that all your children are well again and I embrace them and Yakov Petrovich, too, and I kiss your hands.

Your friend Iv. Turgenev

Letter 322 (5770). To Ya. P. Polonsky.
May 21/June 2, 1882. Paris.

Paris. 50, Rue de Douai.
May 21/June 2, 1882.

My dear friend Yakov Petrovich,

Yesterday in response to your letter, I sent your wife a telegram advising her not to come[1]—and today I can only repeat what I've written both to her and to you in my last letters. The idea that I will remain alone in Paris in a stuffy and crowded room is utterly fantastic. I have three whole rooms, not one; they're spacious and superbly furnished, and I'm only alone when I desire to be—and no one will go to the country without me. As for that move, which depends entirely on my illness, it keeps getting put off—although there is hope that it will be accomplished next Monday (today is Thursday). They'll lift me up like a suitcase, carry me to the carriage, deliver me right to my little house—and then again lift me by hand and carry me to my bed. I'll really be glad then! I'll let you know just as soon as that happens.

As to what will happen from then on in, the Lord alone knows. But the result turns out to be that I and everyone who is well-disposed toward me will have to wait patiently. "Patience! Patience!" Belogolovy[2] kept repeating to me, "there is *no other* medicine for your illness." And so I'm practicing patience.

I've already written you about *The Grasshopper*.[3] Patience is necessary in that matter, too.

In closing I embrace you all and remain

Your Iv. Turgenev.

Letter 323 (5794). To M.G. Savina.
June 7/19, 1882. Bougival.

Dear Maria Gavrilovna,

Your letter from Siva[1] fell on my gray life like a rose petal on the surface of a muddy stream. My moving here from Paris hasn't brought the expected beneficial change; on the contrary: my health has worsened significantly—and I'm now in the same condition as the day you said good-bye to me; as soon as I was able to walk—the gout in my legs passed—the pains in my chest and shoulder grew even stronger—and I'm almost condemned to immobility—I can't raise my arm level with my face and so on. I don't know whether the reason for this is the vile, damp weather that we've had here since I arrived (it will soon be two weeks ago) or whether my illness in general is one of those that are incurable—of which I'm nearly convinced—but the fact remains a fact. Any vigor of spirit has disappeared in me; I try not to glance into the future—and no longer allow myself to dream of seeing you. On the other hand I rejoice with my whole heart—as much as a half-alive person can rejoice—that things are well with you and that you're relaxing in body and spirit. As for your plans (marriage and so on)[2]—I'm certain that you possess sufficient intelligence and quick-wittedness to select the best path, as they say, and to make the best decision for yourself. You did well to conclude a contract for two years.[3] When does it begin? In September?

As for my letters—you may do with them as you please . . .[4] The same thing that you could do with me, if . . . if . . . I'll let you finish the sentence. I know for certain that when I chat with you, I'm chatting with you alone; but an alien hand might brush these pages without your knowledge . . . But that's all nonsense—and I repeat: do as you wish.

My dear friend, I have become so meek in spirit that I don't even allow myself to ponder the meaning of the following words in your letter: "Try to recall sometimes how difficult it was for me to say farewell to you in Paris,[5] *what I went through then!*" I know for certain that had our lives collided earlier . . . But what's the point of all this? Like my Lemm in *A Nest of Gentlefolk,* I'm gazing into a coffin, not a rosy future.

Forgive me for writing you such cheerless things; but it's impossible for me to pretend with you. Remember that throughout all of this one thing is obvious: that I love you very, very much.

You didn't write me of your "military man."[6] What's happened? Did he appear before you again in Petersburg? I hope that you managed to dissuade him. Are there any roles being prepared for you? I keep thinking that you haven't yet found a real author—one worthy of you. You probably flew through Moscow and didn't see anyone there. (Did you know that although poor Maslov[7] recovered, he's become an idiot because of softening of the brain?) And did you see Strepetova[8] in the role of Mary Stuart?

Well, my darling, farewell. Write me at least once more from your far remove. I kiss your hands a thousand times—and everything that you will allow me to kiss, and I remain forever

Your faithful friend I.T.

Letter 324 (5907). To Pauline Bruère.[1]
August 30/September 11, 1882. Bougival.

(Seine-et-Oise). Bougival. Les Frênes.
Monday, Sept. 11, 1882.

Dear Pauline,

I just received your letter and am going to answer you. I caution you that this time I am seriously displeased with you and here is why.

It is not for having told me the gossip that I had asked for anyway. I didn't learn anything new; but I leave that gossip in the mud where it was born—just as I do the porter's drivel which, like a real provincial—you call the neighborhood noise. I do not lower myself to rectify all these lies.[2]

My principal complaint against you is that you allowed yourself to name Mme Viardot as your teacher.[3] In the first place, that was very imprudent and could have allowed your true situation to be discovered; secondly, after the black ingratitude which, due to the influence of the stupid and limited Mme Innis, you have been shown guilty of toward Mme Viardot, *you should not have dared to pronounce her name* and ought to have held your gossipy tongue. You are quite as ungrateful, stupidly ungrateful, with regard to Mlle Arnholt, who has done nothing but render you services and who has always evinced interest in you. By what right do you declare that you *cannot bear her!* (Another remark of a provincial petit-bourgeois.) Your *friends* (which you underline) have declared that person to be *false.* Why the devil would she be false toward you and what profit could she possibly derive from so doing? Who are you—a princess or a capitalist whom she would like to exploit?!!! Collect yourself a bit and judge a little better. One doesn't act falsely toward an indifferent person or a stranger—which at bottom you are for her—and the interest she shows you has no source other than the fact that you are my daughter. Mlle Arnholt was quite right to protest when you permitted yourself to speak of the gifts that I make to the Viardot family—for whose sake I am ruining myself, etc. You ought to have swallowed your tongue rather than pronounce these words. First of all—don't I have the right to make whatever outlays I please? And then, shouldn't you be the last person to speak of that—you, for whom I've done ten times what I should have? If anyone has ruined me—it's surely you and your husband—since you're the ones to whom I've given half my fortune, if not more. The calculations for that can be done quickly. With your dowry of 200,000 francs (with what I paid and gave you later), the 100,000 that I've given from hand to hand (Chamerot's debt, the 25,000 francs, etc.), the 70,000 francs of capital for your children, and the capital of 100,000 francs, the interest on which you're receiving—that turns out to be nearly a half a million. And you weren't afraid to recriminate! And note well that it's not through Mlle Arnholt ("whom you cannot bear")—and who has never said a single word of ill will about you, that I learned of all of this, but from you yourself. It is well that I don't attribute all of this to your heart, which isn't bad—but to your head, which is stuffed with petty and worthless things, suspicions, ridiculous grudges and prejudices, gossip, absurd sympathies and antipathies—and especially to your tongue, which makes you chatter like a magpie, at random—and always to your detriment.

You complain of your situation, but after all, who has created it, if not you? Who was it, after all, who repulsed an honorable man, M. Lambert,[4] only because he was a friend of Mmes Sand and Viardot—and accepted that stupid brute with whom you are aggrieved—and for whom, loathing him and having decided to leave him, you made even more absurd sacrifices, right up to ceding him your children's bread? You went to Switzerland of your own free will—and now you're bored and complain! What do you want me to do? With the money that I give you—and to which I am incapable of adding a sou, you and your children can live well. My conscience gives me no cause for reproach; try to have yours leave you equally at ease.

With the thoughtlessness that is natural for you, you speak of going to Italy, Germany, England. I don't know what else! Of giving lessons, etc.

That's perfect; but if you want to teach French, try to attend to your orthography a bit and not write "je veux étudié, être digne d'interets, être allité," etc.

That's enough of this. I don't want to occupy myself with all of this anymore—and I ask, I demand that in your response there be neither *excuses* nor *explanations*. Profit by the distressing things which I have had to write you; reflect, if that's possible, and don't prattle any more either with your pen or your tongue.

Your music will be on its way today; the books will follow soon. I don't have the time to answer Jeanne and Georges immediately, I'll make do in the meantime by embracing them—and you too.

Your Iv. Tourguéneff.

Letter 325 (5925). To Ya. P. Polonsky. September 10/22, 1882. Bougival.

(Seine-et-Oise.) Bougival. Les Frênes.
Friday, Sept. 10/22, 1882.

My dear friend Yakov Petrovich!

Here's an answer to your long "landscape" letter.[1]

1) The paper cut-out that I'm including represents the exact height of a tree that stands 75 paces from a canvas which is viewed from a distance of one-and-a-half arshins (that's the very least for a viewer; and the artist himself ought to paint at the distance).

2) Corot's[2] first sketches are never from closer than *150* paces; if I spoke of a *half-verst*—then I was referring to the center of the picture—that is, to the central point *between the foreground and the horizon*, which in Corot's pictures is often at a distance of 2 or 3 versts.

3) Even at 75 paces *there are no* distinct outlines in the foliage; there are masses and *spots*.

4) The depiction of trees in camera obscura is an *artificial* concentration of light—and in the artistic respect—as the reproduction of a natural impression—is ugly and deformed; and that ugliness and deformity have been transferred completely to the so-called German school of the

Achenbachs[3] and Calames,[4] who in fact have always painted from camera obscura—not from live nature.

5) It's precisely the *sky* that none of the recent landscapists can paint as accurately and marvellously as *Corot*; in *that* instance he reminds one of Ruysdael.[5]

Dixi et animam meam salvavi [I spoke and saved my soul]!

In closing I clasp your hand cordially and remain

Your Iv. Turgenev.

**Letter 326 (5945). To M. Ye. Saltykov-Shchedrin.
September 24/October 6, 1882. Bougival.**

(Seine-et-Oise.) Bougival. Les Frênes.
Sept. 24/Oct. 6, 1882.

Dear Mikhail Yevgrafovich, I received your letter—and soon after it the September issue of *Notes of the Fatherland*. I immediately read your "Contemporary Idyll"[1]—and found that your innate vis comica has never been manifested with greater brilliance. No! It will be a long time yet before you may retire your pen. If only the censorship doesn't devour you. But you're substantial; it will chew you a bit—but won't be able to swallow. I also read Mikhailovsky's[2] article about Dostoevsky.[3] He has accurately noted the basis characteristic of his art. He could have recalled that there was a similar phenomenon in French literature as well—namely, the notorious Marquis de Sade. The latter even wrote a book, *Tourments et supplices,* in which he dwells with special pleasure on the perverted bliss brought by the infliction of refined tortures and torments. In one of his novels Dostoevsky too paints a fancier's pleasure in detail...[4] And just imagine, all the Russian bishops read offices for the dead for that de Sade of ours and even read little sermons about the all-love of that all-man.[5] We truly are living in a strange time!

It's bad that you're not well (and who could know that and appreciate it better than I); but you're wrong to complain of the hatred of certain people who even turn pale at the mention of your name. Whoever evokes hatred evokes love as well. If you were merely the hereditary noble M. Ye. Saltykov—none of this would be the case. But you're Saltykov-Shchedrin, a writer who was fated to make a great imprint on our literature, and so you're hated—and loved, depending on whom you're talking about. And in regard to the "result of your life," about which you speak, you can be pleased with it. As for loneliness and isolation—who on earth—after the age of fifty—isn't in essence lonely, a "fragment" of the older generation? There's nothing to be done about that; it's death preparing us gradually so that we won't be so sorry to part with life.

As regards our common friend P.V. Annenkov, you are unjust. I know what a high opinion he holds of you. He doesn't regard anyone haughtily or ironically—and he's not about to start with you! You may not perhaps have noticed that he is an extremely shy and even timid person. You didn't make that out under his affected familiarity. Of course he's a contemporary of Gogol's and Belinsky's; but he feels himself just as much a contemporary of Yazykov's and Maslov's—and doesn't reject that in the least.

I'll be remaining here another six weeks or so. Then I'll move to Paris...and when I'll get to Russia—only the gods know that, if they occupy themselves with such triviality.

I clasp your hand firmly and remain

Your sincerely devoted Iv. Turgenev.

P.S. Is it true that V. Garshin[6] sent a povest to *Notes of the Fatherland*?[7] That man has an indubitable and original talent.

Letter 327 (5984). To L.N. Tolstoy.
October 19/31, 1882. Bougival.

(Seine-et-Oise.) Bougival. Les Frênes.
Oct. 19/31, 1882.

Dear Lev Nikolayevich,

I received your letter and I thank you for your promise to send the piece.[1] I'll be waiting for the arrival of Mrs. Olsufieva,[2] with whom I think I am already acquainted, by the way—if this is the same Olsufieva whom I used to see in Paris at Mrs. Rakhmanova's.[3] And there's no question but that I'll read your piece in just the way that you desire. I know that it was written by a very intelligent, very talented, and very *sincere* person; I may disagree with him—but first of all I will try to understand him, to put myself quite in his place ... That will be more instructive and interesting for me than measuring him by my own yardstick or seeking to find what comprises his differences with me. *To be angry*, however—is quite unthinkable—the only people who get angry are young folk who imagine that they are the center of the universe ... and I'll be 64 in a few days. A long life teaches one not to doubt everything (because doubting everything means to believe in oneself), but to doubt oneself, i.e., to believe in something else—and even to need it. That's the spirit in which I'll be reading you.

I'm very glad that you've knit a nest for yourself and that things are so good for you and all your family. But the Lord only knows when I'll see you! My condition is most peculiar. A man is quite healthy ... only he can't *stand*—or *walk*—or *ride* without unbearable pain in his left shoulder, as though from a rotten tooth. It's a thoroughly absurd situation, as a result of which I'm condemned to immobility. And how long this will go on—no one knows that either. I'm gradually growing accustomed to this idea—but it is difficult. Recently, however, I've set to work again.

How happy I would be if I found out that you too had done that! You're right, of course: before anything else one needs to live *as one should*; but after all, the one thing doesn't contradict the other.

In a few days I'll send you a very short story, "The Quail"—you remember, I promised to write it for your children's journal.[4]

I'll remain here about a month.

I send my regards to all your family and clasp you hand firmly.

Your sincerely loving Iv. Turgenev

Letter 328 (6007). To D.V. Grigorovich.
October 31/November 12, 1882. Bougival.

(Seine-et-Oise.) Bougival. Les Frênes.
Sunday, Oct. 31/Nov. 12, 1882.

My dear friend Dmitry Vasilievich, again you failed to display your address, again I have to write to you in care of Polonsky! If you would at least display your official address—your school's address on Malaya (or Bolshaya?) Morskaya Street![1]

I congratulate you on the conclusion of your duties in connection with the Exhibit, at which you may look back with pride;[2] I congratulate you—and the public—on the resumption of your literary activity (I see that *Field* is announcing your povest—along with mine, which hasn't even been begun, and probably will not be finished very soon).[3] The Polonskys, who have heard your povest, have high praise for it. And what's the *comedy* of Petersburg life with its main hero, Figaro-Polovtsev,[4] doing?

One can only wish a speedy end for I.I. Maslov, if he has a vague notion of his condition, as often happens with people who are struck by such an ailment; if not—then may he continue his vegetable existence! Of course—only as long as he isn't suffering.[5] I too am now leading a life that is somewhat similar to that of a birch tree's or an oyster's, thanks to the immobility to which I'm condemned. But it really is all right. It sometimes happens that I don't even desire anything better.

A few days ago a very nice Moscow lady[6] brought me L. Tolstoy's "Confession," which was forbidden by the censorship. I read it with great interest: it is a piece remarkable for its sincerity, truthfulness, and force of persuasion. But it's built entirely on faulty premises—and in the final analysis it leads to the most gloomy negation of all vital, human life . . . This too is nihilism of sorts. I wonder why it is that Tolstoy, who rejects art, among other things, surrounds himself with artists—and what they can gain from his conversations. And still and all, Tolstoy is perhaps the most remarkable person in Russia today!

Do you know anything about the "Pushkin Assembly" that recently made me an honorary member, and do you participate in it? And also—what is the "Pushkin Circle"? Is it an expression of the need to concentrate *our widely dispersed literature*—or does it exist just so, from lack of anything to do? Do you continue to be a member of the Committee of the Society for Assistance to Needy Writers and Scholars? If yes, support an appeal of mine that was sent off a few days ago to your chairman Tagantsev.[7]

Give my cordial regards to your spouse. I clasp your hand firmly.

Your devoted Iv. Turgenev

Letter 329 (6025). To M.N. Stasyulevich.
November 12/24, 1882. Paris.

Paris. 50, Rue de Douai.
November 12/24, 1882. Friday.

Here are the two proposals, dear Mikhail Matveyevich, which I mentioned in yesterday's letter:

a) A povest by L. Ya. Stechkina[1] is being sent to you with today's mail. This poor woman is in an extremely difficult situation here. She has a very bad case of consumption, the doctors suggest that she go to the south—and she doesn't have a farthing. But I recommend her povest for *The Messenger of Europe*—I am not at all guided by a feeling of pity alone—and I'm not begging for alms for her. This povest seems to me quite worthy of appearing in *The Messenger of Europe*. Please be so kind as to read it—and if you find the appraisal of it accurate—and you accept the povest—*then send part of the payment now* (this is what my request consists of)—in advance. In so doing you will save this woman, who deserves complete sympathy—both for her talent and for her character. In any case do not delay in answering—do this for me.[2]

b) And here is my second proposal. The young novelist Guy de Maupassant, of whom you know, and who is indisputably the most talented of all contemporary French writers, has written a novel which, beginning February 15, will be published in *Gil Blas*—as a series of feuilletons. I'm acquainted with the content of this novel—it is not the least bit lewd, as are certain other of his works. A few days ago he read me several lengthy excerpts—and I was absolutely thrown into ecstasy: since the appearance of *Madame Bovery* there has been nothing such as this. It doesn't resemble Zola and the like. I know that I have earned a reputation as a too lenient judge and critic—but either I don't understand a thing—or Maupassant's novel is an outstanding phenomenon, a *capital thing*. He would be amenable to selling it in manuscript form—on the condition that the translation appear no earlier than February 3/15 of next year—i.e., the first part; the second could appear a month later—i.e., in the March issue of *The Messenger of Europe* (assuming that the first part comes out in the February issue). If I'm not mistaken, up until now *The Messenger of Europe* hasn't undertaken such arrangements—but, I repeat, this is an extraordinary work and it will make a strong impression. Maupassant would let you have it for 600 silver rubles. I could find a good translator here—and I would check the translation myself.[3] Think it over—and give me an answer, also as soon as possible.

That's what I had to tell you.

The novel's title is *Une vie*. It's the entire life of an honest, good life,[4] an entire intimate drama, portrayed by a first-class artist. The novel's size does not exceed that of *Madame Bovary*.

I wrote you yesterday that I agree to rechristening "After Death" as "Klara Milich."

I clasp your hand cordially and remain

Your devoted Iv. Turgenev.

Letter 330 (6090). To P.V. Annenkov.
December 29, 1882/January 10, 1883. Paris.

Paris. 50, Rue de Douai.
Dec. 29/Jan. 10, 1883. Wednesday.

Three days from now, on Sunday, to be precise, dear Pavel Vasilievich, I undergo surgery for the removal of a *neuroma*—not a lump or a cyst. This gentleman, whose name was unknown to me up until now, is nasty in that since he consists of an entire cluster of tangled nerve threads, he must be forcibly extracted or removed—while after being struck by the knife the cyst spills out all its insides. The danger is not in the operation itself, painful and long as it may be, but in the chance for the following two complications: erysipelas or an inflammation of the abdominal cavity. For that reason I'll have to lie motionless for about two weeks after the operation. But I'm not despondent: "le vin est tiré—il faut le boire" [the wine has been drawn—it must be drunk], as the French say—and besides, I'll be in skilled hands.[1] But think about me with sympathy on Sunday—between 11 and 1.

This, however, doesn't prevent me from wishing you a Happy New Year, nastily as it's beginning. The death of Gambetta alone is an incalculable loss! I saw his funeral from my window—and I've never seen anything like it in my whole life.[2] It was quite as though all of France, the whole race, the whole nation were accompanying its best son and leader to his grave. I have never seen such a *spectacle* either.

And what peace and joy we Russians are having! Mikhailovsky and Shelgunov[3] have been exiled from the capital,[4] Feoktistov has been given rule over the press,[5] Kavelin is terribly ill again, Goncharov has gone blind in one eye, Pobedonostsev[6] isn't going to the monastery, although his wife has made him a cuckold, the ruble is worth less than 2 francs 50 . . . Marvellous!

Since one ought to foresee anything as much as possible—especially all the bad things—you'll find included in this letter a note from me to you by force of which you have the right, in the event of my death, to sort out my correspondence—and take for yourself anything that you find interesting. I have notified my friends the Viardots about this.

In closing, I wish you all the best, embrace all your family, and remain

Your devoted Iv. Turgenev.

Letter 331 (6143). To Ya. N. Polonsky. March 12/24, 1883. Paris.

50, Rue de Douai. Paris.

Dear friend,

I'm so late with my bulletin because for the last week I've felt very bad, and only today am I better, thanks to the heroic dosages of quinine prescribed by my doctors. I don't know whether this will last long, but I hope that at least the severe chest pains will torment me less. I can't move, of course.

The operation on my neuroma, which in fact was only a subcutaneous tumor, has had no effect on my illness. By the way, you express surprise that English surnames can end in *oe*, but how could you, the official reader of English works,[1] forget *Robinson Crusoe* and its author Defoe?

In closing I embrace you and all you family.

24/III/83

Ivan Turgenev

Letter 332 (6155). To Zh. A. and Ya. P. Polonsky.
May 12/24, 1883. Bougival.

> Bougival.
> May 12/24, 1883. Thursday.

I haven't written to you for a long time, by dear friends, but what was there to write about? Not only is my illness not slackening, it's getting worse, with constant and unbearable torments—in spite of the marvellous weather—there's no hope. The craving for death keeps growing—and all I can do is ask that you too, on your part, wish for the realization of your unfortunate friend's wishes.

I embrace you all.

> Your devoted Iv. Turgenev

Letter 333 (6168). To L.N. Tolstoy.
June 29/July 11, 1883. Bougival.

> Bougival.
> Les Frênes.
> Chalet.
> The beginning of July Russ. st.
> Bougival. 1883.

Dear Lev Nikolayevich!

I haven't written to you for a long time because, speaking frankly, I've been and *am* on my death bed. I cannot recover—there's no point even in thinking of that. I'm writing you, in fact, to tell you how glad I was to be your contemporary—and to express to you my last, sincere request. My friend, return to literary activity! After all, that gift comes to you from where all else does, too. Oh, how happy I would be if I could think that my request will have that effect on you!! I'm a finished person—the doctors don't even know what to call my disease, névralgie stomacale goutteuse [gouty stomach neuralgia]. I can't walk or eat or sleep or anything! It's boring even to repeat all this! My friend, great writer of the Russian land, heed my request! Let me know if you receive this note, and allow me once more to heartily, heartily embrace you, your wife, and all your family. I can't go on anymore, I'm tired.

Letter 334 (6175). To N.A. Shchepkin.[1]
August 17/29, 1883. Bougival.

Nikolay Alexandrovich Shchepkin, Spasskoye, City of Mtsensk, Oryol Province, Russia.—Have you sent the papers immediately to the Gintsburg Office in Petersburg,[2] reply by telegram. Turgenev.

NOTES

Letter 166.

1. Annenkov had written to Turgenev about rumors that Turgenev was to be called up by a Senate Investigative Commission to testify about his relations with the London exiles (Herzen and Ogaryov). The rumors were true, though Turgenev was allowed to answer questions in writing from Paris. Eventually he had to go to Petersburg, however. See letter affair had no repercussions for Turgenev.

2. Critical reaction to *Fathers and Sons* was extraordinarily hostile on the part of *The Contemporary,* for instance.

3. See letters 159, 161, 162, and 164.

4. Baron Andrey Fyodorovich Budberg (1817-1881), the Russian Ambassador in Paris from 1862 to 1868.

5. Count Pavel Dmitrivich Kiselyov (1788-1872), Russian Ambassador in Paris from 1856 to 1862.

Letter 167.

1. The original of this letter is in French.

2. *Nouvelles scènes de la vie russe* (Paris, 1863).

3. *Les Pères et les Enfants* (Paris, 1863).

4. Turgenev and Flaubert were soon to become very good friends. Turgenev did everything within his power to further Flaubert's reputation in Russia and Germany.

Letter 168.

1. The 1840s and 1850s witnessed a flood of didactic stories and tales "for the people."

Letter 169.

1. Nikolay Vasilievich Shcherban (1834-1893), journalist and editor of *Le Nord,* a newspaper published in Brussels by the Russian government.

2. Aurelieu Scholl (1833-1902) took over the journal *Le Nain Jaune* in 1863 and turned it into a literary magazine.

3. See note 1.

4. The French newspaper *Patrie* published a spurious document in which the Tsar allegedly ordered "the extermination of all the Catholics" in Livonia. Shcherban exposed the document as a forgery.

5. Since French troops had taken the Mexican city of Pueblo, Turgenev expected French military involvement there to come to an end, thus freeing France to attack Russia because of the Polish Uprising.

6. Vladimir Vasilievich Stasov (1824-1906), art critic and historian, ideologue for "The Wanderers" and "The Mighty Five." Stasov was a propagandist for Russian national art.

7. The conclusion of Chernyshevsky's novel *What Is to Be Done?* was printed in the May, 1863 issue of *The Contemporary.*

8. Because Dostoevsky's journal, *Time,* was closed down by governmental decree on May 24, 1863 (the reason was an ambiguously worded, but actually pro-government article on Poland), "Phantoms" was ultimately published in Dostoevsky's second journal, *Epoch* (nos. 1, 2, 1864).

9. Turgenev had originally promised "Phantoms" for Katkov's *Russian Messenger.* Katkov took Turgenev's "Faust," published in *The Contemporary* in 1856, to be a revised version of "Phantoms" and made of this a public tempest in a teapot, as a result of which Turgenev no longer felt obliged to give Katkov "Phantoms" at all.

10. *Smoke.*

11. Vera Yosifovna Shcherban (d. 1910).

Letter 170.

1. The newspaper *The Day* had published a claim that Turgenev intended to disseminate a joke about two Russian soldiers who quarrelled because one of them ate Polish children with French mustard, the other with English mustard. In an article entitled "We Don't Believe It" (July 10, 1863), Herzen reacted to this piece of "news" with ambiguous disbelief.

2. See letters 159, 161, 162, and 164.

3. Herzen complied with Turgenev's request.

4. Ivan Sergeyevich Aksakov, the editor of *The Day.*

Letter 171.

1. Moritz Hartmann (1821-1872), Austrian poet, and journalist. He translated several of Turgenev's works into German. The original of this letter is in German.

2. M.A. Bakunin, the anarchist.

3. Sergey Petrovich Gerken, an acquaintance of Turgenev's and Hartmann's, suffered from a severe psychic disorder.

4. Princess Olga Fyodorovna Trubetskaya, née Moren (1812-1882). '

5. Berta Hartmann.

6. See letter 167, note 3.

Letter 172.

1. Turgenev had been without money and was anxiously awaiting 5,000 rubles that his uncle had sent him through Fet.

2. Botkin and Sons, a trading firm whose members included Vasily Petrovich Botkin.

3. Akhenbakh was the co-owner of the Moscow banking office of Akhenbakh and Kolli.

4. Zakhar Fyodorovich Balashov, a former serf, Turgenev's personal servant.

5. See letter 169, note 8.

Letter 173

1. The original of this note is in French.

Letter 174

1. The French original of this letter seems not to be extant. Pauline Viardot set the translations of several Russian poems, including Pushkin's "The Bird," to music.

2. Friedrich Bodenstedt (1819-1893), German poet and specialist in Slavic literatures, provided German translations of the Russian poems that Mme Viardot set to music.

3. August Fyodorovich Iogansen (1829-1875), a St. Petersburg music publisher who issued a number of collections of Viardot's settings of Russian poetry.

4. Turgenev means his story "Phantoms." See letter 169, note 8.

5. A Monsieur Pinet, the civil servant in question, was a potential bridegroom for Turgenev's daughter.

6. Anna Petrovna Markova-Vinogradskaya, née Poltoratskaya (1800-1879), better known as Anna Petrovna Kern (her first husband's name), inspired one of Pushkin's greatest love lyrics. To what extent the poet was really in love with her, however, is open to question, since in private correspondence he referred to her as "the Whore of Babylon."

Letter 175

1. In connection with Turgenev's having been summoned by the Senate Investigative Commission to answer questions about his relations with the London exiles (see letter 166), Herzen published in *The Bell* a rather acid note about "a grey-haired Magdalene (of the male sex) who had written the Emperor... that he had lost his hair and teeth... because of the agony caused by the Emperor's not knowing of his repentance, as a result of which 'she had severed all ties with the friends of her youth.'"

2. Turgenev is referring to his two-year exile at Spasskoye under Nicholas I (see letter 171).

3. In his answers Turgenev played down his friendship with Herzen and failed to mention meetings with Bakunin.

4. Turgenev has in mind the abolition of serfdom and the accompanying reforms.

Letter 176.

1. Turgenev was later to come to the conclusion that in order to write about Russia an author did in fact need to live there.

Letter 177.

1. Turgenev did not have a chance to fulfill his promise: Dostoevsky's journal *The Epoch* folded in February, 1865.

2 Dostoevsky's journal, *Time*, was closed by government decree in May, 1863; his first wife died in April, 1864; and his brother, Mikhail Mikhailovich Dostoevsky, died in July of the same year.

Letter 178.

1. Turgenev was building a house in Baden. By "redemption" Turgenev means the government's post-Reform policy of paying landlords for the land which was distributed to the peasants after their liberation from serfdom.

2. Nikolay Nikolayevich Turgenev.

3. Apollon Alexandrovich Grigoriev (1822-1864), a poet and critic whose notions of "organic criticism" brought him close to the moderate wing of the Slavophiles. His article, "Phenomena in Literature that are Dying Out," was published in Dostoevsky's *The Epoch* (No. 7, 1864).

Letter 179.

1. The original of this letter is in French.

2. Valentine Delessert, née Countess de Labord (1806-1894), an acquaintance of Turgenev's, was close to French literary circles. She introduced Pauline Turgeneva to her future husband, Gaston Bruère.

Letter 180.

1. This letter and Turgenev's arrangements for the dowry in general were occasioned by the fact that since Pauline Turgeneva was illegitimate, she did not have the legal right to inherit her father's property; according to the law, it would pass into the hands of his brother, had his brother survived him. N.S. Turgenev apparently gave his consent to the arrangement proposed in the letter.

2. The phrase occurs in Scribe's play *L'Ours et le Pacha* (1820).

3. Anna Pavlovna Turgeneva, née Shvarts (d. 1872), N.S. Turgenev's wife.

Letter 181.

1. The original of this letter is in French.

Letter 182.

1. Ludwig Pietsch (1824-1911), German artist, illustrator, and writer. It was through Pietsch that Turgenev met many of the leading German literati. The original of this letter is in German.

2. Minna Anstett (1818-1900), Turgenev's Baden landlady from 1863 to 1867.

3. Eduard Mörike (1804-1875), German poet and novelist, generally regarded as somewhere below the first rank of talent.

4. Probably a reference to Mörike's wife Margarete and sister Klara.

5. The second volume, *Erzählungen,* was published in October 1865.

Letter 183.

1. Nothing is known of the child's fate. See letters 59, 82.

Letter 184

1. The original of this letter is in French.

Letter 185.

1. The complete text of this letter is not extant.

2. The moderately radical journal *The Russian Word* was closed down by official decree in February/March, 1866.

3. Nikolay Ivanovich Trubetskoy.

4. In earlier letters Turgenev had waxed very enthusiastic over *Childhood.*

5. See second paragraph of letter 174.

Letter 186.

1. The motif of giving up writing is a common one in Turgenev's correspondence.
2. Turgenev owed Katkov 300 rubles.
3. *Lazarillo de Tormes* (1554) is the prototypical picaresque novel. Of its French successors, Le Sage's *Gil Blas* (1715) was the most popular.

Katkov accepted Turgenev's proposal, but he never received the translation, ostensibly because Turgenev was too busy with his novel *Smoke*. One wonders whether the translation was ever really begun, let alone finished.

4. *Crime and Punishment.* Turgenev disliked the later chapters.

Letter 187.

1. Dmitry Vladimirovich Karakozov (1840-1866) made an attempt on Alexander II's life in April, 1866.
2. Karakazov at first claimed that his name was Alexey Petrov.
3. Turgenev's story "The Dog."

Letter 188.

1. William Ralston (1828-1889), English folklorist, critic, and literary historian. He played a major role in popularizing Russian literature in England. The original of this letter is in French.
2. Alexey Vasilievich Koltsov (1809-1842), poet noted for his stylized folk poetry. Ralston's article about him, "A Russian Poet," appeared in *The Fortnightly Review*, No. 6, 1866.
3. "National" in the sense of *narod*, i.e., the folk, the people.
4. George Henry Lewes (1817-1878), English philosopher and writer, author of *The Life of Goethe* (1855).

Letter 189.

1. Turgenev's birthday was October 28/November 9.
2. Turgenev was working on *Smoke*.
3. *Erzählungen von Iwan Turgenjew* (Munich, 1864-1865).
4. Karl Mayer (1786-1870), German poet, literary historian, and publisher.
5. Maria Vladimirovna Velikhova, née Rashet, N.N. Rashet's daughter.

Letter 190.

1. The original of this letter is in French.
2. Pauline Bruère's father-in-law and mother-in-law.
3. Paul Bruère, Gaston's younger brother.

Letter 191.

1. *Smoke*.
2. Turgenev read the manuscript to V.P. Botkin and P.V. Annenkov, among others.
3. Turgenev did not arrive in Moscow until March, 1867, and *Smoke* was published in the March issue of *The Russian Messenger*.

Letter 192.

1. The complete French original of this letter is not extant; only this partial Russian translation is known.

2. Turgenev was suffering from an attack of gout, an ailment that was to accost him regularly for the rest of his life.

3. The German sculptor Reinhold Begas (1831-1911) apparently had read *Smoke* and reacted to it positively.

4. Rossini's *Otello* (1816).

5. N.N. Turgenev, the estate manager at Spasskoye

Letter 193.

1. Nikita Alexeyevich Kishinsky (d. 1888), Turgenev's estate manager from 1867 until 1876, when Turgenev fired him for embezzlement.

2. N.N. Turgenev, the incompetent estate manager whom Kishinsky replaced.

3. The transfer of control to Kishinsky was a long, painful, and ugly process that ultimately cost Turgenev a great deal of money.

Letter 194.

1. The French original of this Russian translation is not extant.

2. The reference is to *Smoke*.

3. Erneste Héritte de la Tour, Louise Héritte-Viardot's husband.

4. Louise Héritte-Viardot (1841-1918), the Viardots' eldest daughter. A pianist, composer, and teacher of singing, she published very biased memoirs (1907) that portrayed Turgenev in a negative light.

5. E. Gérard, a French music publisher who issued Pauline Viardot's *Six Melodies* for violin and piano.

6. Nicolaus Lenau (1802-1850), Austrian poet. Nothing is known of the song mentioned by Turgenev.

Letter 195.

1. Turgenev lent his name, a few translations, and an introduction to a Russian volume of Charles Perrault's (1628-1703) *Contes de Fées* that was largely the work of N.V. Shcherban. The stylistic error—*seraya loshad's yablokami*, instead of *seraya loshad'v yablokakh*—was apparently Turgenev's own.

2. *Razvivat' deyatel'nost'*, "to unleash activity," is no longer a Gallicism, but simply a cliché.

3. *Smoke*. Fet did not like the novel.

4. *Works of I.S. Turgenev* (Moscow, 1868-1871).

5. Turgenev is referring to his gout.

6. N.A. Kishinsky.

7. Fet had expressed his displeasure over Turgenev's decision to replace his uncle, N.N. Turgenev, with Kishinsky.

8. N.S. Turgenev.

9. Polonsky married Zhozefina Antonovna Ryulman in June, 1866.

Letter 196.

1. The mistake (1867 instead of 277) is Turgenev's.
2. Lambert was active in various Petersburg charities.
3. Whether Akhenbakh went to see Lambert and whether she helped him are not known. Turgenev himself occasionally sent the man money.
Smoke.

Letter 197.

1. Dmitry Ivanovich Pisarev (1840-1868), a radical critic whose sense of humor and literary acumen set him off from most of his coevals. Pisarev was the only leading radical to have reviewed *Fathers and Sons* favorably.
2. Pisarev responded that the scene in question had not offended him in the least, although the novel as a whole was not to his liking.
3. A quotation from Goethe's "Künstlers Fug and Recht."
4. *The Cause* [Delo] was the moderately radical journal in which Pisarev's articles appeared.

Letter 198.

1. Turgenev had moved to his new house in Baden.
2. *Smoke.*
3. Tyutchev wrote both a poem, "Smoke," and an epigram, "Even the Fatherland's smoke is sweet and pleasant to us," apropos of Turgenev's novel.
4. In April 1867 an ethnographic exhibit opened in Moscow. Sixty nationalities living within the Russian Empire were represented, but the Slavic nationalities were set off in a special section. Pisemsky thought the exhibit was absurd.
6. Anton Berjozowski, a Polish revolutionary, made an attempt on Alexander II's life in Paris on May 25/June 6, 1867.
7. Pisemsky wanted to publish some plays abroad, but was afraid of the possible consequences.
8. Turgenev wrote the preface, but did not mention the Slavophiles.
9. Yekaterina Pavlovna Pisemskaya, née Svinina (1829-1891).

Letter 199.

1. Pierre Jules Hetzel (1814-1886), French publisher and children's writer. Almost all of Turgenev's works written after 1862 appeared in French translations in Hetzel's editions.
The original of this letter is in French.

Letter 200

1. Prince Avgustin Petrovich Golitsyn (1824-1875), author and translator who lived in Paris.
The original of this letter is in French.
2. The first chapters of Golitsyn's French translation of *Smoke* appeared in the July 25, 1867 issue of *Correspondant.*
3. The understanding was that Golitsyn was to send proofs to Turgenev, who would then forward them to Mérimée. Mérimée found the editing rather more work than he had

expected, since Golitsyn's command both of Russian and French was shaky and because he kept throwing out "morally objectionable" passages which Mérimée then had to reinstate.

Letter 201.

1. Vera Pavlovna Annenkova (b. 1867).
2. Between 1867 and 1871 Pauline Viardot wrote operettas with librettos by Turgenev: *Trop de femmes, Craquamiche ou le dernier sorcier,* and *L'ogre.*
3. N.N. Turgenev, recently displaced as Turgenev's estate manager (see letter 193), demanded a great deal of money—largely as an act of vengeance. In order to raise the sum, Turgenev had to sell his brand-new home in Baden to the Viardots. For more details on the unpleasantness accompanying the change of managements, see letters 207 and 209.
4. The article was probably written by Berthold Damcke, a German music critic residing in Paris.

Letter 202.

1. Prince Vladimir Fyodorovich Odoyevsky (1803-1869), writer, critic, composer, and musicologist. Examples of his writings may be found in *Russian Romantic Prose,* Carl Proffer, editor (Ann Arbor, 1979).
The original of this note is in French.
2. Eugene Schuyler (1840-1890), American diplomat, author, and translator. He was the American consul in Moscow from 1866 until 1868; from 1868 until 1876 he was secretary of the Embassy in St. Petersburg. Schuyler's translation of *Fathers and Sons* was published in New York in 1867 and went through several editions.

Letter 203.

1. Maxim Du Camp (1822-1894), French author and traveller. He and Turgenev broke off relations after the Franco-Prussian War and Du Camp's rift with Flaubert.
2. Yelizaveta Nikolayevna Akhmatova (1820-1904), author, translator, and the editor and publisher of *The Anthology of Translated Novels, Novellas, and Short Stories* (1856-1885).
3. For details on Pauline Viardot's operettas see letter 201, note 2.
4. Fyodor Mikhailovich Reshetnikov (1841-1871), a Populist writer whose *People of Podlipov* came out in St. Petersburg in 1867.
5. The author of *The Notes of a Hunter from Eastern Siberia* (St. Petersburg, 1867) was Alexander Alexandrovich Cherkasov (1834-1895).

Letter 204.

1. The original of this letter is in German.
2. Editions of the works of Pushkin, Lermontov, and Nekrasov had been published abroad.
3. *Smoke.*
4. Stuhr's did not publish *Smoke* after all, though because of the lack of a copyright convention between Russia and Germany, it often published Russian works without remuneration to the authors.

Letter 205.

1. Turgenev is polemicizing with Herzen's "Prolegomena," in which Herzen argues that Western European civilization has lost the capacity for social progress and that only in Russia, thanks to the peasant commune, can socialism be born.

2. With his French edition of *The Bell* Herzen hoped to persuade the Western European public that not all Russians were reactionaries.

3. A quotation from a Latin transcription of Aesop's "The Braggart."

4. For the journal edition of *Smoke* Katkov insisted upon the removal of a number of phrases and passages whose tone he found too radical. Turgenev did not in fact reinstate all of these omissions.

Letter 206.

1. Dmitry Dmitrievich Minayev (1835-1889), satirical poet and translator. He was a regular customer to the more radical journals of the day.

2. Turgenev is referring to an earlier letter in which he objected to certain lines in Polonsky's "The Eagle and the Snake."

3. Nikolay Nikolayevich Strakhov (1828-1896), conservative philosopher and critic.

4. Polonsky's second wife, Zh. A. Polonskaya.

Letter 207.

1. Nikolay Nikolayevich Turgenev.

Letter 208.

1. Turgenev's letter to the editor was in reaction to a short article that had been published in the same newspaper about Artur Benni (1840-1867), a "repentant radical" who had recently died.

2. Annenkov's article on *War and Peace* was published in *The Messenger of Europe*, No. 2, 1868.

3. Emperor Alexander I (1777-1825).

4. Count Mikhail Mikhailovich Speransky (1772-1839), one of Alexander I's leading advisors during his liberal period.

5. See letter 203.

6. Prosper Mérimée, "Alexandre Pouchkine," *Moniteur universal*, No. 20 (January 20, 1868); No. 27 (January 27, 1868).

Letter 209.

1. The original of this letter is in French.

2. Gaston Bruère was experiencing financial difficulties.

Letter 210.

1. The original of this letter is in German.

2. *Smoke.*

Letter 211.

1. The French original of this letter is not known to be extant.
2. Maria Schröder-Hanfstängel (b. 1848), one of Pauline Viardot's pupils.
3. Pauline Viardot had had great success at the Théâtre Lyrique in Gluck's *Orfeo*.
4. Henri Puget (1813-1887), French tenor.
5. Léon Carvalho (1825-1897), director of a number of Paris theaters.
6. The "Renaissance," a Paris theater.
7. Marie de Mohl, wife of Jules de Mohl, French Orientalist.
8. Antoine Laugel (b. 1830), French author.
   Pierre Lanfrey (1828-1877), French historian.
   Edmond Scherer (1815-1889), French theologian.
   Pierre Dupont (1821-1870), French poet and composer.
   Andrew White (1832-1918), American diplomat and author.
   Erneste Renan (1823-1892), French historian and philosopher.
9. Turgenev is referring to the French translation of *Smoke*.
10. Richard Liebreich (1830-1917), German oculist.
11. Hermann Helmholtz (1821-1894), German scientist.
12. Louis Pomey (1831-1901), French artist, translator, and poet. He was on good terms with Turgenev and the Viardot family.
13. The reference is to Pauline Viardot's operetta, *L'ogre*.
14. Ambroise Thomas (1811-1896), French composer, occasionally remembered today for his opera *Hamlet*.

Letter 212.

1. The original of this letter is in French. See letter 211, note 14.
2. Guillaume Augier (1820-1889), French poet and playwright.
3. Turgenev apparently knew of Thomas' plan for an opera, *Francesca da Rimini*. The opera was written later, in 1882.
4. Thomas did not use Viardot's libretto.
5. Jules Barbier (1822-1901) and Michel Carré (1819-1872), team of French playwrights whose best-known effort remains the libretto for Gounod's *Faust*.

Letter 213.

1. Mikhail Vasilievich Avdeyev (1821-1876), minor writer with radical leanings whose literary style was influenced by Turgenev's.
2. Avdeyev had written to ask Turgenev where the French translation of two of his novels, *The Reef* and *Between Two Fires*, could be published.
3. Antoine Droz (1832-1895), author of the novel *Monsieur, Madame et Bébé* (1866), which had gone through 175 editions by the end of the century.
4. A.K. Tolstoy's novel was not published in French until 1872.
5. Anna Fyodorovna Chekuanova, née Kryukovskaya (1818-1889), translator and pedagogue.
6. The reference is to "The Story of Lieutenant Yergunov" (1868), which Avdeyev criticized for its lack of ideas.
7. Avdeyev's *Between Two Fires* (1868).
8. Avdeyev had mentioned in his letter that *War and Peace* contained some marvellous scenes, but that the historical personages were portrayed from the point of view of a lackey.

Letter 214.

1. See letter 201, note 2.

2. 25° Réamur is about 90° Fahrenheit.

3. Nikolay Mikhailovich Stromilov (b. 1841), a young Russian without a position whom Turgenev had offered half-hearted help in finding employment.

Letter 215.

1. A reference to an incident from Plutarch's *Lives.*

2. In a recent letter Turgenev's uncle, N.N. Turgenev, had referred to himself more or less in those terms.

3. Mikhail Ivanovich Zhikharyov (b.1820), P. Ya. Chaadayev's nephew and the author of memoirs about him.

4. Pyotr Yakovlevich Chaadayev (1794-1856), early Westernizer whose *Philosophical Letters* (1836) caused him to be declared legally insane. See Peter Yakovlevich Chaadayev, *Philosophical Letters & Apology of a Madman,* translated with an introduction by Mary-Barbara Zeldin (Knoxville, Tenn., 1969).

Letter 216.

1. The original of this letter is in German.

2. Georg Anstett (d. 1868) owned the house in Baden in which Turgenev lived before building his own.

3. Berthold Auerbach (1812-1882), German writer whose works Turgenev helped arrange to have published in Russia.

4. Turgenev agreed to write a Russian preface to Auerbach's *House on the Rhine.* Pressed for time, Turgenev asked Pietsch to write the preface, which Turgenev then translated into Russian, reworking it slightly.

5. *Alceste,* opera by Gluck (1767).

Letter 217.

1. The anonymous letter accused Kishinsky of a variety of shady transactions and begged Turgenev to come to Spasskoye to sort things out.

Letter 218.

1. Charles Sainte-Beuve (1804-1868), French critic and poet. The original of this letter is in French.

Letter 219.

1. The original of this letter is in French.

2. The reference is to *A Sentimental Education.*

3. Turgenev uses the word *bouquin,* i.e., an old, used, second-hand volume; he is referring to *Smoke.*

4. Caroline Flaubert (1793-1872).

Letter 220.

1. The original of this letter is in German.
2. Richard Pohl (1826-1896), German composer, poet, and music critic. Four of his poems were translated into Russian by Turgenev and set to music by Pauline Viardot.
3. Karl Friedrich Lessing (1808-1880), German painter.
4. Albrecht Breuer (1830-1897), German painter.
5. Ludwig Riefstahl (1827-1888), German landscape artist.
6. Alfred Woltmann (1841-1880), German art historian.
7. Claudie Viardot.
8. Berthe Viardot, one of Louis Viardot's three sisters.
9. Turgenev is referring to "The Unfortunate One."
10. Aglaya Organi (stage name; her real name was Anna von Görger; 1843-1926), German soprano, pupil of Pauline Viardot.
11. Adolf Menzel (1815-1905), German artist.
12. Julian Schmidt (1818-1886), German critic and literary historian. He devoted a number of works to Turgenev.
13. Karl Eckert (1820-1879), composer, conductor, and accompanist for Pauline Viardot. Kate Eckert (d. 1881), his wife.

Letter 221.

1. Turgenev means Wagner's opera *Die Meistersinger.*
2. Alexey Mikhailovich Zhemchuzhnikov (1821-1908), poet and one of the creators of the popular and fictitious poet Kuzma Prutkov.
3. M.V. Velikhova.
4. Yelena Vladimirovna Rashet (d. 1889), N.N. Rashet's daughter.

Letter 222.

1. "Recollections of Belinsky" was published in the April, 1869 issue of *The Messenger of Europe.*
2. Fyodor Ivanovich Salayev (1820-1879), Moscow publisher who issued three collected editions of Turgenev's works.
3. Belinsky died May 26/ June 7, 1848.
4. *The Precipice,* anti-nihilist novel by I.A. Goncharov.
5. I.A. Goncharov.
6. Nekrasov, a hero for the radicals, a man whose poetry focused on the poor and the downtrodden, was a member of the posh English Club.

Letter 223.

1. The original of this letter is in French.
2. See letter 201, note 2.
3. The opera was not written.
4. Claudie, Marianne, and Paul Viardot, children of Louis and Pauline Viardot.
5. Turgenev's daughter had been hostile to Pauline Viardot in 1863, when the former visited Baden.

Letter 224.

1. The original of this letter is in German.
2. Turgenev's *Literary Memoirs* were published in 1869.
3. Turgenev is referring to Pietsch's series of sketches entitled "Eine Stangensche Orientfahrt" (1869).

Letter 225.

1. Nikolaus Friedreich (1825-1882), well-known Heidelberg doctor.
2. Turgenev's symptoms passed before long, and the doctors declared his "disease" not serious.
3. See letter 222, note 1.
4. Fet had been re-elected a judge in his district.
5. See letter 222, note 4.
6. Pyotr Ivanovich Borisov.

Letter 226.

1. Pyotr Petrovich Vasiliev (1840[?]-1883), a bibliographer and ethnographer from Kazan.
2. P.P. Vasiliev, *A Bibliographical Note on Translations of I.S. Turgenev's Works into Foreign Languages* (Kazan, 1868).
3. Bernhard Behre (1832-1881), Riga publisher.
4. William Ralston (1828-1889), British translator and popularizer of Russian literature.

Letter 227.

1. Fet did not go to Baden.
2. Pyotr Ivanovich Borisov.
3. Borisov recommended not building a new house in Spasskoye for the time being.
4. Turgenev attended the unveiling of a Goethe monument in Munich on August 16/28, 1869.
5. It has long been suspected that part of Ludwig II's attraction to Wagner may have been sexual. Turgenev may be hinting at that here.
6. The details are too complicated to go into, but in essence Wagner sabotaged the performance that Ludwig II had insisted upon. Turgenev did not follow up on his wish to write about this incident.

Letter 228.

1. Turgenev had misinterpreted one of Fet's letters and wrongly concluded that Fet would be coming to Baden-Baden. Fet apparently had apologized for the confusion.
2. Fet was a justice of the peace. There is a pun here on the words *mirovoy* and *mirny*, the former meaning "justice of the peace," the latter "peaceful."
3. Fet may have meant that Shakespeare was a fool in the sense that his talent was an unconscious one.
4. V.P. Botkin died October 10/22, 1869. Fet was present for the funeral.
5. An inexact translation from a German translation of *The Iliad*.
6. The wordplay is only a little more successful in Russian.

Letter 229.

1. See letter 228, note 4.
2. Botkin left nothing in his will for the Society for Assistance to Needy Writers and Scholars (Literary Fund).
3. Turgenev is referring to Nikolay I, nineteenth-century Russia's most militaristic and reactionary Emperor.
4. The reference is to "A Literary Evening at P.A. Pletnyov's" in *Literary Memoirs*.
5. Pyotr Ivanovich Bartenyev (1829-1912), archeologist and literary historian. "A Literary Evening at P.A. Pletnyov's" was first published in Bartenyev's journal *The Russian Archive* (1869).

Letter 230.

1. Alexandra Vasilievna Pletnyova, née Shchetinina (1826-1901), P.A. Pletnyov's second wife.
2. See letter 229, final paragraph, as well as note 4.
3. The Russian word *shchastie* suggests both happiness and luck.

Letter 231.

1. Civic-minded critics very nearly hounded lyric poetry out of the literary journals of the 1860s.
2. Turgenev's article was published in *The St. Petersburg News,* January 8/20, 1870.
3. *Chalygin's Confessions* (1867), novel by Polonsky.
4. In 1859 N.A. Dobrolyubov published an article in which he argued that Aksakov's *Family Chronicle* (1856) could no longer arouse anything but mockery among contemporary readers.
5. Alexander Anfimovich Orlov (1791-1840), an extraordinarily unprincipled writer whose career was mired in scandal.
6. Viktor Ipatievich Askochensky (1813-1879), arch-reactionary author and editor.

Letter 232.

1. Herzen died January 9/21, 1870.
2. Alexander Alexandrovich Herzen.
3. Natalya Alexandrovna Herzen (1844-1936).
4. Maxime DuCamp.
5. Jean Traupmann (1849-1870), a notorious murderer guillotined in Paris on January 19, 1870.
6. A quotation from Shakespeare's *Macbeth,* Act V, Scene 5.
7. Turgenev's article, "The Execution of Traupmann," was published in *The Messenger of Europe* (No. 6, 1870) and subsequently included in his *Literary Memoirs*.
8. See letter 231, note 2.
9. The article was an unpleasant shock for Polonsky, since it contained an attack on Nekrasov.

Letter 233.

1. Marguerite Artôt (1835-1907), Belgian mezzo-soprano, student of Pauline Viardot's.
2. Fet had withdrawn from the Literary Fund, allegedly on the grounds that it subsidized laziness; the real reason was probably Fet's legendary stinginess.

Letter 234.

1. The original of this letter is in German.
2. The reference is to the performance of Pauline Viardot's operetta *Le dernier sorcier* in Carlsruhe in January, 1870.
3. Philip Devrient (1801-1877), director of the Court Theater at Carlsruhe.
4. Jozif Hauser (1829-1902), singer.
5. In both instances Turgenev greatly exaggerates and distorts the newspaper reviews.
6. Gluck's opera *Orfeo*.
7. Claudie Viardot.
8. Charles Verlat (1824-1890), Belgian artist.
9. Otto Lewald, a Berlin lawyer who had requested Turgenev's autograph.

Letter 235.

1. The poem, "On the Death of Vasily Petrovich Botkin," contained an attack on Westernizers and a concealed polemic with Turgenev.
2. Victor Noir (1848-1870), a French journalist, had come to the palace as a second for Pascal Grousset. In that capacity he was shot by Prince Bonaparte, and the former's funeral turned into a mass demonstration against Bonaparte.
3. Maria Petrovna Fet.

Letter 236.

1. The Franco-Prussian War broke out on July 19, 1870.

Letter 237.

1. François Bazaine (1811-1888), French military leader.
2. Marie MacMahon (1808-1893), French military leader and statesman.
3. Prince Sergey Semyonovich Urusov (1827-1897) published an article in which he outlined what he felt were the necessary steps for securing France's victory in the Franco-Prussian War. He was indeed an intimate of Tolstoy's.
4. Yelizaveta Dmitrievna Shenshina, a relative of Fet's.
5. Pyotr Ivanovich Borisov.

Letter 238.

1. The reference is to the story "A King Lear of the Steppe."
2. Mikhail Matveyevich Stasyulevich (1826-1911), historian who in 1856 began publishing *The Messenger of Europe*, a journal to which he tried to attract leading Russian and Western European writers.
3. That character in LeSage's novel suffers a stroke and loses his gift of eloquence.
4. Nikolay Alexeyevich Milyutin (1818-1872), statesman who played a leading role in the preparations for the abolition of serfdom in 1861. He was a close friend of Turgenev's.

Letter 239.

1. The brothers Alexander Osipovich and Roman Osipovich Livan.

2. Alexander Fyodorovich Berg (1803-1884), Russian Consul in London in 1870. His brother, Fyodor Fyodorovich Berg (1793-1874), was the Governor of Poland.

3. The story "Knock...Knock...Knock!..." was published in *The Messenger of Europe*, No. 1, 1871.

4. Leon Gambetta (1838-1882), French politician and model liberal with whose views Turgenev greatly sympathized.

Pierre Pelletan (1813-1884), liberal French journalist.

Vladimir Nikolayevich Leontiev, K.N. Leontiev's brother.

5. The reference is to the seventh chapter of Pypin's *Intellectual Movements after 1815 and Their Consequences*, in which Pypin made use of information published abroad by N.I. Turgenev.

6. Professor Alexander Nikolayevich Engelhardt (1832-1893), a radical sympathizer, was arrested in 1871 and exiled to his family estate. His wife was Sofia Vladimirovna Engelhardt, née Novosiltsev (1828-1894).

7. Alexander Ivanovich Rubets (1837-1913), composer. The reference is probably to his *Album of Ukrainian Folk Songs* (1870).

Letter 240.

1. The French original of this letter is not known to be extant.

2. Nikolay Grigorievich Rubinstein (1835-1881), pianist, director, composer, had invited Pauline Viardot to teach at the Moscow Conservatory, which he founded.

3. See note 2.

4. Anton Grigorievich Rubinstein (1829-1894), composer pianist, and director of the Russian Music Society.

5. Joseph Servais (1850-1885), French violinist.

6. Servais had participated in the Weimar production of Pauline Viardot's operetta *The Last Sorcerer* in 1869.

7. The artists in question were Nikolay Nikolayevich Gé (1831-1894) and Konstantin Yegorovich Makovsky (1839-1915).

8. Adelina Patti (1843-1919), one of the major Italian sopranos of the nineteenth century.

9. Turgenev probably means himself. The reason for his not going was likely his artistic loyalty to Pauline Viardot.

Letter 241.

1. The original of this letter (in French) is not known to be extant.

2. The reference is to an album entitled *Six Poems by Heine, Mörike, and Pohl, Translated into Russian by I. Turgenev and Set to Music by Pauline Viardot-Garcia* (St. Petersburg, 1871).

3. Louise Héritte-Viardot.

4. Anton Grigorievich Rubinstein; the organization's activities were terminated after two meetings.

5. Ivan Mikhaylovich Sechenov (1829-1906), physiologist, professor at a number of Russian universities.

Letter 242.

1. The French original of this letter is not known to be extant.
2. Turgenev is referring to the proclamation of the Paris Commune and the start of civil war in France.
3. A quotation from Horace's seventh epode.
4. Claudie Viardot.

Letter 243.

1. Pauline and Gaston Bruère needed money for the renewal of the lease on their factory.
2. The reference is to Turgenev's estate Kadnoye, which was not sold until 1881.

Letter 244.

1. Marya Ageyevna Milyutina, née Abaza (1834-1903), wife of N.A. Milyutin and friend of Turgenev's from the 1850s on.
2. Lev Alexandrovich Mei (1822-1862), relatively minor poet with a distinctly Romantic bent.
3. N.A. Milyutin.
4. Turgenev was rumored to have said that he despised the Russian people just as much as he despised himself.

Letter 245.

1. Maria Malibran, née García (1808-1836), the most celebrated soprano of her time. Her career was tragically short, but she left a permanent impression on musical history.
2. See letter 241, note 2.

Letter 246.

1. M. Ye. Saltykov-Shchedrin criticized Polonsky's collection of poems, *Sheaves*, in the February, 1871 issue of *Notes of the Fatherland*. Saltykov's objection to Polonsky's poetry was that it was not useful. Polonsky's reply was included as an appendix to the volume *Sheaves*.
2. Karmazinov in Dostoevsky's *The Possessed* is a malicious, but sometimes painfully accurate caricature of Turgenev.

Letter 247.

1. Mark Matveyevich Antokolsky (1843-1902), sculptor whose talent Turgenev greatly admired.
2. The reference is to "Spring Freshets."
3. Ilya Yefimovich Repin (1844-1930), master of realistic and historical canvasses. Repin is perhaps the best-known Russian artist of the nineteenth century.
4. See letter 93, note 3.

Letter 248.

1. The reference is to "Spring Freshets."

2. Annenkov objected to the story's conclusion, with its hero, Sanin, abandoning a "pure love" for the "depraved" Polozova.

3. Turgenev did not alter the conclusion.

4. The reference is to a short essay on hunting in the Scottish Highlands that Turgenev had promised to A.N. Nikolayev's *Hunting Journal.* Annenkov had informed Turgenev that the journal, whose editor he mistakenly called Ivanov, had collapsed, but that there would be a new journal under the editorship of Alexander Stepanovich Gieroglifov (1825-1900).

5. Hortense Schneider (1837-1920), French operetta singer best known for her liaison with Napoleon III.

Letter 249.

1. Viktor Petrovich Burenin (1841-1926), journalist, poet, and literary critic. He was a frequent contributor to the *St. Petersburg News.*

2. Burenin's article in the January 8, 1872, issue of *The St. Petersburg News* criticized "Spring Freshets" for its absence of a social message.

3. Alexander Nikolayevich Serov (1820-1871), composer and critic. Valentina Semyonovna Serova, née Bergman (1846-1924), his wife, was also a composer and critic.

4. Prince Pyotr Andrevevich Vyazemsky (1792-1878), poet whose ultimate claim to fame is the fact that he was Pushkin's closest friend.

5. See letter 250, note 2.

6. Letnev was the pseudonym of Anna Alexandrovna Lachinova (c. 1832-1914).

7. Turgenev had several times asked for a copy of the score of A.S. Dargomyzhsky's *The Stone Guest.*

Letter 250.

1. This letter to Ralston, written in English, provides a good idea of Turgenev's impressive but eccentric command of the language.

2. Henry Chorley published an obituary of Turgenev in the January 19, 1872 issue of *Orchestra.* See letter 249.

3. Chorley noted that Turgenev was an enchanting, but exhausting conversationalist.

4. "Spring Freshets."

Letter 251.

1. The original of this letter is in German.

2. Turgenev has in mind German critics who, by and large, adopted a sharply negative attitude toward Turgenev after his move from Baden to Paris.

3. "Spring Freshets."

Letter 252.

1. Jules Simon (1814-1896), French statesman; he was Prime Minister in 1876-77.

2. Louis Thiers (1797-1877), statesman and historian; head of the French government 1871-1873.

Letter 253.

1. Edmond de Goncourt (1822-1896), distinguished French writer. From 1872 on Flaubert, Turgenev, Goncourt, Daudet, and Zola dined together on a regular basis.
The original of this letter is in French.
2. The reference apparently is to Princess Mathilde Bonaparte (1820-1904).
3. *Charles Demailly*, by Edmond and Jules de Goncourt (1863).

Letter 254.

1. Vladimir Alexandrovich Shenshin (1814-1872), a close friend of Fet's, had died suddenly.
2. Fet's remarks about Alexander Nikolayevich Afanasiev (1826-1871) are not known. Afanasiev was an ethnographer, literary historian, and folklorist. This passage in the letter is a continuation of Turgenev's polemic with Fet about the Literary Fund. See letter 233, note 2.
3. Reference to Horace's poem bearing the same opening line. Fet apparently evaluated himself as a poet in a letter that seems not to be extant.
4. Fet had decided to build a hospital because of the fearsome spread of syphilis in the Mtsensk District.

Letter 255.

1. See letter 249, note 6.
2. Ary Scheffer (1795-1858), French artist who was extremely popular in the 1840s and 1850s.
3. Wilhelm Kaulbach (1805-1874), German neo-Classical artist.
4. Stasov had suggested that Delacroix was overrated.
5. The reference is to Repin's picture "Slavic Composers."
6. Faust's student in Goethe's work—not the German composer.
7. Quotation from *Faust*, Part I, Scene I.
8. Mily Alexeyevich Balakirev (1837-1910), composer and moving force behind the "Mighty Five," whose members originally worked for the development of a distinctly national Russian music.
9. Nestor Vasilievich Kukolnik (1809-1868), second-rate Romantic playwright who was enormously popular in the 1830s.

Letter 256.

1. The original of this letter is in French.
2. Turgenev is referring to Cicero's "Cato the Elder, or About Old Age," where he speaks of the advantages of old age over the other periods in man's life.
3. In June-July, 1872, the French government issued two bonds in the total amount of five billion francs.
4. Jeanne Bruère (1872-1952). In adult life Turgenev's granddaughter taught music and foreign languages.

Letter 257.

1. The original of this letter is in French.
2. Claudie and Marianne Viardot.

211

3. Aurore Sand, George Sand's granddaughter.
4. Elzéar Blaise (1786-1848), French writer.

Letter 258.

1. Varvara Alexandrovna Tsurikova (1851-?), resident of Oryol Province. Turgenev wrote her a number of encouraging letters, and she published several stories after his death.

Letter 259.

1. The original of this letter is in French.
2. Ernesta Grisi, Italian mezzo-soprano. Left in great poverty after the death of Théophile Gautier, she hoped that Pauline Viardot would participate in a fund-raising concert.

Letter 260.

1. The complete original of this letter, in German, is not known to be extant.
2. *Virgin Soil.*

Letter 261.

1. Pyotr Lavrovich Lavrov (1823-1900), one of the leaders of Populism and a member of "The People's Will," a party that included political terror in its program. Turgenev contributed sums of money to Lavrov, somehow failing to understand that he was an active revolutionary.
2. Grigory Nikolayevich Vyrubov (1843-1913), positivist philosopher who lived abroad from 1864 on.
3. The colony of Russian revolutionaries in Zurich had split into two camps—the followers of Bakunin and those of Lavrov. Arguments between representatives of the two groups were known to end in fist fights.
4. Turgenev was unpopular among the young Russian revolutionaries of the early 1870s. He was going to Zurich to meet young revolutionaries abroad in order to gather material for *Virgin Soil.* Most of them refused to have anything to do with him.

Letter 262.

1. "Turgenjew in Deutschland," *Europa,* No. 22 (1872).
2. Turgenev is referring to the article "The Unretouched Old Days," (*The Deed,* No. 12 [1872] by P.N. Tkachev (pseud. Postny). Though the article is fiercely critical of Turgenev, it does not contain the phrase cited in this letter.
3. *The Messenger of Europe* received a second warning for V.I. Likhachov's "The Recasting of the Court Statues," (no. 28 [1873]), which allegedly undermined respect for the government.

Letter 263.

1. Fet apparently had quoted the following from Faust, Part I, (Prolog im Himmel):

Er [der Mensch] scheint mir, mit Verlaub von Euer Gnaden,
Wie eine der langbeinigen Zikaden,
Die immer fliegt und fliegend springt
Und gleich im Gras ihr altes Liedchen singt;
Und läg er nur noch immer in dem Grase!
In jeden Quark begräbt er seine Nase.

[The (man) seems to me, with the permission of your Excellency,
Like one of the long-legged cicadas,
Which always flies, and flying, leaps,
And sings his old song here in the grass.
And if only he always lay in the grass!
He sticks his nose into all sorts of rubbish.]

2. A.S. Khomyakov.
3. The reference is to a very Slavophile poem by Khomyakov.
4. *Fathers and Sons,* Chapter XXI.
5. In 1792 France was declared a republic, while in 1789 all class privileges were abolished.
6. A reference to revolutionary events in Spain.
7. Some of the leading Russian radicals were priests' sons.
8. A reference to the Russian generals depicted in Turgenev's *Smoke.*
9. Mikhail Nikolayevich Longinov (1823-1875), historian of literature, bibliographer, who, though close to radical circles in the 1850s, had become an arch-conservative by the late 1860s.
10. Paul Viardot.
11. *Anna Karenina.*
12. P.I. Borisov, whom Fet looked after following the death of I.P. Borisov.

Letter 264.

1. Pyotr Nikolayevich Polevoy (1839-1902), writer, literary historian, and author of a biography of Turgenev.
2. False Dmitry (d. 1606), claiming to be the son of Ivan IV (the real son was dead), led a Polish army into Moscow during the so-called "Time of Troubles." The events, treated in a historically inaccurate light, are the subject of Musorgsky's opera *Boris Godunov.*
3. As a part of Peter the Great's campaign of Westernization, boyars (nobles) were required to cut off their beards.

Letter 265

1. Prince Nikolay Sergeyevich Dolgoruky (1840-1913).
2. Princess Alexandra Sergeyevna Albendinskaya, née Dolgorukaya (1836-1913), lady-in-waiting to Empress Maria Alexandrova and Alexander II's mistress.

3. Baron Louis d'Anthès-Heeckeren (1843-1902), officer and son of Baron Georges d'Anthès-Heeckeren (1812-1895), who was responsible for A.S. Pushkin's death in a duel in 1837.

4. See note 3.

Letter 266.

1. Stasyulevich originally accepted the proposal. When he actually read the work, however, he refused to publish it, on the grounds that there would be difficulties with the censorship. Turgenev simply told Flaubert that his novel had been forbidden by the censors.

Letter 267.

1. The original of this letter is in French.

2. Turgenev had given his daughter a regular pension up until the time of her marriage.

Letter 268.

1. *The Pool,* an album published to aid the starving population of Samara Province, included contributions by most of the leading Russian authors of the day.

2. The reference is to the story "Living Relics."

3. The famine year was 1840, not 1841.

Letter 269.

1. Annenkov's son, Pavel Petrovich, had been seriously ill.

2. "Living Relics."

3. Turgenev excised a passage in which Lukeria relates a dream where she saw herself as an intercessor for the Russian people.

4. A reference to the wedding of Claudie Viardot and Georges Chambord.

Letter 270.

1. Little is known about Alexandra Vladimirovna Sorneva except that even after Turgenev's negative evaluation of her work, she continued to insist that he help her find a publisher.

2. This letter is typical of the care that Turgenev took to respond to any and all requests for advice and help. As in this case, he regularly received pleas and manuscripts from complete strangers.

Letter 271.

1. Alexey Sergeyevich Suvorin (1834-1912), journalist and publisher. Her is perhaps best known in Russian literary history for the encouragement that he gave Anton Chekhov.

2. In his feuilleton Suvorin made fun of the article, "I.S. Turgenev's Current Stay in Petersburg" (*The Russian World* [August 4, 1874]) and its author, the anonymous P.B.

3. Suvorin called Turgenev the most brilliant conversationalist among Russian writers.

4. Fyodor Fyodorovich Trepov (1812-1889), military governor of Petersburg from 1886 until 1878.

5. Suvorin's wife was murdered in a St. Petersburg hotel.

Letter 272.

1. Stasyulevich was experiencing censorship difficulties with *The Messenger of Europe.* Longinov was the head of the Office of Publishing Affairs.

2. Gervais Charpentier (1805-1871), French publisher.

3. Zola's novel (in translation) appeared in the first three issues of *The Messenger of Europe* for 1875.

4. The first complete Czech edition of *Notes of a Hunter* was published in Prague in 1874.

Letter 273.

1. Boleslav Mikhailovich Markevich (1822-1884), novelist and journalist. An arch-conservative, he and Turgenev were on very bad terms by the 1870s.

2. Prince Vladimir Petrovich Meshchersky (1839-1914), arch-conservative writer and journalist.

3. P.I. Borisov, Fet's ward.

4. According to Fet's memoirs, he heard Turgenev say to the youths: "Je vous félicite, messieurs, en votre qualité de lycéens. Le gouvernement ne manquera pas de vous recevoir à bras ouverts."

5. Turgenev may be alluding to an unknown letter from Fet.

6. Relations between Fet and Turgenev were re-established in the late 1870s, but on a rather formal level.

Letter 274.

1. The German original of this letter is not known to be extant.

2. The issues of *Wiener Zeitung* contained Schmidt's reviews of Zola's first four novels.

3. This is probably a reference to "Tatyana Borisovna and Her Nephew," part of *Notes of a Hunter.*

Letter 275.

1. Yury Nikolayevich Milyutin (1856-1912), the same boy mentioned in letter 273.

2. Alexey Alexandrovich Kharlamov (1842-1922), artist, portraitist, and illustrator for a number of Turgenev's works.

Letter 276.

1. Alexander Vasilievich Toporov (1831-1887), a close friend of Turgenev's who carried out all manner of assignments for him in Petersburg.

2. Louise Arnholt, a housekeeper for the Viardot family.

3. *The Citizen* was a fiercely conservative journal to which Turgenev subscribed in Arnholt's name.

4. Turgenev means that Toporov need not subscribe to the journal for him.

5. Yevgeny Ivanovich Ragozin (1834-1906), writer, and close friend of Turgenev's from 1870 on.

6. See letter 174, notes 1 and 3.

7. *The Demon,* opera by A.G. Rubinstein.

8. *Anna Karenina.*

9. Turgenev later revised upward his estimation of the novel.

10. *Virgin Soil.*

Letter 277

1. Semyon Afanasievich Vengerov (1855-1920), critic, historian, and bibliographer.

2. The reference is to Vengerov's *Russian Literature in its Contemporary Representatives: Ivan Sergeyevich Turgenev,* Part I (Petersburg, 1875), in the preface to which Vengerov announced his intention to examine writers' biographies against the backgrounds of the age which they embody.

3. An inaccurate citation from Horace's *Ars poetica* (lines 372-373).

Letter 278.

1. The original of this letter is in French.

2. Turgenev is referring to Jules Verne's novel, *Michel Strogoff,* the manuscript of which Hetzel had asked Turgenev to check over for howlers.

Letter 279.

1. The original of this letter is in French.

2. The reference is to a Russian translation of Zola's *Son excellence Eugène Rougon.*

3. *Renée Mauperin* was not published in *The Messenger of Europe.*

4. Edmond de Goncourt.

Letter 280.

1. Danilova was Saltykov's landlady in Nice.

2. Danilova liked to gamble at Monte Carlo.

3. Saltykov did in fact use the sketch "A Family Tribunal" as the first chapter of his novel *The Golovlyov Family* (1872-76).

4. The reference is to Saltykov's satrical bent, especially as evidenced in a work such as *Pompadours and Pompadouresses.*

5. Salkykov had been present at the reading of a new play by V.A. Sollogub. The former was so irritated by the comedy (not extant) that he had something like a fit of hysterics.

6. Betel Henri Strusberg (1823-1884), a railway entrepreneur whose insolvency led to the collapse of a Moscow commercial bank in 1875.

Letter 281.

1. Saltykov did not enlarge on the fragment.

2. The reference is to *Virgin Soil.*

3. Saltykov had written that in view of Turgenev's excessive tolerance, he was surprised that Turgenev was not the tutor to the heir apparent.

4. Saltykov apparently had called Goncharov an entertaining author.

Letter 282.

1. The original of this letter is in French.

2. The reference is to Taine's *Les origines de la France contemporaine.*

Letter 283.

1. Herzen's wife, Natalya Alexandrovna, née Zakharina (1817-1852) had an extended affair with Herzen's close friend George Herwegh. For the details of this domestic tragedy, see E.M. Carr, *The Romantic Exiles* (London, 1968), 43-107.
2. Emma Herwegh (1817-1904).
3. Natalya Alexandrovna Herzen (1844-1936).
4. Annekov read the manuscript and agreed with Turgenev's opinion.
5. There had been French elections on January 30, 1876.
6. Louise Héritte de la Tour.

Letter 284.

1. The original of this letter is in French.
2. Approximately 103° Fahrenheit.
3. Approximately 12° Fahrenheit.
4. Sand died June 7, 1876.
5. *Figaro,* the conservative Paris newspaper.
6. Turgenev was translating Flaubert's "La Légende de St. Julien l'hospitalier."
7. A reference to recent events in Turkey.
8. Erneste and Caroline Commanville.

Letter 285.

1. Vladimir Ludvigovich Kign (1856-1908), minor writer.
2. Alexander Mikhaylovich Skabichevsky (1838-1910), critic and literary historian.
3. Gleb Ivanovich Uspensky (1843-1902), Populist writer.

Letter 286.

1. Turgenev's "Croquet in Windsor Park" (1876), apropos the Bulgarian uprising against the Turks, was forbidden by the Russian censorship, but circulated from hand to hand. It was soon translated into English, French, and German.
2. *Virgin Soil.*
3. A reference to the strained period immediately preceding the Russo-Turkish War (1877-78).
4. Anna Davydovna Baratynskaya (1814-1889), poet and translator.
5. Count Vladimir Petrovich Orlov-Davydov (1809-1882), translator.
6. I.S. Aksakov helped organize a campaign to raise funds for the Bulgarians. He himself contributed considerable sums of money to the cause.
7. V.A. Cherkassky was appointed head of the Red Cross units within the Southern Army.

Letter 287.

1. *Virgin Soil* was being set for *Messenger of Europe.*
2. On December 10, 1869, *The Voice* published a Russian *translation* of Turgenev's "A Strange Story," which had first appeared in a German translation in the journal *Salon* and was then supposed to be published first in the Russian original in Stasyulevich's journal.

3. Yelena Ivanovna Blaramberg (pseud. Ye. Ardov; 1843-1923), writer and translator whose early work Turgenev liked.

4. Blaramberg's story, "Apollon Markovich," was not accepted by Stasyulevich.

5. See letter 284, note 4.

6. Characters in *Virgin Soil.*

Letter 288.

1. The reference is to Richard Wagner's *Eine Kapitulation, Lustspiel in antiker Manier* (1871).

2. *Virgin Soil.*

3. Turgenev's information was incorrect. By the start of the war Russia had mobilized 257,000 men against Turkey's 180,000.

Letter 289.

1. The original of this letter is in German.

2. Presumably Turgenev means a photograph of Adolf Menzel.

3. Kate Eckert.

4. Paul Viardot.

5. Paul Viardot had given a violin concert in Berlin and Pietsch apparently had reviewed it.

6. See letter 274.

7. Theodor Storm (1817-1888), one of the best-known German writers of his age. He was an admirer of Turgenev's work.

Letter 290.

1. Sofia Konstantinovna Bryullova, née Kavelina (1851-1877), teacher, historian, and critic. She and Turgenev corresponded with some regularity from 1871 until her early death.

2. Konstantin Dmitrievich Kavelin.

3. The reference is to *Virgin Soil.*

4. In his letter to Kavelin of December 17/29, 1876, Turgenev said, in essence, that in *Virgin Soil* he had not devoted much attention to "progressive" peasants because he was out of touch with them.

5. Pavel Alexandrovich Bryullov (1840-1914), an artist.

Letter 291.

1. Alexey Petrovich Bogolyubov (1824-1896), Russian artist and entrepreneur for the arts.

2. Sergey Ivanovich Taneyev (1856-1915), distinguished Russian composer and teacher.

Letter 293.

1. Emile Durand (1838-1900), French writer and translator. The first French translation of *Virgin Soil* was Durand's.

2. See letter 246 for some of the details on the events leading to the rupture in Turgenev's relations with Dostoyevsky. For a fuller account of this long story, see Schapiro, 50-51, 213-217.

Letter 294.

1. The reference is to Polonsky's "To I.S. Turgenev."
2. Pauline Viardot.
3. See note 1.

Letter 295.

1. The original of this letter, here reproduced, is in Turgenev's own English.
2. It is not certain to what article Turgenev refers.
3. Turgenev is referring to the so-called "Trial of the Fifty," which involved Populists arrested in Moscow, Tula, and other cities. The trial lasted from February 21-March 14 (O.S.) 1877. Contemporary observers found remarkable parallels between the testimony at the trial and the thematics of Turgenev's *Virgin Soil.*
4. Characters from *Virgin Soil.*
5. Lydia Nikolayevna Figner (1853-1920), a Populist revolutionary.
6. Note that Figner did not die until 1920.
7. Solomin, one of the male protagonists in *Virgin Soil.* Who Zsvilenef was and what letter Turgenev is describing remain matters of conjecture.

Letter 296.

1. The original of this letter is in French.
2. Mme Delessert's friends, monarchists, did not come to power.

Letter 297.

1. Adelaida Nikolayevna Lukanina, née Rykacheva (1843-1908), a doctor and writer.
2. The story was accepted and Mrs. Lukanina continued publishing in *The Messenger of Europe* until 1886.
3. V.V. Stasov.

Letter 298.

1. Heine was long bedfast because of paralysis.
2. Countess Natalya Alexandrovna Merenberg, née Pushkina (1836-1913), the poet's daughter, entrusted Turgenev with the publication of a number of her father's letters. They appeared in *The Messenger of Europe,* after which Turgenev received a letter alerting him that Pushkin's sons were planning to give him a drubbing. Nothing of the sort took place, of course.
3. The French Army was defeated near Sedan on September 2, 1870.
4. Théodore Rousseau (1812-1867), French painter whose work Turgenev greatly admired.
5. Baroness Yulya Petrovna Vrevskaya (1841-1878), a close friend of Turgenev's and a nurse during the Russo-Turkish War. She died of typhus January 24/ February 5, 1878, in a Russian hospital in Bulgaria where she was working. Polonsky's poem to her was entitled "Under the Red Cross."
6. Pavel Alexandrovich Gaydeburov (1841-1893), the editor of *The Week,* had made verbal criticism of Polonsky's povest *Accidentally.*
7. Mikhail Grigorievich Chernyayev (1828-1898), Commander-in-Chief of the Serbian Army during the Serbo-Turkish War (1876).

8. Vladimir Viktorovich Chuiko (1839-1899), literary historian, critic, and one of Polonsky's friends.

9. Parmen Petrovich Zabello (1830-1917), sculptor.

Letter 299.

1. Tolstoy's letter was dated April 6/18, 1878.

2. See letters 136, 137, 138.

Letter 300.

1. See letter 273 for the explanation of the rupture in Turgenev and Fet's relations.

2. Fet bought the estate Vorobiovka in 1877.

Letter 301.

1. Tolstoy had complained that he had been mentally unwell. The years 1878-1880 were a period of personal crisis for Tolstoy.

2. Tolstoy had written that the mention of his writings made him fear that people were laughing at him.

3. Eugene Schuyler's translation of *The Cossacks* was published in London in 1873.

4. Baroness Yelizaveta Ivanovna Mengden's French translation of *The Cossacks,* undertaken without Tolstoy's authorization, was published in *Journal de St-Petersbourg* in 1878.

5. No separate French edition of the book came about.

6. Turgenev had visited his friend William Henry Bullock-Hall (1836-1904).

7. Turgenev has in mind British hostility toward Russia in connection with the Russo-Turkish War.

8. The libretto was composed by Chaikovsky and his brother Modest Ilich.

9. Lensky has no such line in the opera, but Turgenev's remark is nonetheless generally accurate.

10. A series of four concerts of Russian music were organized by N.G. Rubinstein at the Trockadero Concert Hall in Paris in September, 1878.

Letter 302.

1. A. Ya. Turgeneva.

2. Maria Gavrilovna Savina (1854-1915), one of the most distinguished actresses of her time. She and Turgenev became quite close: one might plausibly call Savina Turgenev's last great love. For his full correspondence to her see Nora Gottlieb and Raymond Chapman, *Letters to an Actress* (London, 1973).

3. Yekaterina Nikolayevna Vasilieva, née Lavrova (1829-1877), an actress at Moscow's Maly Theater.

4. The first performance of the play took place on January 13/25, 1872.

5. Karl Beggrov was a commissionaire in the St. Petersburg art market. He had sold a painting from Turgenev's collection, and Turgenev wanted to know the details.

6. The Samarsky family was headed by Vladimir Vasilievich Samarsky-Vykhovets (1837-1902), a lawyer whose services Turgenev often employed.

Letter 303.

1. The original of this letter is in French.
2. See letter 302.
3. Pauline apparently had asked her father to try to find a position for her husband.

Letter 304.

1. Porfiry Konstantinovich Malyarevsky (d. 1896), N.S. Turgenev's estate manager and husband of his wife's niece.
2. See letter 302, note 6.

Letter 305.

1. Turgenev is referring to the warm reception that he found in Russia. See letter 304.
2. Little is known about the cited documents, although they would seem to have been expressions of admiration and respect for Turgenev.
3. An attempt was made on Emperor Alexander II's life on April 2/14, 1879.
4. Saltykov-Shchedrin was noted for his satirical exposes of corruption, bribery, and the like. Turgenev apparently encountered a good deal of chicanery in connection with the probate of his brother's estate.

Letter 306.

1. Turgenev was awarded the honorary degree of Doctor of Civil Law by Oxford University on June 18, 1879.
2. Because of conflicting Russian and British interests in the Balkans, anti-Russian feeling was running high in England.
3. See *The Times,* June 19, 1879.
4. Louis Napoleon, the son of Napoleon III, was killed on June 1, 1879, in a skirmish with Zulus in Cape Colony (South Africa).
5. A quotation from the last line of Gogol's story "The Nose."

Letter 307.

1. The original of this letter is in French.

Letter 308.

1. The identity of the Russian in question is not known with any real certainty. It may have been a man named Bronsky.

Letter 309.

1. The Pushkin Commemoration, held in connection with the unveiling of the Pushkin Monument in Moscow, was delayed until June 5/17, 1880. The event was an epochal one in Russian literary life. See letters 310, 313.
2. Alexey Antipovich Potekhin (1829-1908), minor writer.
3. Nikolay Savvich Tikhonravov (1832-1893), distinguished literary historian.

4. The reference is to the ouster of Count Dmitry Andreyevich Tolstoy (1823-1889), from his posts as Minister of National Enlightenment and Over-Procurator of the Holy Synod.

5. Tolstoy did not participate in the Pushkin Commemoration.

Letter 310.

1. Viktor Pavlovich Gayevsky (1826-1888), literary historian and activist in Russian literary circles. He edited the first (posthumous) edition of Turgenev's letters.

2. See letter 309, note 1.

3. Sergey Andreyevich Yuriev (1821-1888), translator and critic.

4. Yakov Karlovich Grot (1812-1893), literary historian, linguist, and translator.

5. Turgenev is referring to M.N. Katkov, publisher who was an arch-conservative by the 1870s.

6. Goncharov was unable to attend, due to ill health.

7. Ivan Vasilievich Samarin (1817-1885), actor at the Maly Theater.

8. Erneste Commanville, French businessman and relative of Flaubert's through marriage.

9. Count Matvey Vladimirovich Sollogub (1852-1894), son of V.A. Sollogub.

Letter 311.

1. The original of this letter is in French.

2. The reference, as the following line makes clear, is to the death of Gustave Flaubert.

3. Flaubert's *Bouvard et Pécuchet* was published in late 1880 and early 1881 in the journal *Nouvelle Revue*.

Letter 312.

1. In May, 1880, Savina was on her way from Petersburg to Odessa. Turgenev met her at the Mtsensk train station and on May 16/28 accompanied her as far as Oryol. In a letter of May 17/29, Turgenev confessed to her that just as her train was about to pull out of Oryol he had been seized by the desire to carry her off and have his way with her.

2. The reference is to Turgenev's letter of May 17/29, 1880, one in which the expression of his feelings for Savina is no less intense, but more coy.

Letter 313.

1. Dostoyevsky's speech was given on June 8/20, 1880, and was greeted by thunderous applause, hosannas, cries of "Prophet!" and similar expressions of wonderment. In Dostoyevsky's messianic interpretation, Pushkin had provided universal models of manhood and womanhood. In a word, Pushkin had provided Russian models for Europe and the world.

2. Aleko is the tragic hero of Pushkin's narrative poem "The Gypsies."

3. Tatyana, the heroine of Pushkin's novel-in-verse, *Eugene Onegin*.

4. Turgenev's citation is not quite accurate.

Letter 314.

1. Vsevolod Vladimirovich Krestovsky (1840-1895), the author of a number of crude anti-nihilist and anti-Polish works, one of them being *Petersburg Slums*.

2. The reference is to a medicine for gout.

3. Turgenev and Savina met in Paris at the end of August 1880, and their former friendship was quickly renewed.

Letter 315.

1. Turgenev had drafted a letter to his publisher Stasyulevich in which he explained, rather lamely, that if he broke his vow not to publish anything ever again, Stasyulevich would have to bear the responsibility for that.
2. Annenkov apparently had urged Turgenev to make Ivan in "Old Portraits" a murderer *and* a suicide.
3. Turgenev's "A Desperate Fellow" was published in 1882.

Letter 316.

1. Konstantin Nikolayevich Boborykin (1829-1904), Governor of Oryol Province.
2. Yakov Isayevich Zilberman, a sculptor in his own right, was also M.M. Antokolsky's assistant.
3. Boborykin replied that he would do everything possible to help Zilberman's sisters.

Letter 317.

1. The reference is to a French prose translation, as of then still unpublished, of Pushkin's *Eugene Onegin,* done by Vladimir Mikhailovich Mikhailov (1811-?). The translation eventually appeared in Paris in 1884.
2. Turgenev's letter to Mikhailov seems not to be extant.
3. The translation was published in *Revue Nationale et Etrangère,* Vol. XIII (1863).
4. Probably a reference to Paul Béeson's French translation of *Eugene Onegin* that was published in Paris in 1868.
5. Mikhailov's Russian translation of Heine's "Deutschland" was published in Leipzig in 1875, with an introduction by Turgenev.
6. See note 1.
7. Gambetta had been forced to resign as the head of the French government.
8. A not quite accurate quotation from V.I. Maikov's "Ode on the World's Vanity" (1775).
9. An inaccurate quotation from Pushkin's "Who Raised Theocritus' Tender Roses on the Snow?"
10. Marianne Viardot-Duvernoix.

Letter 318.

1. At a dinner during the Pushkin Commemoration (June 8/20, 1880), Turgenev declined M.N. Katkov's attempt to clink glasses with him.
2. The reference is to Turgenev's letter of December 16/28, 1881 to D.V. Grigorovich. The discussion of Bernhardt was occasioned by her appearances in Petersburg in December 1881. A.S. Suvorin's feuilletons about Bernhardt were published in *New Time,* Nos. 2074, 2079-82, and 2098 (Dec.-Jan., 1881-1882). In the latter issue Suvorin made reference to the negative evaluation of Bernhardt given in Turgenev's letter to Grigorovich.
3. M.M. Stasyulevich was the publisher and editor of the journal *The Messenger of Europe* and the newspaper *Order.*

Letter 319.

1. Pauline Bruère left her husband at the beginning of March, 1882. Turgenev sent her and her children off to a hotel in Soleure, Switzerland.

Letter 320.

1. The original of this letter is in French.
2. See letter 319, note 1.
3. Georges Chamerot (b. 1845), publisher and husband of Claudie Viardot from 1874 on.

Letter 321.

1. This was the beginning of the illness that was ultimately to take Turgenev's life. Modern medical authorities familiar with the record suggest that the disease was cancer of the spine, not angina pectoris.
2. Jean Charcot (1825-1893), French doctor and member of the Parisian Academy of Sciences.
3. Nikolay Alexandrovich Shchepkin (1850-1914), Turgenev's estate manager from 1876 until the time of Turgenev's death.
4. Ya. P. Polonsky.
5. Turgenev was trying to arrange a second illustrated edition of Polonsky's narrative poem, *The Grasshopper Musician* (a first edition, with illustrations by V.A. Hartman, was published in Petersburg in 1863). The plan came to naught.

Letter 322.

1. Zhozefina Antonovna Polonskaya, imagining that the Viardots might go to Bougival and leave Turgenev alone in Paris, wanted to come to Paris to look after him.
2. Nikolay Andreyevich Belogolovy (1834-1895), one of Turgenev's doctors during the last year-and-a-half of his life.
3. See letter 321, note 5.

Letter 323.

1. Siva was N.N. Vsevolozhsky's estate in Perm Province. See note 2.
2. Savina married Nikita Nikitich Vsevolozhsky (1846-1896) in 1882. The marriage was annulled in 1891.
3. Savina had signed a two-year contract with the Imperial Theaters.
4. Savina kept almost all of Turgenev's letters. They remain in her archive to this day.
5. Savina visited Turgenev in April, 1882.
6. A reference to General Mikhail Dmitrievich Skobelev (183-1882).
7. I.I. Maslov.
8. Polina Antipievna Strepetova (1850-1903), actress.

Letter 324.

1. The original of this letter is in French.
2. It is likely that the gossip had to do with the relations between Pauline Viardot and Turgenev.

3. Pauline Bruère had apparently named Viardot as her singing teacher in response to praise for her singing.

4. Yosif Karlovich Lambert.

Letter 325.

1. Polonsky's letter is not extant, but it apparently was part of an on-going polemic about landscape painting.

2. Camille Corot (1796-1875), French landscapist.

3. Andreas Achenbach (1815-?), German landscape painter.

4. Alexandre Calame (1810-1864), Swiss landscape painter.

5. Salomon Ruysdael (c. 1600-1670), Dutch landscape painter.

Letter 326.

1. Chapters XII-XV of *A Contemporary Idyll* were published in *Notes of the Fatherland,* No. 9, 1882.

2. Nikolay Konstantinovich Mikhailovsky (1842-1904), sociologist and literary critic with a socialist bent. His influence among the radical intelligentsia in the 1870s and early 1880s was enormous.

3. Mikhailovsky's "A Cruel Talent" (1882) characterized Dostoyevsky as a writer whose theme was wolves eating sheep. In his early works, according to Mikhailovsky, Dostoyevsky portrayed the process from the sheep's point of view, in his later works from that of the wolves. See N.K. Mikhailovsky, *A Cruel Talent,* translated by Spencer Cadmus (Ann Arbor, 1978).

4. It is unclear what work of Dostoyevsky's Turgenev had in mind.

5. See letter 313 for the reference to the "all-man."

6. Vsevolod Mikhailovich Garshin (1855-1888), mentally unstable but talented minor writer who greatly admired Turgenev's art. Turgenev took a lively interest in Garshin's work and tragic life, helping him with advice and allowing him to stay at Spasskoye in the summer of 1882.

7. Apparently a reference to Garshin's story "From the Memoirs of Private Ivanov" (1882).

Letter 327.

1. Tolstoy's "A Confession." For Turgenev's reaction to Tolstoy's work, see letter 328.

2. Alexandra Grigorievna Olsufieva, née Yesipova, was a neighbor of Tolstoy's. She delivered Tolstoy's "A Confession" to Turgenev.

3. Yelena Sergeyevna Rakhmanova, née Volkonskaya (1835-1916).

4. Instead of appearing in the journal *Children's Relaxation,* Turgenev's story was issued in a separate book edition along with Tolstoy's "What Men Live By" in 1883.

Letter 328.

1. In 1878-79 Grigorovich organized a School of Drawing on Bolshaya Morskaya Street in Petersburg.

2. Reference to the All-Russian Industrial Art Exhibit that closed in October 1882.

3. *The Field,* No. 43 (1882) announced a new povest by Turgenev for 1883, along with Grigorovich's "The Guttapercha Boy."

4. Anatoly Viktorovich Polovtsev (1849-1905), archeologist, jurist, journalist, and high-ranking bureaucrat.

5. See letter 323.

6. A.G. Olsufieva.

7. Nikolay Stepanovich Tagantsev (1843-1923), jurist and professor at Petersburg University.

Turgenev's appeal to Tagantsev, which was written the *same* day as the present letter, concerned Nikolay Petrovich Tsakin (1851-1904), a revolutionary who lived in Paris from 1878-1888.

Letter 329.

1. Lyubov Yakovlevna Stechkina (1851-1901), writer. Turgenev not only tried to arrange for her works to be published, but gave her financial asssistance as well.

2. Stechkina's povest was not published in *The Messenger of Europe*. The manuscript seems to have been lost in the mail.

3. Maupassant's *Une Vie* was not published in *The Messenger of Europe,* because Turgenev was not satisfied with N.P. Tsakin's translation.

4. The phrasing is Turgenev's, though it no doubt represents a slip of the pen.

Letter 330.

1. The operation, performed without anesthesia, was successful.

2. Gambetta's funeral was held January 5, 1883.

3. Nikolay Vasilievich Shelgunov (1824-1891), journalist, literary critic, and colleague of N.K. Mikhailovsky's.

4. N.K. Mikhailovsky and N.V. Shelgunov were exiled to Vyborg on December 27, 1882 (O.S.). The unofficial and real reason for their exile was their links to "The People's Will," a revolutionary party.

5. Yevgeny Mikhailovich Feoktistov (1829-1893), an extremely conservative figure, was the head of the Main Office for Press Affairs from early 1883 on.

6. Konstantin Petrovich Pobedonostsev (1827-1907), Over-Procurator for the Holy Synod and influential advisor to Alexander III and Nicholas II. Pobedonostsev, an ardent foe of reform, was the leading conservative statesman of his time.

Letter 331.

1. Polonsky was a censor for the Committee on Foreign Literature.

Letter 333.

1. As a result of his philosophico-religious crisis in the early 1880s, Tolstoy had renounced literature. He continued writing until the end of his life, however.

Letter 334.

1. This telegram, sent in French, is Turgenev's last known written communication.

2. Turgenev wished to empower David Goratsievich Gintsburg (1857-1910) to sell or lease Spasskoye.

INDEX TO VOLUME II

The numbers following names in this index refer to letter numbers, not pages. Italics indicates that the given person was the letter's addressee. An asterisk indicates that the name occurs in Volume I as well. Biographical information can usually be found in the notes to the first letter in which a person's name appears. Thus, if the name is followed by an asterisk, such information will be in Volume I.